The RSVPeople

The RSVPeople

Paul Chronnell

With essential contributions from
Sarah-Louise Young

The RSVPeople
By Paul Chronnell & Sarah-Louise Young

First edition.

For more information: thersvpeople@gmail.com

Disclaimer:
Old copies of music magazines are freely available to buy. They contain full names and addresses of people who put them there willingly. All the people in this book are real. The events surrounding them in the quest of the book are recorded entirely as they were experienced by the authors. However, most of their names have been changed to respect their privacy. So too their road names and numbers and most of the districts and towns. Any similarity, now, between these fictitious names at their fictitious addresses, and actual people, is neither intended nor, frankly, likely.

Permissions:
Lazermall book cover and Filthy Loot logo used with permission from Filthy Loot.
Top Up The Generator album cover used with permission from W. Barratt.

Cover design by Justin David (inkandescent.co.uk)
Cover photographs by Angus Stewart (angusstewart.me)
Cover photo styling by Thom Shaw

www.TheRSVPeople.co.uk

For Mama Chronnell

'She had beautiful handwriting that danced across the page.'

She would have been thrilled to know this book exists.
She'd have written a letter saying how proud she was -
and that she'd found a typo everyone else missed.

And for Papa Chronnell

As a retired GP, his handwriting is pretty much illegible, but nonetheless, his eternal support and unfailing ability to listen to my wittering and never, ever saying I should give up and get a proper job, has been invaluable the whole of my life.

With thanks...

Much as we'd love to pull a Spike Milligan, claiming we have no one to thank because we did it all ourselves, we can't. Because it would be a lie.

So, in no particular order, we'd like to thank everyone who helped us along the way - Andrew Fingret, Kate Burdette, Kate Millner, Michael Shaw, Ilka Cook, Richard Cook, Charlie da Gama, Jack Chronnell, Joe Chronnell, Angus Stewart, Justin David, Miles Moss, Fred Johanson, Pun Kai Loon, Thom Shaw, Dr. Steve Young, Matt Connell, Alex Bates, Russell Lucas, Sophie Brigstocke, Frank, Lily and Wilf.

It goes without saying we couldn't have got past the first week of January without all The RSVPeople who replied, wrote, commented and wanted to play.
You're all brilliant and although your names have been changed in this book, you know who you are.

Friday 1st January 2021

Happy New Year!

35 years ago a group of young people wrote brief pen pal requests and sent them off to Smash Hits magazine in the hope of making friends and sharing thoughts with like-minded teenagers. How do we know this? That's a very good question. And here's a very good answer: seven days ago that very copy of Smash Hits was gifted to Sarah by her brother, as a tongue-in-cheek Christmas present and throwback to their childhood.

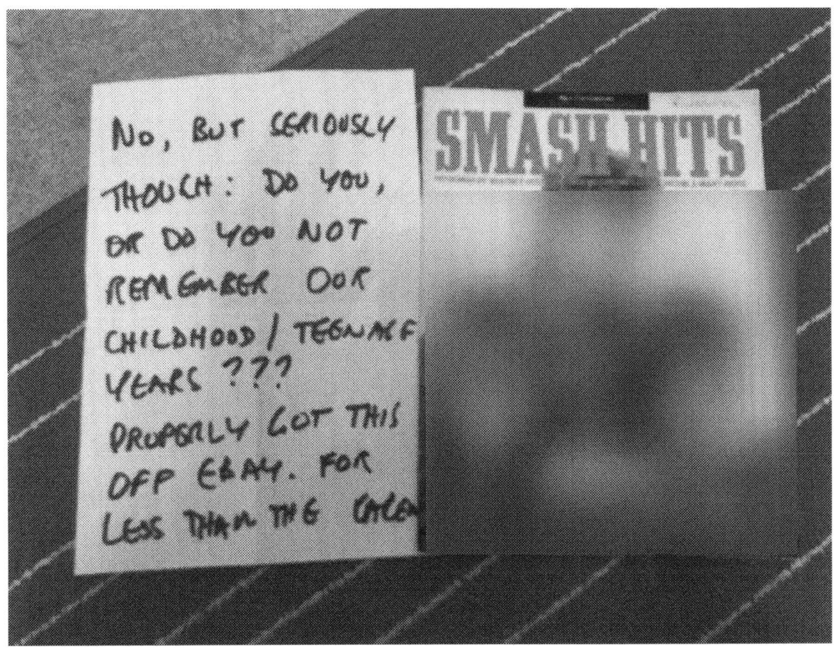

(Obviously, in 1985, teenage magazines didn't come with hi-tech, weapons-grade data protection systems, infused with NATO supported paranoia and anxiety. So we've put this sort of shower screen in front of the mag, to keep everyone safe. You're welcome.)

And deep within its pages, there they all were…

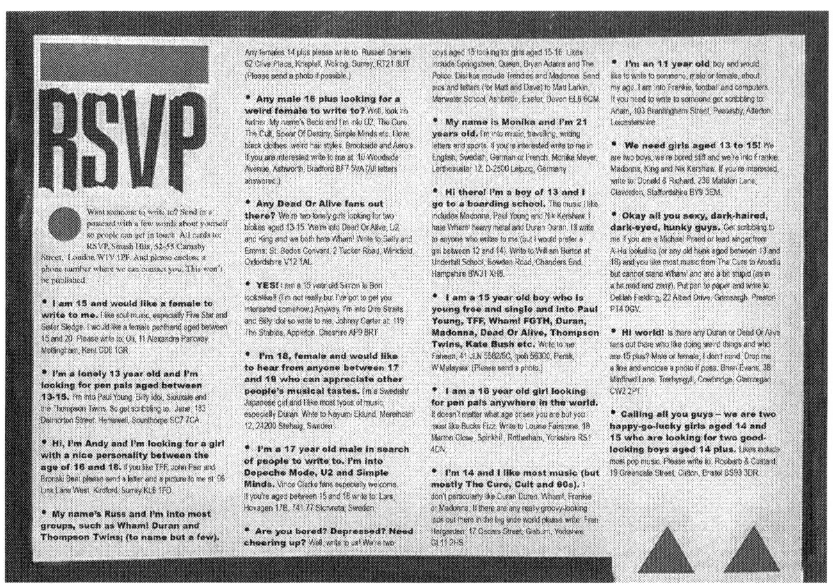

RSVP

Want someone to write to? Send in a postcard with a few words about yourself so people can get in touch. All cards to: RSVP, Smash Hits, 52-55 Carnaby Street, London W1V 1PF. And please enclose a phone number where we can contact you. This won't be published.

• **I am 15 and would like a female to write to me.** I like soul music, especially Five Star and Sister Sledge. I would like a female penfriend aged between 15 and 20. Please write to: Oli, 11 Alexandra Parkway, Mottingham, Kent CD6 1GR.

• **I'm a lonely 13 year old and I'm looking for pen pals aged between 13-15.** I'm into Paul Young, Billy Idol, Siouxsie and the Thompson Twins. So get scribbling to: Jane, 183 Dalmorton Street, Hemswell, Scunthorpe SC7 7CA.

• **Hi, I'm Andy and I'm looking for a girl with a nice personality between the age of 16 and 18.** If you like TFF, John Parr and Bronski Beat please send a letter and a picture to me at 96 Link Lane West, Kirdford, Surrey KL6 1FO.

• **My name's Russ and I'm into most groups, such as Wham! Duran and Thompson Twins; (to name but a few).** Any females 14 plus please write to: Russell Daniels, 62 Clive Place, Knephill, Woking, Surrey, RT21 8UT (Please send a photo if possible.)

• **Any male 16 plus looking for a weird female to write to?** Well, look no further. My name's Becki and I'm into U2, The Cure, The Cult, Spear Of Destiny, Simple Minds etc. I love black clothes, weird hair styles, Brookside and Aero's. If you are interested write to me at: 10 Woodside Avenue, Ashworth, Bradford BF7 5VA (All letters answered.)

• **Any Dead Or Alive fans out there?** We're two lonely girls looking for two blokes aged 13-15. We're into Dead Or Alive, U2 and King and we both hate Wham! Write to Sally and Emma, St. Bedes Convent, 2 Tucker Road, Winkfield, Oxfordshire V12 1AL.

• **YES!** I am a 15 year old Simon le Bon lookalike!! (I'm not really but I've got to get you interested somehow.) Anyway, I'm into Dire Straits and Billy Idol so write to me, Johnny Carter at: 119 The Stables, Appleton, Cheshire AP9 8RT.

• **I'm 18, female and would like to hear from anyone between 17 and 19 who can appreciate other people's musical tastes.** I'm a Swedish/Japanese girl and I like most types of music, especially Duran. Write to Nayumi Eklund, Mereholm 12, 24200 Stehaig, Sweden.

• **I'm a 17 year old male in search of people to write to. I'm into Depeche Mode, U2 and Simple Minds.** Vince Clarke fans especially welcome. If you're aged between 15 and 18 write to: Lars, Hovagen 17B, 741 77 Slotvreta, Sweden.

• **Are you bored? Depressed? Need cheering up?** Well, write to us! We're two boys aged 15 looking for girls aged 15-16. Likes include Springsteen, Queen, Bryan Adams and The Police. Dislikes include Trendies and Madonna. Send pics and letters (for Matt and Dave) to Matt Larkin, Marwater School, Ashbrittle, Exeter, Devon EL6 6QM.

• **My name is Monika and I'm 21 years old.** I'm into music, travelling, writing letters and sports. If you're interested write to me in English, Swedish, German or French. Monika Meyer, Lerthesustar 12, D-2500 Leipzig, Germany.

• **Hi there! I'm a boy of 13 and I go to a boarding school.** The music I like includes Madonna, Paul Young and Nik Kershaw. I hate Wham! heavy metal and Duran Duran. I'll write to anyone who writes to me (but I would prefer a girl between 12 and 14). Write to William Burton at: Underhill School, Bowden Road, Chanders End, Hampshire BW31 XH8.

• **I am a 15 year old boy who is young free and single and into Paul Young, TFF, Wham! FGTH, Duran, Madonna, Dead Or Alive, Thompson Twins, Kate Bush etc.** Write to me: Faheem, 41 JLN 5582/5C, Ipoh 56300, Perak, W Malaysia. (Please send a photo.)

• **I am a 16 year old girl looking for pen pals anywhere in the world.** It doesn't matter what age or sex you are but you must like Bucks Fizz. Write to Louise Fairstone, 18 Martin Close, Spinkhill, Rotherham, Yorkshire RS1 4DN.

• **I'm 14 and I like most music (but mostly The Cure, Cult and 60s).** I don't particularly like Duran Duran, Wham!, Frankie or Madonna. If there are any really groovy-looking guys out there in the big wide world please write: Fran Helgarden, 17 Oscars Street, Gisburn, Yorkshire GL11 2HS.

• **I'm an 11 year old** boy and would like to write to someone, male or female, about my age. I am into Frankie, football and computers. If you need to write to someone get scribbling to: Adam, 103 Brantingham Street, Peasenby, Allerton, Leicestershire.

• **We need girls aged 13 to 15!** We are two boys, we're bored stiff and we're into Frankie, Madonna, King and Nik Kershaw. If you're interested, write to: Donald & Richard, 236 Malden Lane, Claverdon, Staffordshire BY9 3EM.

• **Okay all you sexy, dark-haired, dark-eyed, hunky guys.** Get scribbling to me if you are a Michael Praed or lead singer from A-Ha lookalike (or any old hunk aged between 13 and 18) and you like most music from The Cure to Arcadia but cannot stand Wham! and are a bit stupid (as in a bit mad and zany). Put pen to paper and write to Delilah Fielding, 22 Albert Drive, Grimsargh, Preston PT4 0GV.

• **Hi world!** Is there any Duran or Dead Or Alive fans out there who like doing weird things and who are 15 plus? Male or female, I don't mind. Drop me a line and enclose a photo if poss. Brian Evans, 38 Minfrwd Lane, Trethyngyll, Cowbridge, Glamorgan CW2 2PT.

• **Calling all you guys – we are two happy-go-lucky girls aged 14 and 15 who are looking for two good-looking boys aged 14 plus.** Likes include most pop music. Please write to: Roobarb & Custard, 19 Greendale Street, Clifton, Bristol BS93 3DR.

* **I am 15 and would like a female to write to me.** I like soul music, especially Five Star and Sister Sledge. I would like a female penfriend aged between 15 and 20. Please write to: Oli, 11 Alexandra Parkway, Mottingham, Kent CD6 1GR.

* **I'm a lonely 13 year old and I'm looking for pen pals aged between 13-15.** I'm into Paul Young, Billy Idol, Siouxsie and the Thompson Twins. So get scribbling to: Jane, 183 Dalmorton Street, Hemswell, Scunthorpe SC7 7CA.

* **Hi, I'm Andy and I'm looking for a girl with a nice personality between the age of 16 and 18.** If you like TFF, John Parr and Bronski

Beat please send a letter and a picture to me at: 96 Link Lane West, Kirdford, Surrey KL6 1FD.

* **My name's Russ and I'm into most groups, such as Wham! Duran and Thompson Twins; (to name but a few).** Any females 14 plus please write to Russell Daniels, 62 Clive Place, Knaphill, Woking, Surrey RT21 8UT. (Please send a photo if possible.)

* **Any male 16 plus looking for a weird female to write to**? Well, look no further. My name's Becki and I'm into U2, The Cure, The Cult, Spear Of Destiny, Simple Minds etc. I love black clothes, weird hair styles, Brookside and Aero's. If you are interested write to me at: 10 Woodside Avenue, Ashworth, Bradford BF7 5VA. (All letters answered.)

* **Any Dead Or Alive fans out there?** We're two lonely girls looking for two blokes aged 13-15. We're into Dead Or Alive, U2 and King and we both hate Wham! Write to: Sally and Emma St. Bedes Convent, 2 Tucker Road, Winkfield, Oxfordshire V12 1AL.

* **YES!** I am a 15 year old Simon Le Bon lookalike!! (I'm not really but I've got to get you interested somehow.) Anyway, I'm into Dire Straits and Billy Idol so write to me, Johnny Carter at: 119 The Stables, Appleton, Cheshire AP9 8RT.

* **I'm 18, female and would like to hear from anyone between 17 and 19 who can appreciate other people's musical tastes.** I'm a Swedish/Japanese girl and I like most types of music, especially Duran. Write to Nayumi Eklund, Mareiholm 12, 24200 Stehaig, Sweden.

* **I'm a 17 year old male in search of people to write to. I'm into Depeche Mode, U2 and Simple Minds.** Vince Clarke fans especially welcome. If you're aged between 15 and 18 write to: Lars, Hovagen 17B, 741 77 Storvreta, Sweden.

* **Are you bored? Depressed? Need cheering up?** Well, write to us! We're two boys aged 15 looking for girls aged 15-16. Likes include Springsteen, Queen, Bryan Adams and The Police. Dislikes include Trendies and Madonna. Send pics and letters (for Matt and Dave) to Matt Larkin, Marwater School, Ashbrittle, Exeter, Devon EL6 6QM.

* **My name is Monika and I'm 21 years old.** I'm into music, travelling, writing letters and sports. If you're interested write to me in English, Swedish, German or French: Monika Meyer, Lertheauster 12, D-2600 Leipzig, Germany.

* **Hi there! I'm a boy of 13 and I go to a boarding school.** The music I like includes Madonna, Paul Young and Nik Kershaw. I hate Wham! heavy metal and Duran Duran. I'll write to anyone who writes to me (but I would prefer a girl between 12 and 14). Write to William Burton at: Underhill School, Bowden Road, Chanders End, Hampshire BW31 XH8.

* **I am a 15 year old boy who is young free and single and into Paul Young, TFF, Wham! FGTH, Duran, Madonna, Dead Or Alive, Thompson Twins, Kate Bush etc.** Write to me: Faheen, 41 JLN 5582/5C, Ipoh 56300, Perak, W.Malaysia. (Please send a photo.)

* **I am a 16 year old girl looking for pen pals anywhere in the world.** It doesn't matter what age or sex you are but you must like Bucks Fizz. Write to Louise Fairstone, 18 Marton Close, Spinkhill, Rotherham, Yorkshire RS1 4DN.

* **I'm 14 and I like most music (but mostly The Cure, Cult and 60s).** I don't particularly like Duran Duran, Wham!, Frankie or Madonna. If there are any really groovy-looking lads out there in the big wide world please write: Fran Hargarden, 17 Cedars Street, Gisburn, Yorkshire GL11 2HS.

* **I'm an 11 year old** boy and would like to write to someone, male or female, about my age. I am into Frankie, football and computers. If you need to write to someone get scribbling to: Adam, 103 Brantingham Street, Peatesby, Atterton, Leicestershire.

* **We need girls aged 13 to 15!** We are two boys, we're bored stiff and we're into Frankie, Madonna, King and Nik Kershaw. If you're interested, write to: Donald & Richard, 236 Maltden Lane, Claverdon, Staffordshire BY9 3EM.

* **Okay all you sexy, dark-haired, dark-eyed, hunky guys**. Get scribbling to me if you are a Michael Praed or lead singer from A-Ha lookalike (or any old hunk aged between 13 and 18) and you like most music from The Cure to Arcadia but cannot stand Wham! and are a bit stupid (as in a bit mad and zany). Put pen to paper and write to: Delilah Fielding, 22 Albert Drive, Grimsargh, Preston PT4 0GV.

* **Hi world!** Is there any Duran or Dead Or Alive fans out there who like doing weird things and who are 15 plus? Male or female, I don't mind. Drop me a line and enclose a photo if poss: Brian Evans, 38 Minffrwd Lane, Trerhyngyll, Cowbridge, Glamorgan CW2 2PT.

* **Calling all you guys - we are two happy-go-lucky girls aged 14 and 15 who are looking for two good-looking boys aged 14 plus.** Likes include most pop music. Please write to: Roobarb & Custard, 19 Greendale Street, Clifton, Bristol BS93 3DR.

There was: Russ from Woking, Jane from Scunthorpe, Brian from Cowbridge, Faheen from Malaysia, plus many others. Strangers with different musical tastes, yet bound together by an identical hope of connection. Connection not by email, text or tweet, not by DM, GIF or emoji, but the old fashioned way - by letter. With a pen. Pens! Remember them?

Back then, in 1985, you couldn't hide behind an invented email address (im_mad_me@email.com). You couldn't have a social media account with a picture of your daft dog, disguising your true identity. No, back then, you had a name: Oli, for instance or Donald or Monika. Names, sometimes with surnames, but always real… apart from 'Roobarb & Custard' from Bristol - some people are just ahead of their time.

As well as names, their ads all shared something that today is almost obsolete - a complete geographical address. Their house, or in some cases their school, written out in full! So if you wanted to go to Leicestershire to find Adam, you could head straight to Peatesby, find his address (in an A-Z) and throw stones at his window until his Mum called the police (on a landline). I mean Sarah and I wouldn't do that, not with all the crazy people around. And I'm sure you wouldn't either (unless you're one of those crazy people). But the '80s were different, there were no bad people around then at all. Just big hair and pop stars wearing make-up. Not like today, when you have to change your password every thirty-eight seconds to something you can't remember for fear someone will steal your identity, your life or, God forbid, your collection of old music mags in the garage.

The world is not what it was.

Sarah and I are not what we were either. Since 1985 we've aged quite a lot, grown a fair bit too, finished our education, left home, met each other and arrived here today having forgotten virtually everything that happened along the way of the last three and a half decades. If you're our age, you're probably the same.

One thing we've become though, is fascinated by stories. Sarah writes, sings, acts, teaches, makes, directs, dramaturges, tours and is basically a force of nature. I write. And I make coffee. And I buy biscuits. And I eat them.

Anyway, much of our time is spent throwing ideas around and around and around, then tinkering with them, then sometimes sending those ideas out into the world. Sometimes the ideas are not so much worked on as 'stared out the window at' until it's time for lunch or dinner or bed. By me, I hasten to add. When Sarah's out taking a bow - I'm more likely to be taking a break.

I think it's safe to say the last nine months have been pretty hard. We've all been trying to keep one step ahead of Covid, staying home, socially distancing with the cleanest hands the world has ever known. This has also meant Sarah and I have spent more time than ever talking to each other, around each other, at each other, over each other - often till our ears bled or one of us was near to tears begging the other to shush for a minute. It's just cabin fever brought on by a plague.

Thankfully, since the arrival of these historic magazine invites to communicate, the questions we've been throwing around every day have been sans bleeding ears. For example: did anyone ever respond to these message-in-a-bottle type cries for attention? What happened to these Paul Young and Duran Duran fans seeking similar? And might any of them still be looking for pen pals?

On a normal day in a normal world between normal people you'd imagine these questions would just fade and turn to dust - without the faintest chance of getting answered. However it's anything but normal at the moment. So 1985's plaintive call keeps echoing through our heads: the films, the music and the fact no one thought twice about putting a kid's complete address in a hugely popular music magazine for anyone to see. And those ads don't know it's 2021, they're still there, frozen in time, still hopeful, still keen. Our ears are not deaf to their call. So we've made a decision - we've decided to try and get some answers - by responding to each and every one of them.

So here we are - with a decision and a vague plan.

There's a lot to think about before putting pen to paper - for a start there's 'finding paper' (we'd like bright and fun). And a pen (Sarah prefers a four-colour biro). First decision we made - we've decided we'll both sign off on each letter, as a couple. Paul & Sarah. These days a lone individual, especially a lone male individual reaching out across the years might be seen as odd or creepy.

Hang on, is it still creepy, even if we both do it? Strangers writing to strangers. Adults writing to teenagers, who aren't teenagers anymore. Is that creepy? I'm not sure. Is 'creepy' in the eye of the beholder? I'm even more not sure. I don't like being not sure. I ask Sarah...

Me: *Sarah, is it a bit creepy, what we're planning to do?*
Sarah isn't sure either.

I like it even less when Sarah's not sure.

We go for a walk in the crisp New Year chill. Ah, the families, the fresh air, the large groups who have entirely missed the social distancing memo. It's good to be out. The moment we're sure no one is close enough to eavesdrop, we discuss the 'creepy' conundrum. It doesn't take long, we quickly decide, without a shadow of doubt - hell, NO! It isn't creepy.

Me: *It's fun! Hell, yes! And if anyone finds it creepy, well they're creepy. Fact. So there, Creepy McCreepy.*

Sarah's looking at me sideways. She isn't immediately sure if my 'creepy' logic stands up, so we move on. Anyway, she says, maybe we won't hear back from a single soul, so it won't matter.

Eh?

But she's right, what if we don't hear back from anyone? A silence passes between us. Are we wasting our time, is the project over before it's begun?

Someone needs to be in charge of problem solving.
I nominate Sarah. I second Sarah. Sarah is duly elected.
Over to Sarah, Head of Problem Solving…

After fewer than six or seven steps Sarah gives birth to another excellent idea: to solve the problem of no replies we'll include a stamped-addressed envelope in each of the initial letters. This is no guarantee, but surely it increases the probability of a response?
Excellent idea.

Then, as if I'm standing exactly where troublesome idea lightning strikes, another troublesome thought: what if the person no longer lives at their Smash Hits address? No number of SAEs are going to solve that problem.

Me: *Sarah? What if they don't live there anymore?*
Sarah doesn't so much as break stride.
Sarah: *We put a 'please return to sender' message on the back.*

Of course! She's two for two. Quite brilliant. This is precisely why I elected her. But she's not finished.

Sarah: *In fact, let's say 'if not contactable at this address, please return to sender', to throw down the detective gauntlet.*

Then a thunderstorm of troublesome thoughts: what if *none* of them still live at their childhood address? Not one? At best we'll get twenty returned letters on our doormat by the end of January?

Oh.

I put this to Sarah, it is her job after all. She agrees that although it's slightly negative, it's still a good point. And it is - my teenage home has been bought and sold several times in the last 20 years. But, she reminds me, her Mum still lives at hers.

So, that would seem to give us a 50/50 chance of a letter finding someone who at least still knows the whereabouts of the intended RSVPer? I'm not a professor of mathematics or anything but even I can see we may need to conduct this scientific research on a bigger pool of people before making assumptions?

I scoff like a professor of mathematics might when a suggestion is too stupid for his enormous brain. Sarah asks me why I'm making such an unpleasant sound. People are staring. I stop scoffing. People continue to stare. I look at the floor. We walk on.

For the next few minutes we go through people we know and whether they could still be found via their address from 35 years ago. We reckon there's a better than average chance. Excellent. Better than average will do for me.

More lightening... but even if they can be found and even if our letters don't go astray, might they not think it weird and creepy to be contacted out of the blue by complete strangers - by post? (Who does that?)

Oh.

As we stroll, we make up the potential letter and try it out on each other, to see what we'd think if it dropped onto our mat. To see if it feels weird or creepy. Or both. And we agree there are two possible truths at work here - either we are both weird *and* creepy or it's a great idea. We'd love it if someone did the same for us - and we'd reply, without hesitation! So long as everyone is of exactly the same mindset as us, we'll be fine.

Lightening. Whoa there, hang on just one second. We know we're not weird or creepy, but what about them? Even after we've written to them, they'll still be strangers to us, and after 35 years they could be literally anyone. Liking Five Star in the '80s does not guarantee you've not evolved into a sociopath today!

So how do we feel about giving our address to these potential murderers or members of parliament or whoever? I mean, we know who we are, but who's vouching for them? Who knows what doors to terror and crazy we might be opening? Gah! It's an impasse. Sarah's newly elected position looks suddenly suspect as her face registers nothing but furrows.

Getting a post office box to hide behind simply wouldn't be playing fair, so we can't do that. And anything other than honest, hand-written letters, posted with a stamp seems to taint the purity of the idea. Yes, purity, it's a pure idea. Like a religion, sort of.

We're tense, the park seems colder. Nearby dogs are sniffing the air, what are they smelling? It might be our fear. This must be exactly how Neil Armstrong felt just before he stepped out of the big tin box that got him to the moon - on the verge of something brilliant, but what if the moon wasn't as he expected? What if the suit didn't work? What if gravity was a myth? What if huge invisible monsters were waiting on the other side of the door? Identical to how we're feeling right now.

But you know what, if an 11 year old Frankie Goes To Hollywood fan wasn't scared to put his address out into the world for all to see back in 1985 - then neither should we be today.

And, frankly, all these people are now middle aged and have probably worked through most of their crazy by now. And if not, and things go sour, we'll shove Buzz Aldrin out in front of us and move house. Excellent idea! Walk over, job done.

Back home, kettle on, we share a Mars Duo (another Christmas present from Sarah's brother, he sent 40 in a huge box - some small, some big, some 'proper' presents and other, sillier, childhood related stuff) and we begin to write. Sarah, over there, crafting the essential content of a letter that needs to hit all the right notes, to get strangers to write to strangers. And me, over here, waffling any old nonsense.

A match made in heaven. Well, South London.

Saturday 2nd January 2021

Where the hell is the year going?

Never fear, as this post-Brexit, stay-home world is doing its thing, ticking along, so too, are we.

We photocopy the RSVP page 20 times, highlighting the specific ad for each person, just in case they don't remember ever writing it. (As if such a momentous moment could be forgotten?)

Then on to the letters themselves…

Today we'll also write 20 letters in reply to the 20 ads. 20 addresses but actually 24 people because a few ads were posted by friends, two people, not one: Sally & Emma; Donald & Richard; Matt & Dave; Roobarb & Custard.

Those last two might prove problematic. Makes you think though, were those cartoon characters lifelong nicknames or simply fleeting silliness? (Maybe a cynical pink cat really did have an overly enthusiastic green dog as a friend? They might have done.) Do the adults those kids turned into still go by those names today?

Or, wait a minute, maybe it's actually Roobarb and his nemesis! Surely stranger things have happened than two animated characters looking for friends with similar tastes in music?

Oh. Sarah says they haven't.

Sally and Emma might be tricky too - their address is a convent school. There's a pretty high probability they don't live there any more, unless they became teachers? Or nuns? But if they've moved on, and the nuns at the convent school get our letter, are they likely to open it if it's not addressed to them? 'Nosey Nuns' isn't a well-known phrase around convent towns as far as we're aware. We shall see.

You may remember, as it was only yesterday, that originally the plan was to write the letters by hand, to be more authentic? However, we've realised it would take almost until the end of time to do that. And who writes by hand these days anyway? And why does it hurt so much to pen more than 26 words in a row? That's not how it used to be.

So, instead I type almost 500 words. (See? To write it 20 times would have been more words than I produced for my, mostly-copied-out-of-textbooks, university dissertations.)

So, I type almost 500 words…

Actually that's not quite accurate. Sarah wrote a brilliant first draft last night, in about half an hour. Starting after breakfast I've already spent the best part of six hours tinkering with it, changing it, then changing it back, then personalising it for each of our recipients.

Six hours!

Me: *Sarah, what's the definition of 'anally retentive'?*
Sarah: *A perfectionist.*

She's being kind. We both know she's just being kind.

This here, is one of our letters.

2nd January 2021

Dear Oli,

Happy New Year!

About 35 years ago (in 1985) you sent an RSVP into Smash Hits. I've enclosed a photocopy of your ad, just in case you've absolutely no recollection of doing so.

You might be asking, 'so what?' Or 'why?' Both very good questions...

To explain - entirely randomly, at Christmas, a vintage copy of that specific Smash Hits was gifted to us as a nostalgic reminder of our long-gone teenage years: AHA, Nik Kershaw, Marillion, Paul Young and even Cliff Richard, and WAY more adverts than we ever remembered.

Reading through the pen pal section, all those young people looking for connections (including you!), we couldn't help wondering what might have happened. Did any of you actually hear back from anyone? Maybe you made friends? Maybe you're still in touch? Or maybe the whole thing was a disaster or a complete waste of time? And post 1985, where did you end up? That kind of thing. Twenty pen pal posts, twenty potential stories.

And, although it's ages since you wrote it, are you, by any chance, still looking for a 'pen friend' and who knows, maybe you're still a fan of 'soul, Five Star and Sister Sledge'?

Strange as it may seem, we'd love to know!

Now, before you edge closer to your recycling bin, let us introduce ourselves (like people used to, 35 years ago). We're Sarah and Paul. We're both writers. Based in London.

And OK, you may be thinking that we need to get out a bit more, and we probably do, but that's not happing, for any of us at the moment so here we are - contacting all 20 of those Smash Hits RSVPers - just to see what happens, to see what we might find.

By way of full disclosure (and historical social data sharing) back in 1985 we were 10 (Sarah) and 17 (Paul). And although we didn't meet till 2017 we found we both had roots in the same 1980s culture: The Cure, The Smiths, The Breakfast Club, Blackadder, The Young Ones to name a few.

Obviously, after 35 years we've both changed a bit, there's a pretty good chance you have too.

You're probably very busy, so thank you for reading this far, but after a year when people have been more separated than ever, we're interested to discover whether people still find pleasure in letter writing and communicating with strangers - simply because they say 'hello'.

We would love to hear from you, not only about your experience from posting an ad in Smash Hits, but well, anything you like. The door is open and in hopeful anticipation of your reply, we've even included an SAE.

We look forward to hearing from you.

Kind regards

Paul & Sarah

It's Oli's letter, we put his name at the top and everything, so he'd know it was especially for him…

I think that was my idea..?

Halfway through the process we re-listen to the Christmas Day messages we exchanged with Sarah's brother, Steve: he who brought that specific copy of Smash Hits into our lives. Listening to all our excited voices we are hearing the kernel of the idea being born. Its conception, if you like. If this were a documentary, I'd insist the recording be inserted here, for all to hear. But it went on for ages and ages and feels like an awful lot of extra work, so here's the one particular phrase of Steve's that sticks in our heads...

> **Steve**: If you don't make the Smash Hits pen pals 'show', someone else will!

And he may have a point. I mean, I'm not suggesting that on day two of the project we branch out into affiliate programmes and franchises or anything, but if I tell you Sarah is an Olivier Award-winning improviser, has done 17 Edinburgh Fringes in the last 25 years, including 12 self-written shows, there's a chance this, whatever it is, whatever it turns into, could be treading boards near you sometime in the future. Don't panic, we'll reserve you seats.

But I digress. When contacting these strangers we've tried very hard to adopt a wonderfully warm and cosy and gorgeously harmless lilt to our words. Not that we don't have that already, we do. But they don't know that. For all they know we kick kittens on the weekend. Which we don't. Not ever. But if we ever did, it would be entirely by accident and we'd be very upset. We'd give them treats. And catnip. Guilt catnip. Even so, when writing the letters it feels like we're walking a wavy line, trying to sound more Wallace and Gromit than Weirdo and Goebbels.

The process of writing all the letters takes ages, which might not matter so much if we didn't have other things to do too. Sarah measured our sofa and listed it for sale, and I put River Phoenix in an envelope. We're moving soon, and selling stuff. River's gone to a better home.

While I'm tippy-tapping, Sarah orders nice envelopes, because nowhere in the high street proved helpful. We stuck to our plan and included stamped SAEs to strong-arm people into replying. Then Sarah points out four of the letters are going abroad. Two to Sweden, one to Germany and another to Malaysia. A UK stamp won't work when posting from abroad. Oh well, not sure there's time to bring about a universally approved method of stamp-sharing for the whole world, so an un-stamped envelope will have to do.

Naturally all this faffing makes us notice we've missed the last Saturday post, and suddenly there's not quite the rush or urgency to get to the post box. So now on Monday, twenty letters will leave us for who knows where? (Well, we know where they're going first - it's written on the front of the envelopes.) It's a little like a pigeon fancier throwing open the door to his loft, watching the feathered ones go, and waiting for their safe return. Although, in our case, there's a better than average chance our pigeons are entirely without a sense of direction. It may be a long wait.

Sunday 3rd January 2021

I did my tax today and discovered I'd made so little money last tax year, I was due a sizeable rebate. All things considered, filling in the self-assessment form online was some of the best paid work I've had in a while.

Sarah nearly sold the sofa.

Maybe life could be more rock 'n' roll than this, but I can't see how…

I made dinner. We both ate dinner. I cleared up after dinner. Sarah wrote some envelopes. I imagine the division of power in our house could be more unfair than this, but I just can't see how…

Monday 4th January 2021

Can't sleep, up stupid early. Combination of things. Moving house, moving on, packing up, changing addresses etc. Changing addresses - so people know where we are. But only the right people. The bank, Amazon, friends and family - but in reality, those last two are only for Christmas cards in 12 months' time. We have no expectation of a letter or an anti-lockdown visit any time soon, more's the pity.

These days we're obsessed with our information getting into the 'wrong' hands. But whose hands are wrong? The people telling us to protect our data, like new parents watching over their first-born, are the very people who harvest our information, aren't they? Modern day child catchers, loading all our details into the back of a van for some unspoken but insidious purpose?

And then we go on social media anyway and voluntarily share every last detail about our real children, their schools, our holidays (so the thieves know when to break in) and even our darkest thoughts (so our friends can say, 'Aw babe,' without even checking what the matter is). A million cries for help on the never-ending noticeboard. 'Like', 'heart', 'sad'. Emoji after emoji and three seconds later we've forgotten about it. It's not really connection is it? It's barely even 'social', but I've got almost a 1000 Facebook friends, so that makes me like, really popular, yeah? I can even remember who a few of them are…

Do you know what's better? Much better? Getting a colourful envelope (we're sending orange, yellow, red, blue and green ones so they can't be missed when they flop down onto excited door mats across the world) in the post from someone you've never heard of, offering themselves as a pen pal. Honest, old-fashioned, uncynical. Absolutely.

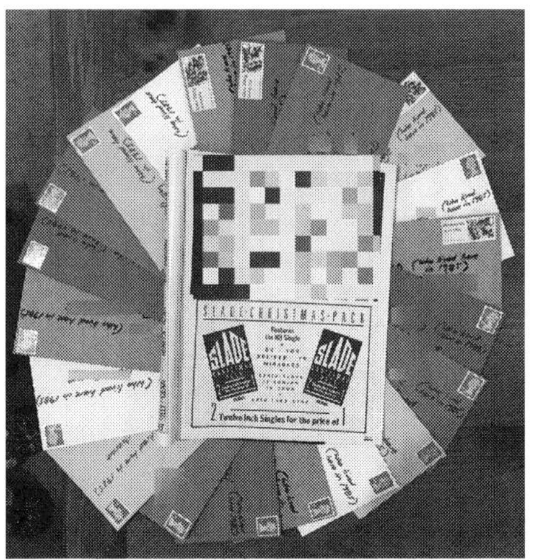

But the world has changed a lot since old-fashioned was 'in'. Sarah and I think long and hard (about three minutes) and decide that although we want these people to share themselves with us, we don't want too much of ourselves shared with them too soon.

So we decide to keep our surnames secret. Mine is quite unusual. (Everyone with it is either a blood relative or married to one - clearly something weird went on with the family name some while ago but no one's sure exactly what. Maybe one day I'll find out the name's history and who burnt down that old Irish church destroying all the records.) If you Google Sarah's name, on the other hand, you'll discover a famous namesake, still very popular but now retired from the Adult Entertainment Industry and you might want to delete your search history if it's a shared computer. Now, although this revelation could increase our chances of a response - it would be for all the wrong reasons.

Hang on, does that mean a surname is more intimate than an address? It feels like a long shot that a person might travel hundreds of miles to an address, where they might find an empty house and a fruitless search, whereas the Internet gives everyone the tools to be a Detective-Stalker...

When I first saw Sarah she was smiling at a dog called Murphy. Of course, at the time I didn't know that was her name, or Murphy's, as Sarah was 'WorkInProgress1975' and I was 'FairlyOddFeatures'.

It should be said it was in a photograph, there was nothing odd going on in the park or anything. It was on the, now defunct, pre-swiping, dating site, Guardian Soulmates. (You needed a credit card to be on there, which gave the assumption the players would think twice before signing up.) GSM was a shop window for people. I usually got home from work quite late, picked up my 'potential relationship' shopping basket, poured a large glass of wine and wandered down the aisles looking for interesting faces. With it being pre-swipe, everyone had to write about themselves. Most people wrote a variation of the following:

Most People: *Gosh...* (everyone was Hugh Grant-esque) *Well, this is weird... my best friend put me up to this, so what do I have to lose? I work hard but love to have fun, whether it's going out or cosying up with a bottle of red at home in front of a good film, with the right person. I love to travel* (go on holiday) *and can't wait to take the next adventure - with the right person. I'm happy alone but have reached a time of life when I think things would be more fun sharing it all with the right person.*

I'm sure all those ladies were absolutely lovely, they just weren't great at writing about themselves. (I have no doubt the guys were just as bad, but their aisles were not the ones I was shopping in. As it were.) But why should anyone be good at it? It's completely unnatural and forced. I mean, when you're on a paid-for dating site, isn't it a given the 'right person' is who you're hoping to find? But it probably didn't matter because that first introductory 'about yourself' paragraph was bait, nothing more. Intentionally popped on the hook of possibility.

I always wrote fairly long, bespoke messages based on whatever a person had written in their profile. Most of my messages were ignored (printed and framed and still hanging on walls somewhere, I'm sure, but ignored). Sarah's profile was unusual. It was funny and honest and brilliant - and she looked amazing smiling at dogs. I wrote, she replied briefly, saying she was 'caffeinating friends' but would be back in touch soon. And she was.

Over the next three days we sent literally hundreds and hundreds and hundreds of WhatsApp messages and photos and stuff. By the time we met, we were both ready to fall in love - there was just the 'chemistry' test to pass. We met, we passed, we've been together ever since. Three and a half years. I've just checked and on WhatsApp we've shared 8043 'media, links and docs', basically photos. Of everything and anything. 8043?! That's roughly 193.8 photos a month. Wait, so that's an average of more than six a day! Every single day. If I weren't already sitting down, I think I'd need a chair…

8043 - which, considering we've lived together for more than two years and for the last nine months have barely been apart because of the coronavirus, that's scary. But not half as scary as how many actual messages we've sent… Tens. Of. Thousands.

But that goes to show what we hoist up our flagpole as the most important ingredient of our relationship - communication. We used messaging as a way to chit-chat through our days before we actually lived under the same roof, sharing the similarly light-hearted, incessant chatter, that we now share in actual spoken-out-loud words.

I guess the above, rather extended, aside throws some light on why we've undertaken this RSVP Challenge - people can be fascinating - but you'll only know if you reach out and say hello.

So, today we start the process of saying 'hello' to 24 people at 20 long ago addresses. Makes you wonder who they might be now?

Like with internet dating, can assumptions be made on very little information? Of course they can, we can assume anything about anything.

Based on nothing other than their brief pen pal ad, this is who Sarah and I expect to find at the other end of this search, and how likely we think they are to reply - in a four division index thing. Like the four football leagues. But completely different.

DIVISION 1 (no Premiere League here, this is old school).
Easy-peasy finds.

Oli:
Sarah: Mum still lives in Mottingham and Oli goes back every Christmas, still loves Five Star. Has married his childhood sweetheart.
Paul: Particular, precise, definite. Runs his own business or works in a lab. Helped create the Oxford vaccine. Married with kids.

Becki:
Sarah: Tattooist or civil servant. Still loves chocolate.
Paul: Social services or a 'helping/supportive' occupation. Drinks pints. Has tattoos. Is afraid of heights.

Johnny:
Sarah: Easiest person to find and thrilled to play along. Crazy hair.
Paul: Publican. Loves his job. Has an earring. Refs Sunday league football.

Faheen:
Sarah: Multilingual. Fervent RSVPer. Still in touch with pen pals and keen to help us. Came to London to see Kate Bush in 2014.
Paul: Businessman. Lives in UK. Works in tech. Has a collection of Smash Hits magazines in pristine condition.

Delilah:
Sarah: Stayed local. Big deal with Preston am-dram. Plays lottery with the same numbers every week and loves a scratch-card. She wins more often than probability should allow.
Paul: Still lives in Preston. Landscape gardener. She once ran as a candidate for the Green Party.

DIVISION 2.
Confident we'll find them, but the workload might be a smidge heavier.

Jane:
Sarah: Emotionally intelligent. Works in local politics. Huge Bake Off fan.
Paul: A writer. Currently a happily single Mum. Can't bear the colour grey or horse racing.

Nayumi:
Sarah: Music journalist living in New York. Achingly cool.
Paul: Computers/creative design. Knows how to make more than a dozen cocktails from scratch.

Matt & Dave:
Sarah: Friendship broke up because Matt kept all the best letters for himself.
Paul: Both farmers or work outside. Still go drinking together. Their ambition at 18 was to double-date twins. They failed.

Adam:
Sarah: Owns a start-up company but has lots of connections in publishing, thinks we should turn this into a book.
Paul: Store manager. Excellent at his job, high flier. Always organises the Christmas party at work. Has never photocopied his own bum.

Brian:
Sarah: Still does weird things. In a shed. Inventor. 6 kids. Big jumper. Round glasses, even rounder face.
Paul: Works in education. Lives alone. Keeps fish. Says 'I'm mad me'.

DIVISION 3.
We'll need a bit of luck, a following wind, crossed fingers and, maybe, prayer.

Lars:
Sarah: Still lives at this address. He replied to Nayumi's ad, but she never wrote back.
Paul: Happily attached. Works in a hotel. Favourite film is The Shining. Knows the difference between tangerines, clementines and satsumas on sight.

Monika:
Sarah: Brexit negotiator or a primary school teacher.
Paul: Is either a fashion designer or works for Google. Way too busy to be married. No kids, never wanted them, her nieces and nephews are more than enough. Keeps a meticulous diary.

Louise:
Sarah: Works with Medicines San Frontiers in Africa.
Paul: Works as a therapist. Confident, quiet, happy. Was Head Girl at school. Still has the badge.

William:
Sarah: Rediscovered Wham! after hearing Frank Turner's 'Last Christmas'. He is content.
Paul: Head teacher. Married. Owns two dogs called George and Ridgeley. Never wears t-shirts.

Roobarb & Custard:
Sarah: Lost contact after thwarted love triangle. Reunited when we get in touch to find they led identical parallel lives.
Paul: Both work in personal care. Both love karaoke because they both have great voices. Once entered Britain's Got Talent as a duo. Simon Cowell wasn't impressed.

DIVISION 4.
Possibly punching above our weight with this lot.

Andy:
Sarah: Lives abroad with his internet bride. Sensitive.
Paul: A performer/creative. Divorced with kids. Bald.

Russell:
Sarah: Having a wonderful friend called Russell makes negative thoughts almost impossible. Even so… he's a player. Very rich with ties to a protection racket. No baby photos exist of him.
Paul: Works in an office. Lives unmarried with a partner who wishes he were just a little bit taller.

Sally & Emma:
Sarah: One works at the convent. Still in touch. Godmothers to each other's kids.
Paul: Still friends, but only on Facebook. Both teachers. One modern languages, the other English.

Fran:
Sarah: Mystery person. We never find them despite Google-friendly name.
Paul: Sings in a band with her partner. Mostly covers from the '80s.

Donald & Richard:
Sarah: Both in prison (they work there - probably).
Paul: Have no recollection of writing to SH. No longer in touch. One of them dated the other's sister. Competitive.

(Although based on unbelievably extensive scientific research, the above assumptions have been judged to have a margin of error of roughly plus or minus 100%.)

Who knows who we'll find, who'll reply or what they'll say? But the envelopes are on their way…

We shall see…

Tuesday 5th January 2021

If, like me, you're wondering where the year's going, well I'll tell you - right back into lockdown. Boris sat, hands clenched (so we knew he was serious) and told us that although yesterday it had been safe to be in Tier 4, and send all the kids back to school, today it isn't!

And what's the one thing making today different from yesterday? Sarah and I have posted twenty letters to strangers. It has to be that. What else could it be? Boris didn't mention it, but it's clear to me it can't really be anything else. Wow, the power of a letter! Or twenty.

Of course, it now means that if any of those people still live at those addresses, or if anyone who even still knows them lives there, then there's a chance they'll be home! National lockdowns because of global pandemics should never be seen as a good thing, but we're taking any silver linings we can find. And if they're home more, they might have more time on their hands, which means they might sit at home wondering what to fill the extra hours with, and their eyes might once more fall upon the colourful envelope that dropped through their door. And they might ignite into action!

Well, they might. We'll have to wait and see about that too.

Did you know there's such a thing as a Dead Letter Office? A place where undeliverable letters go? A quick search reveals about 10 billion letters are posted in the UK each year. Of those, about 14 million end up at the Dead Letter Office. Mostly because we (and by 'we' I mean 'you') addressed them incorrectly. And because we (ditto, see above) didn't put return addresses on. We (and here I mean Sarah and me) were guilty of neither of these heinous crimes. We copied the addresses carefully from Smash Hits, we checked them and checked them again, so one way or another we should be hearing back from them all.

Unless they're ignored. That's the ultimate insult. A letter for a Dead Or Alive fan simply left 'on the side' because the addressee is not known at the address. That's mean and I'm not going to entertain such unpleasantness.

A second unpleasantness, so far unmentioned, is that half a million letters are 'lost' every year. 500,000, give or take. That's a lot of paper to slip down the back of somewhere. That won't happen to our hardy and determined envelopes of fun! Unless it does. In which case we'll never know. And what you don't know, can't hurt you, can it? Unless it's a piano, falling out an upstairs window as you wander in the street below. But I'm wandering off topic.

Sarah and I are the sort of people who, upon receiving one of our envelopes, would immediately get on board with the possibilities and the adventures suggested by its arrival. A letter, addressed to someone who lived at our house 35 years ago! We'd get very excited about what it might contain.

But would we return it to sender? Or would we open it? A modern dilemma. The 'right' thing to do is obvious, but what of the adventure? Would we open it? Would other people open it? Would you open it? We ask Facebook:

Hypothetical dilemma/social experiment:

A brightly coloured hand-written envelope is delivered by post through your door addressed to someone you don't know. It states next to their name that they lived there in 1985. On the back is written: 'If not contactable please return to sender' plus an address, but no name.

What do you do? Be honest. There are no wrong answers. With thanks from Sarah-Louise Young and me.

Facebook is split.

Well, on my page they're split - half want to open it, half want to return it. (Note to self: percentage of dodgy people on my FB is much higher than I expected. Cull required soon.)

Sarah's friends are clearly a better class of person. Only two suggest opening it. (Maybe I should add them as friends of my own? Then cull them.) Five times as many want the right thing doing.

But what's even more interesting is about a third of her friends (creative types, as opposed to the criminal element of my friends) suggest adventure!

My two favourites are:

Sarah's Friend (going to heaven): Become a sudden Private Investigator, track the person down, documenting all the dead-ends, adventures and pitfalls along the way, then triumphantly befriend the recipient, reunite them with the sender, watch them rekindle a long-lost flame, agree to officiate their wedding and THEN write an award-winning musical about the whole experience. Turn it into a film. Star in the film as whichever character you prefer. I might have got carried away... But what else are you doing this year? xx

My Friend (going to hell): Want to open it. Leave it on the side. Look at it every time I pass by. Know it's best to return it. Avoid taking it to the postbox. Open it. Feel bad.

I have to hope that the envelopes, if not delivered to the intended recipients, or someone who knows them, fall into the hands of people cut from Sarah's friends' cloth. It may take this project down roads we have yet to anticipate.

Sarah's brother Steve, whose fault this all is, and ever the optimist, sent us the following:

Steve: If any of the girls from Smash Hits, now women of course, are still bored and looking for someone who shares their taste in music, then:

My name's Steve. I like The Smiths, I am prepared to go along with liking A-Ha, and I can definitely take a firm 'I hate Wham!' stance, if that helps. My interests include learning song lyrics, big hair and existentialism.

Any correspondence will be passed on to Steve, naturally.

35 years is a very long time, ask anyone who's 34. It's sobering to think that everyone we've contacted is now middle aged, their Smash Hits reading self, long-gone.

Thursday 7th January 2021

I was up in the night, popping down the hall to the loo (too much information?) Sarah was fast asleep in bed (enough information). And there, sitting on a little step, facing away from me was a woman, bent forward as though tying a shoelace (not enough information).

Except it wasn't a woman. It was, and this is, to my recollection, the first time I have made this mistake, a large Sainsbury's bag. Not a plastic one, a more serious one than that - it can stand open and upright all by itself. Cocky, you know the sort. And it can look like a shoe-tying woman in the darkness of a hallway. Yeah, you know.

But, importantly, it wasn't usually there. The reason it was there was because yesterday a complete stranger came to the flat to collect 'five bags of books' as advertised on Facebook marketplace. (You may remember we're moving soon, and all the charity shops are closed, so giving away is all we've got.) Half the books were mine and a very long time ago I'd stuck address labels in them - maybe in case they got lost so they could show the label to a policeman or taxi driver and be pointed in the direction of home? Actually, I think the address labels were a gift and I realised I'd be dead before I wrote that many letters, so put them to use as book homing devices. But, and this is the point - I had a moment of concern about giving these books away with those labels still in them.

Full disclosure requires I reveal the address is my old family home that I left about 30 years ago, and my parents sold 20 years ago. It's changed hands at least twice since then. No one living there will know me or the family - but still it seemed wrong to put my name and old address into the hands of strangers.

I explained this to Sarah as she transferred my books from bags that look like women, into bags that look like bags. I probably should have been helping, but I was deep in existential crisis about my identity, and what with my back, it was probably better for me just to provide emotional support rather than, well, actual help. I asked her if she thought I should Sharpie out all the addresses.

Sarah: *No.*

I almost voiced that I wasn't sure she needed to sound quite so abrupt, actually, but decided against it. And that was that.

More important is that our letters will have arrived today! Or at least they should have. The UK ones anyway. All those sticky fingers - not sure why they're sticky - opening the envelopes with interest. Hang on, no, that's not going to happen. The chances of any single letter arriving with the Smash Hits teen it's intended for are close to nil. Maybe someone who's moved back in with an elderly parent, or maybe someone who's taken over the family home after the death of a parent, maybe?

I'm going to start that thought again…

More important is that our letters will have arrived today! Or at least they should have. The UK ones anyway. All those sticky eyes - not sure why they're sticky - glancing at the name of someone who doesn't live there, and putting it to one side to deal with later, or possibly forget about, whichever comes first…

Damn.

Remember how a few of the addresses were schools? Well my primary school in Manchester, English Martyrs RC Primary, no longer exists. It's now houses. My secondary school, St Thomas Aquinas, was split over two sites. The lower school no longer exists. It's now houses. The upper school is now called something else. My confidence of the school letters at least opening interesting doors, is suddenly waning.

I'm going to check if those schools still exist… first Sally and Emma's school…

Damn. It operated as a hotel in the 1920s before being sold to a religious order who converted the house into a convent and school called the St. Bedes Convent School. The school closed ages ago and after ten years or so it was demolished and redeveloped into housing.

I can't tell you how depressing that discovery is. Sally and Emma went to that school 35 years ago and now it's houses. Who knew I'd have so much in common with them?
This cannot be a moment for disappointment. It's a moment for discovery and search and internet detecting! So…

The holy order still exists. They have two other schools here in London. It's not a solution, but it is a lead. And there's still a church dedicated to them. I'm not sure how many of the parishioners remain Dead Or Alive fans, it might be a difficult question to ask. Obviously they'll all hate Wham! I mean, doesn't everyone? No, you're right, I rather liked them way back when.

So, Matt & Dave's school, here's hoping for better luck and fewer new build houses…

Damn. Also closed. What's happened to education in this country!? Apparently it was quite an exclusive school, favoured by diplomats and armed services personnel. Now we're talking! Matt & Dave might be semi-famous! War heroes! Tory MPs?

A quick search for an elite school, and there's a Facebook chap called Matt, the right age with a friend called Dave! Could that be him? Oh the urge is too great, I have Matt's full name, I'm going in search of him…

If you remember my dilemma about leaving my old, long gone address in books about to be given away, you can imagine I would feel a certain amount of wariness at going in search of Matt & Dave? Well I did, for about three seconds. The next 20 minutes after the three tricky seconds were much more fun.

The school may be gone but only a few minutes later I've found one of those really long whole-school photos. You know the sort - where legend has it, certain scabby-kneed oiks would stand on the extreme left, then duck down and appear on the far right of the photo too?

Three things to say about that - first, there were no oiks at Matt & Dave's school; second, the photographer may have used a wide lens on his camera (I shall leave it to you to seek out the photographic reality of school photos in the '80s) and third, there on the right of the second row and the left of the third row, no doubt kept apart to stop them attacking 'trendies', are Matt and Dave! Actual RSVPeople. Their teenage faces staring out for all the world to see! They both look extraordinarily rough and ready and not at all like Queen fans. However, once a Springsteen fan, always a Springsteen fan, so maybe The Boss still adorns a bit of wall in a garage or Man Cave somewhere?

Trickier to sit with is how easy it was to find first Matt on Facebook, then Dave (his only friend called David - who went to the same school). Matt is LinkedIn savvy. Dave is more elusive. But what this means without any shadow of doubt is that although the school has gone, we can get a letter to these two, one way or another.

Oh, and if you can believe it, at least a couple of Matt's friends are friends with my FB friends!! Not Matt himself, which is a pity. With social media maybe six degrees of Kevin Bacon will become two degrees of Paul Chronnell?

Anyway, onto the next school, a boarding school, where a 13 year old William penned his Smash Hits ad…

William's school still exists - no doubt the local area has enough housing. I should probably leave it there, but the afternoon is on a roll. I find William very easily. (Does that sound creepy? Mm, it sounds a little creepy.) LinkedIn again. Therefore he can still be reached if his old school isn't as brilliantly organised as their website leads me to believe and don't pass our letter on themselves. What I really want to do is see what someone's actual old address looks like - picking one at random…

Oh no.

Becki, she who liked black clothes, may be impossible to find. Her old house came up on an estate agent's website. It's been sold several times in the last 20 years alone, and is now boarded up.

The estate agent has all the usual photos, but in one of them there appears to be a dog by the garden doors. In a boarded up house? A squatter dog? A very lifelike draught excluder? A real dog?

I'm having a very peculiar realisation. No, not a dog living in a boarded up house, but that this is Becki's actual house. Actual rooms where she wandered. She may have eaten an Aero right there in that back garden. She may have been in that lounge when she wrote her ad.

Like one of those haunted house detective programmes, I'm staring at the screen wondering if her spirit might re-enter the frame. Sarah comes in to get a drink and I tell her about my discoveries and she gets very excited before returning to whatever, none-detective work she's doing in the front room. At the door, she turns.

Sarah: *You're looking at photos, not a TV, nothing's going to enter from anywhere, no matter how long you stare.*

Then she's gone, like a burp in the wind. Spoilsport.

All that from a few clicks on the Internet and a bit of luck that Becki's house is up for sale. There are two things we can discover from this new information. First, finding these people might be really rather hard. And second, 'research' and 'innocent stalking', although not next-door neighbours, appear to be worryingly from the same neighbourhood.

It's easy to spiral down the rabbit hole of information the Internet has about us. All of us.

Completely randomly a friend sends me a link (on Signal, he's suspicious of WhatsApp) to a news story telling that WhatsApp is going to make us agree to sharing our phone numbers with Facebook, or they'll stop us using WhatsApp. His message:

'Just saying.'

So in conclusion: if the information is out there, it's out there to be found, right? That's what Google exists for - to find for us the things we're looking to find? LinkedIn and Facebook are all about sharing, right? So even though everything I've been looking at and detecting is information regarding people I only know exist because of something they did 35 years ago, it's not wrong or bad or evil or unforgiveable, right? It can't be. I was just 'surfing the net'.

Anyway, if the great God of ancient pen pals didn't want me on this crusade, they wouldn't be sending shoelace-tying, shopping bag women to my hall in the dead of night, would they?

Just saying.

Saturday 9th January 2021

It's simply impossible for this to be the second week of January. I mean, New Year feels like a month ago. Time makes no sense at all.

It occurs to me that, as information accrues about the 24 pen pals, the reality of making contact is likely to change. So, on this cold, weekend morning, this is the revised league table of contact-likeliness (I may be able to come up with a title a little more slip-off-the-tonguey, rather than fall-face-first-down-concrete-stepsy). The number in brackets is where they placed previously in the four division malarky, which we ditched because this is much more scientifically accurate. Entirely based on data. And stuff.

1. Matt & Dave - practically family! (2)
2. William - old school still exists when almost all other '80s schools are now housing estates. That must increase our chances? (3)
3. Johnny - Cheshire. Say no more. Confident. (1)
4. Delilah - Preston. A Northerner, a surname, a surety! (1)
5. Russ - Knaphill. No one leaves Knaphill. Very confident. Plus we have his surname. (4)
6. Louise - Rotherham/surname/Bucks Fizz, it's a very potent set of clues. (3)

7. Jane - one of my dearest friends is called Jane, must be a good sign? (2)
8. Fran Hargarden - surely an unusual name? Therefore easier? (4)
9. Brian Evans - a Welsh name amongst 450,000 others no doubt, but the Welsh are fabulous! (2)
10. Monika - surname = good. German = she might hate us because of Brexit. Jury's out. (3)
11. Andy - Surrey. No detective skills yet applied. (4)
12. Sally & Emma - at the new housing estate ex-convent. Tricky but there are leads. (4)
13. Oli - no last name (not detected yet). (1)
14. Donald & Richard - a duo, but no surname. Also tricky. (4)
15. Lars - Sweden. Vince Clarke fans leave a trail. Not easy, but possible. (3)
16. Nayumi - with both Swedish and Japanese DNA she might be anywhere! (2)
17. Adam - Leicestershire. Football and computers makes him different from the rest, but finding him..? (2)
18. Faheen - Malaysia is a very long way away… just saying. (1)
19. Roobarb & Custard! - Oh, for goodness sake! (3)
20. Becki - too early to call anything a dead end, but we're not holding our breath. (1)

A LinkedIn stranger literally just now asked to connect, with the words:

LinkedIn Stranger: Hi Paul,
I hope you don't mind me sending you a connection request. I fully understand if you don't connect with people you have never met…

Normally, I'd nose-dive this straight into the bin. But it seems spookily on-topic with The RSVPeople. The stranger's photo makes her look like she's on the way to a summer garden party - as do the photos of most of her same-company colleagues. Must be a marketing ploy? I wonder if middle-aged women are all being contacted at the same time by handsome chaps in athletic vests? It's a cynical thought, but for a pension/finance company I would have expected less skin.

Mm, there's definitely something about first impressions, how we present to others. We all do it. It's why Sarah and I chose coloured envelopes and why we put the photos we did on our dating profiles.

Another thought occurs - LinkedIn lets you know when someone's looked at your profile. (I'm constantly being patronised by them with emails announcing I'm doing 'really well' because 9 people have viewed my profile in the last 17 years - and they'll even share those secrets with me if I pay a monthly fee! Really? Really?! No, just no. Really.) But, proper LinkedIners, like Matt - he now knows I exist. A writer called Paul. If he gets the letter, sees the letter, or hears about the letter, and LinkedIn have patronised him about how well he's doing, he may put two and two together! Exciting times.

But all things LinkedIn evaporate with the sound of post falling through the door. The post's arrived! And take me to the foot of our stairs - we've got THREE replies!!

Count them: one, two and that one!

Well, sort of. Matt, he of Matt & Dave, was a Return To Sender. Not unsurprising really as the letter was sent to a school that doesn't exist anymore. I wonder who sent it back?

So too William. Which was unfriendly. His old school still exists. It's clearly got a bob or two and I bet there was someone there, on a coffee break, probably with a quality hobnob, who could have taken their interest out of Tupperware and piqued it with a fork or something. Then they might have remembered they've got a wonderful Alumni group (probably, I've no idea) where an enquiry could be made. But no, straight back in the post. Rude! However, it does have a typed address label, for which we are grateful.

Then there's Oli. Oli's letter has come back in a new white handwritten envelope. Addressed to 'Oli's Friend'. We've yet to earn the title of 'friend' but we certainly like the sound of it. The reverse of the envelope declares Oli moved in July 1987, aged 17. This however, is not a kindly, hand-written dead end, oh no...

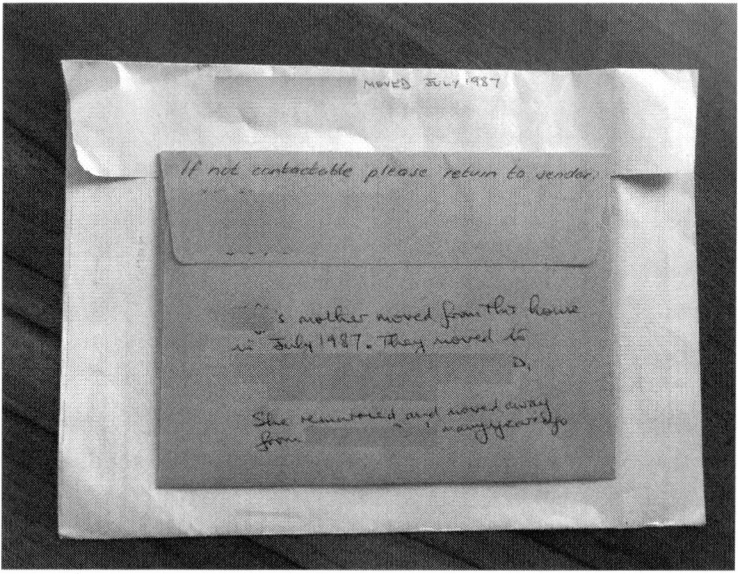

Inside, on the orange paper of our original envelope is a story. The person, who shall forthwith be known as 'Lovely Person', informs us Oli's mother moved from the house in 1987. They also give us Oli's Mum's new address! And then, as an afterthought, in a different pace of writing, there's the fact that Oli's Mum remarried and moved away from this new address 'many years ago'.

Sarah and I grin at each other. Oli had a Mum, who had a forwarding address, then met someone, married them and moved

elsewhere. Who knows, maybe there's a plethora of littler Olis wandering around somewhere, probably all hating Wham!
It's amazing how much information can be gleaned from so little information. I wonder who Lovely Person is? Is it Oli's Dad? Relationship broke up, Mum moved away, but not far, and now they've lost touch? Doesn't ring true. For a start it looks like a woman's handwriting. I have no idea what a woman's handwriting looks like, but Sarah, who is a woman, and infinitely more adept at the recognition of female scribble, seems fairly certain.

Is it Oli's Mum's Mum? Oli's Gran? But if so, why has she lost touch with those two Oli generations? Also doesn't seem likely. Sarah wonders if there's been a family rift. Possible. Families often have rifts. So potentially, Oli's Mum moved down the road with Oli, then there was a rift and she met someone else, maybe someone our Lovely Person didn't like? And they never spoke again? But wouldn't Oli have kept in touch with his Gran? He liked Five Star and Sister Sledge - he had Soul, for heaven's sake, he'd have kept in touch with his Gran, surely?

Unless it's not his Gran. What if the Lovely Person is Dad's current partner? That answers the female handwriting dilemma. But wouldn't she say to Oli's Dad, 'Hey love, shall we forward this to Oli?' And that didn't happen. So maybe Oli's Dad is no longer around in this scenario? Maybe they split up? Maybe he sadly died? That would explain why the Lovely Person still lives there, and why she followed what happened to Oli's Mum until she remarried. No, even that doesn't quite make logical sense. Who would know so much about Oli's Mum's movements but nothing about Oli's? Oh, all this thinking is exhausting!

Saying 'Oli's Mother remarried' is a lot of information to pass on to strangers. Does that smack of a historical sting in the tale? And is 'Mother', rather than 'Mum', a choice to be a little less friendly, or is it just a word that describes the gender of a parent? Of Oli.

And who keeps a forwarding address to a house that the person (Oli's mum) moved away from many years ago? I sometimes have to check on my phone for my own post code! I have an address book I use so infrequently, my thought on opening it is always the same - I wonder if this address is still current..?

Not so the Lovely Person - they got our letter, passed on as much information as would fit on the back of an envelope, and sent it back - in a new envelope with a stamp of their own. The moniker Lovely Person has never, ever been so apt!

But Mrs. Oli's Mum will now be Mrs. Oli's Re-married Mum. That's hard to chase up at the new address that she left 'many years ago'.

No, no, no - wait! We missed it! The best piece of new information is there on the back of the new white envelope. So enormous was our excitement that we missed it. Oli has a surname. Nanson.

Tuesday 12th January 2021

The year! The year! Time! How? How?

The last few days have been busy in a Lockdown-London kind of way. For me that's been: making lists, not completing them, carrying the jobs onto the next day, and the next, and eventually, scrubbing them from the list as though they've been done, and then adding them as a brand new shiny job on a new list a little later.

They say on the day we die, there'll still be a full to-do list we never got round to. Doesn't it make you wonder whether any of the jobs really matter? And with there being so many of them to do all the time, will any of our twenty letter recipients find a sliver of time to reply to us?

Going back to the 'Oli's Friend' letter, even with all the wonderful information about mothers and moving and remarrying, the next step is still unclear. However, finding he is now Oli Nanson, brings another realisation. With the Internet, Google Earth, LinkedIn, Facebook etc. a man like me - Detective Paul Stalker, with way too much time on his hands - could pretty much have a stab at finding anyone, and then walk down their Google Earth driveway and tap on their Google Earth front window without so much as leaving their chair.

Food for thought.

When Sarah and I met, on GSM, she christened me Detective Stalker. Not in a (very) creepy way. I'll explain. Some of her photos were fairly standard ones: smiling, looking at dogs etc. But as Sarah's also a performer, others were just plain weird: being a sperm entering an egg, with a couple of disappointed, slow swimming friends, for example.

But in the middle were a couple of studio photos: Sarah looking rather glamorous and cool for a professional photographer. These photos were watermarked with the photographer's name. To them, it was a copyright protection/advert sort of thing. But to me it was a clue! Don't forget, at this stage her name was a mystery, I only knew her as 'WorkInProgress1975'.

So, I found the photographer's website, scrolled hundreds of photos until I found her photos. Underneath was her full name. Then I checked out her Facebook page and discovered we shared a friend! A very good friend actually, and that friend basically told me I'd be the luckiest man on earth if I started seeing Sarah. And I did and the rest is history…

However, there was a moment when Sarah was a little taken aback that her (very public) information could be discovered and cross-referenced and collated and a romantic Detective Stalker could add one and one together and get pretty much, well, everything.

With the discovery of Oli's surname another dilemma has reared its head. Almost anyone with a surname can be found and if they exist on the Internet they can be contacted on the Internet. And that's at odds with The RSVPeople Project, which is deeply rooted in the pre-Internet world of letters, sharing addresses and using a pen.

So, like Matt (of Matt & Dave) and William, when the initial letter is returned unopened and unread (and without a story about Oli's Mum on the back) Sarah and I have decided we're allowed to use the Internet to find our '80s teenagers, but only to get another possible contact address. Then that address must be written to - with the initial unopened letter, inside a new envelope - so they get the full experience, without explanation. (Come on, keep up…)

Otherwise we'll be in this territory:

Us: *Hello internet stranger!*
Them: *Er, hello internet weirdos.*
Us: *Can we have an address to send something to you?*
Them: *What for? What is it? Who are you?*
Us: *We're really nice and we're not going to tell you. Address please?*
Them: *No.*
Us: *Oh…*

And that would be rubbish.

If we hadn't been so excited at the beginning we might have thought through the rules a little better. But we were, so we didn't. But now we are.

It's now the twelfth day of 2021 and 15% of our letters have returned. Two dead ends. One onward story to explore. Nothing came yesterday. Nothing. Maybe something about council tax to do with our move, but that's not important enough to make it into a story about 1980s pen pals. So I won't mention it.

However, the postman is due again shortly.

Our postman is a nice chap. Ask Sarah. He knows Sarah's name. I suppose that's to be expected when names are on the front of letters and such - you can't help but become familiar with the identities behind the letterboxes on your delivery route. Sarah also knows his name. But he doesn't know mine. He says hello to Sarah in the street. Not me. I know, because I'm with her when he says it. I've experienced it. It's not like he's never seen me. I mean, I open the door, I say thank you for post he hands me. I'm fairly sure I'm not invisible.

I wonder if it's because Sarah's a very attractive woman, and I'm, well, not? Were the shoe on the other foot, I might be the same. However, our postman believes the Covid vaccines contain little processors so Bill Gates can control us all, so maybe him not knowing my name is a blessing in disguise.

It'll be a long time until I get the vaccine, of course, but I wonder, if postie is correct, whether, upon having the vaccine I won't be able to find my printer anymore? I'll go to where it usually is, and it simply won't be findable. Just like it often is to my laptop. Honestly, if Mr. Gates can't get my laptop to find the printer right next to it, I'm not too worried about him being able to control the population via microchips in our blood stream.

I wonder whether our new post person, at our new address, will be barking too?

Whoop whoop! Postie's here - I decide not to hide behind the sofa, so he can't see me, that would be ridiculous - but I do wait in the hallway, out of sight, where the shoe-tying, bag woman was, waiting for the sound of paper to plop on the floor...

Plop!

The RSVPeople Project is probably a long game of waiting and disappointment. Mustn't get hopes up - that plop is more than likely more council tax gubbins. No! It's a white envelope! Addressed to 'Sarah & Paul'. In Sarah's handwriting!

Someone has used our SAE.

SOMEONE HAS REPLIED!!!!!

Sarah and I sit on the couch (not the big one, we sold that last week, but a little sofa bed one) and we grin at each other. A reply.

Sarah: *I hope it's nice.*
Me: *Eh?*
Sarah: *I hope they're not nasty.*

Nasty? I hadn't considered this, that these grown up teenagers might not want to be found, approached, reminded of how much they hated Wham! and loved Paul Young. Then again the best response from a person who wants to remain anonymous, who doesn't want to play, is simply to ignore the letter. A bit like we've been doing with the council tax stuff. It would surely take a very irate annoyance to reply, using our envelope, simply to tell us to bog off. It's like phishing emails that suggest the best thing to do if you don't want to hear from them again is to reply to them (certifying your email address is current and manned) and tell them you don't want to hear from them again (guaranteeing you will be inundated with spam for the next 12 years).

But, we live in a world where everything anyone does invites comment - either by actually commenting on a social media post, or taking to any platform and screaming (often incoherently) about whatever annoys or delights us. So is this envelope in my hands such a 'comment'? Blimey, I wasn't expecting all this to be so stressful. There's only one way to find out.

I'm given the privilege of opening it. I can tell immediately it doesn't contain the words BOG OFF scrawled in dog poo. It contains a handwritten letter.

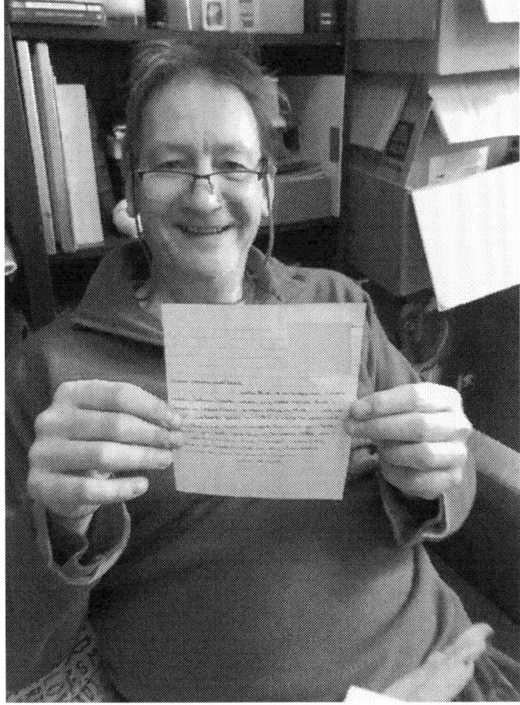

Bingo!

We have a proper reply. From Andy.

Andy? He started as a highly unlikely contact possibility (Division 4) and is currently only at number 11 in the newer table.

Andy? It defies all our logic but here it is. A letter from Andy, not written in dog poo.

Who'd have thought?

(What I particularly like about this photo, is that after editing it using 'auto enhancements' it's made me look remarkably like Brad Pitt! Spooky, huh? Can't see it? Try squinting. And if that doesn't work - I can't help you.)

Andy's letter is on lined notepaper. Black pen, left slanting. The impression is that Andy maybe writes more often than the rest of us. Well, more than me. I often forget how to spell and even form letters with a pen. A piece of paper has no auto-correct.

Andy: Well this is a surprise...

Our grins almost explode at such a jolly opening line!

He tells us his Mum still lives at the old address… and then he carries on writing like an old friend - maybe a new friend?

He hopes we're keeping safe. His musical tastes, not unsurprisingly have changed. He now listens to Capital Gold on his DAB radio.

It's a brief letter, but it's great! He signs off with 'lots of love'. He also mentions…

HE'D LIKE TO KEEP IN TOUCH!!

After some jumping up and down and shrieking, we take a look at what we have:

Andy still lives a six minute drive from his childhood home. His Capital Gold listening, judging by today's playlist, suggests he now likes even older music than when he was 16: Neil Diamond, Chuck Berry, Stevie Wonder and Petula Clark were all playing this morning. Not at the same time - they've not formed a super group. He has a DAB radio. He wanted to tell us that specifically. And good for him. He's a chap who wants his 'Gold' music in beautiful digital quality. Excellent, good man.

Sarah and I set out wondering what we might have in common with our Smash Hits chums. But Andy's made it perfectly clear that we have the pandemic in common. 35 years ago, apart from age and music, our lives were very different. But today, he's living the same cut-off, health-concerned existence we are. Exactly the same as all our RSVPeople. We're connected because, maybe for the only time ever, the whole world is connected. Because of a virus. A microscopic little virus connects us even more than a hatred of Wham! Who knew that's where we'd be all these years later?

Sarah thought Andy might live abroad with an 'off the shelf' bride. How wrong she was. Whether he's a performer, a Dad or bald, remains to be seen. Thanks Andy. Our first reply.

Wednesday 13th January 2021

We're almost halfway through the first month of the year! The Christmas trees are still all strewn around the streets - all the owners got the memo to leave them out for collection, but the same memo hasn't made its way to whoever comes to take them away. It's pine tree carnage.

Except our tree seems to have gone. The only one that's missing from the street. Chances are, a group of South London school kids engaged in some sort of Christmas tree running battle with it, and as ours was small it was used as a melee weapon and is now on another street catching its breath.

But I prefer to think that our tree, Norman (because one should always name a living thing that comes to stay in your house - we have house plants called Tina, Ava and a group called Lady and The Baby Gagas) picked himself up and wandered home, or at least off on an adventure. He wasn't ready to be pulp just yet and it's a good lesson for us all: Be More Norman!

So, as we reach the end of week two of The RSVPeople Adventure, let's take a look at where we're up to with our optimism. A little recap, so we're all on the same page.

1. Andy - he wins! Ready and willing to be our pen pal.
2. Matt (and possibly Dave) - good feelings.
3.Oli - we're already thought of as his friends by a Lovely Person.

4. William - his old school is mean and awful, probably run by hags and monsters.
5. Johnny - still confident, not sure why.
6. Delilah - a Northerner, a surname, a surety! But nothing yet!
7. Russ - I repeat, no one leaves Knaphill. Still Confident. Still have his surname.
8. Louise - she's probably having a Bucks Fizz right now - with excitement.
9. Jane - it's only a matter of time.
10. Fran Hargarden - Fran The Surprised Back Yard? (Ha! Garden? Geddit? No? OK.)
11. Brian Evans - Wales is in full lockdown, maybe he can't get to a postbox?
12. Monika - since Brexit should we have filled out a form before posting?!
13. Lars - may have changed his name to Vince Clarke?
14. Sally & Emma - starting to think this might be a long shot.
15. Donald & Richard - ditto these guys.
16. Nayumi - Sweden? Japan? What were we thinking?
17. Adam - we have a bad feeling already…
18. Faheen - Malaysia is still a very long way away. I checked.
19. Roobarb & Custard - what on earth were they hiding?!
20. Becki - frowning face.

Before starting this project I never had the faintest idea when our postman was due to arrive. At some point letters would appear by the door. But now I know it's often between ten and half past. Which suggests I should start writing earlier in the morning, because he arrived while I was tinkering with the table above. I'd heard a faint plop, but I couldn't go to the door or the table would remain unfinished, and that would be a disaster. So I finished it - lazily just so I could see what had plopped.

Oh, and it was worth it! Two letters!

First Russ. Simple return to sender.

Oh Russ, I expected more from you. Granted, it was a while ago but there was nothing stopping you extending your Royal Mail forwarding service for three and a half decades, was there? Shame on you.

The forwarder looks like they might have stumbled over the 'is it one D or two Ds in ADDRESS?' conundrum but I can forgive that, what with the earth shattering exhilaration of being so close to something so exciting as a 35 year old pen pal letter. Exhilarating excitement, indeed, but sadly, you the kind Return To Sender-er, have not been asked to play. I guess that would effect (or is it affect?) my spelling confidence too!

They also drew a box around 'NO LONGER AT ADDRESS' which just goes to show their disappointment. Oh Russ, you were at number seven, but I think you've sunk a good half dozen places now. All because of a person you don't know. Life is so unfair.

Wherever that puts Russ, it's most certainly below Fran Hargarden.

Why Fran? Because Fran's letter, also an RTS, arrived with more than just a box around a message, it arrived with a note!

Not from an actual person, but literally signed from Good Luck herself. (Apologies for the assumed personal pronoun, luck is probably gender fluid, but I don't want to overcomplicate things. No, wait, what am I talking about - Lady Luck! Everyone stand down, I'm good with 'herself'.)

Lady Luck is sorry to be the bearer of bad news but that scamp Fran Hargarden has moved away.

No great surprise there. But you know Lady Luck, she's not lazy like those evil monsters at William's old school, oh no. Lady Luck only went and checked the deeds of the house!

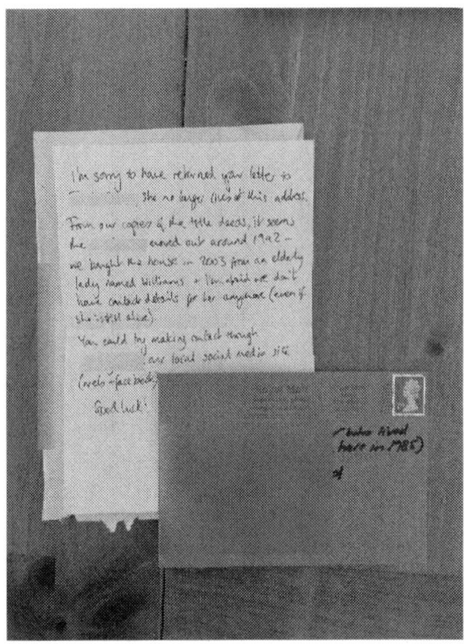

I'm sorry to have returned your letter to
She no longer lives at this address.
From our copies of the title deeds, it seems
the moved out around 1992 -
we bought the house in 2003 from an elderly
lady named Williams & I'm afraid we don't
have contact details for her anymore (even if
she's still alive).
You could try making contact through
our local social media site
(Facebook).
Good luck!

Yep, she dug around, probably in the loft, blew off dust, coughed and reported that 1992 was when Fran's family wandered off in search of pastures new.

A lady called Evans bought the house after that - there's a tiny chance this lady was Brian Evans' Gran, but let's not put money on that. (Or even think about it again.) Lady Luck doesn't know if Grandma Evans is still alive.

At this point Lady Luck realises she has more to be getting on with than scribbling to strangers about ancient history (that's our job!) She probably has horseshoes to polish and four leaf clovers to plant. But she has a thought - Lady Luck knows of a local online group, who we might contact for thoughts and details of Fran's onward journey, or even Grandma Evans'? However, if the older lady has in fact passed on and we're able to get details of that 'onward journey', we'll have an absolute bestseller on our hands that will change the face of humanity forever!

Fran, this particular end may be dead but like many dead ends, there's a path at the end for pedestrians that could lead to further adventures. Path, here we come.

Thursday 14th January 2021

It's my firm belief that all dead ends would rather be new beginnings. Their 'dead end' status makes them unhappy. So let's see if we can't bring a little joy back into the world. Matt, William and Russ all sound like people who deserve joy and happiness more than returned envelopes and tears. So with nothing but the powers of Google, Facebook, Twitter, LinkedIn and my stubborn belief I can find these lovely people, I set to work.

Matt.
Wow. We had his full name and his school. LinkedIn popped right up with a suggestion of a Matt, right name, right school, right age bracket. Must be him. Hello Matt!

I call Sarah and she leans over my shoulder to look. You can always rely on Sarah for wisdom, for insight, for nuance and I await her words with bated breath.

Sarah: *Oooh look, he's all grown up!*
I wait. Nope, that's it, Sarah's finished. Disappointing.

But, although her comments lack her usual pzazz, she's right. He is all grown up. His 35 years look kinder on him than mine feel on me. He doesn't look like a man with a bad back. He's also got a proper job and a proper job title. And you know what proper jobs have?

Me: *Sarah, you know what proper jobs have..?*
She shakes her head. This isn't like her, maybe I need to take her temperature and heat some chicken soup?
Me: *Proper jobs have proper addresses!*
Click, click, click. There it is - Matt's work address. Derby. Easy as that.

William.
Posh school, *Bam*! LinkedIn again. If I paid for it, it would be worth the money already. And talking of money, William's in money - the monsters from his school probably sensed he was way too busy for frivolity, so returned his letter rather than forwarding it on? They no doubt knew his sights were set on more important things (if there *are* more important things than Nik Kershaw, Madonna et al).

Frivolity, yes, but also what I'm sure he needs. LinkedIn reports his firm/business has been rebranded/bought, which is interesting, but we wanted to find him, not write his business biog. I get the feeling William isn't a man who's had time to listen to Paul Young's Wherever I Lay My Hat for a very long time. Interestingly, he isn't listed on the company website. Mm. So although he's part of the organisation, I don't know which bit. Right, in that case, his letter is going straight to head office here in London (looks really posh). The company seem to be worth more than a bob or two, but I'm certain our letter arriving will triple their share price.

Russ.

From Knaphill. Chaps called Russell Daniels are everywhere - sorry Russ, they are - several hundred of them have registered businesses at Companies House. Blimey. He's an unusual one because 35 years ago, Russ was the standard-bearer for Wham! He liked them. Where would a man like that be now? At a Club Tropicana?

Maybe Facebook has a Knaphill group..? Woah! Facebook has only one Russ from Knaphill. He was at the local school at exactly the right time to be writing to Smash Hits. But he's not stayed local. He's in Canada! And a quick look at his rainbow filled profile suggests his teenage self was maybe only platonically interested in the 'females' he hoped would write to him. In fact, his FB lists meeting a rather special chap as one of his 'life events'. I fully expect, when he gets our letter, it will be almost as important.

Friday 15th January 2021

Sarah and I talked this morning. That in itself isn't particularly momentous - we talk, literally, non-stop. All day. And Sarah talks in her sleep too. But I digress. Today we're considering how to reach out to Fran Hargarden. Lady Luck pointed us at the Gisburn Chat Facebook page. Easy. Or at least it would have been 35 years ago - aside from the fact it didn't exist 35 years ago, obviously.

It's made us ponder a few 'modern-day dilemmas'.

Does it make a difference whether our public enquiry on the group is written by a man or a woman? If this were a lonely road at night it might be quite an important difference, but on a sunlit social media page? Sarah's been selling things online and says she always registers a tiny sliver of awareness when she is giving her address to a man, an awareness that isn't there if selling to another woman. So, if I message the group, do we reduce our chances of a response, compared to if Sarah does it? We don't know. We're totally aware that neither of us is a risk to anyone (although, before her first coffee of the day, Sarah can be quite scary) so there isn't a 'danger' factor to our enquiry. But Gisburn Chat don't know that.

Next - what are we expecting? Surely no one will simply give us Fran's address - and nor should they - no one would feel that was the right thing to do. So, at best, we may be pointed in a new direction, or possibly someone will nudge Fran that a 6' 3" stranger is trying to find her. And she will, no doubt, go straight into some sort of pen pal protection scheme and that will be the end of that.

However, if Fran is contacted by someone from Gisburn Chat she'll immediately be able to see my profile. Sarah's privacy settings mean only crime bosses, aliens and The Dead can view the photos she posts of her dinner, which might appear odd to Fran. I, on other hand, can be found and viewed by anyone, so I get the go ahead to take point with the online community.

And should Fran do a little research of her own, she'll see I have kids (my youngest accidentally giving the finger from his high chair about 6 years ago might offend, but frankly, he's not the one sending the message); loads of 'friends' (reminder to self: imminent cull); and absolutely nothing that's less than warm and cuddly.

I post a very carefully worded, non-threatening post, softening our request and making it sound as much like the friendly request it truly is.

Me: Morning all, I wonder if anyone might be able to help me? I'm trying to forward a letter to a lady called Fran, who lived on Cedars Street in the mid '80s but have reached a dead end. After the letter was returned to sender from the old address it was suggested I try this forum to see if anyone can point me in the right direction. Many thanks.

Within about three minutes, a group admin offers up the name of a possible lead.

Admin: Coleen Hargarden might be able to help.

No further details. Just a link to her Facebook page. A sister?

If what Sarah and I are doing is the equivalent of walking down a deserted road behind a lone woman, we are most definitely hanging back, crossing the road, going the long way round, unlike those Gisburn admins who did the equivalent of screaming down that same road wielding a chainsaw, chanting demonic incantations while dressed as Donald Trump.

But I've never been to Gisburn, maybe that's how they roll up there?

I write to Coleen asking for her assistance, and also comment on my own post that Coleen will not be able to read my message because we are not Facebook friends - hoping someone might let her know to check that 'other mailbox', the one that used to be virtually secret and now is virtually just ignored. No one says they'll let her know, the sound of chainsaws is fast receding. So I have to hope that the Gisburn Admin, mentioning Coleen, works like a tag?

It's not long since the last one, but a lot's been happening. So, hands up who wants another Top 20 chart..? Fine, here it is.

1. Andy - very possibly a God.
2. Matt (and possibly Dave) - pastures new.
3. Russ - no one leaves Knaphill. Unless they go to Canada via Australia.
4. William - makes more per week than us per year? Definite pen pal material.
5. Oli - second attempt. On the trail of his Mum - in a good way.
6. Fran - everyone in Gisburn's on the case or Coleen's on the phone, to the police!
7. Johnny - tomorrow, he'll be in touch tomorrow, bettcha bottom dollar.
8. Delilah - I think she may have become a spy, which might be problematic.
9. Louise - she's probably having a Bucks Fizz right now - another one.
10. Jane - we remain confident.
11. Brian Evans - told my Dad (in Wales) we're seeking that name in Wales. He's still laughing.
12. Monika - speaks four languages, will probably deliver her reply to us by hand.
13. Lars - I have a Swedish friend, maybe he knows him? (I have a lottery ticket - maybe I'll win?)
14. Sally & Emma - why, oh why couldn't one of these girls be called Deuteronomy, or something?
15. Donald & Richard - right now, I have a feeling these guys are looking through a shoebox of RSVPs.
16. Nayumi - starting to think Nayumi might be wanted by Interpol.
17. Adam - come on Ad!
18. Faheen - I think Malaysia is actually getting further away?
19. Roobarb & Custard - no idea. Frankly, it's just silly.

20. Becki - I really like the cut of her jib. But she's still at the bottom. I wonder if that dog is still in her old house?

We also contact a lady called Sue. In 1985 she was credited in Smash Hits as being responsible for Reader Services and Lyrics. I've visions of her constantly rewinding a cassette, trying to fathom the words for a garbled pop tune of the day. I wonder if she made any mistakes and we've all been singing those lyrics wrong for 35 years?

Although my pro-writer LinkedIn account has surely impressed her enormously, she still might not reply - it was a very niche enquiry about whether she was in charge of the RSVP pen pal bit all those years ago. Maybe we should contact absolutely everyone credited in that edition of the magazine? Even Neil Tennant, who must have been on the cusp of being a Pet Shop Boy at the time.

I mentioned we're moving. I mentioned we're downsizing. I mentioned Sarah is massively ignoring her share of RSVPeople work, or as she prefers to call it: arranging absolutely everything for a smooth transition to our new place. Unbelievably selfish.

One of her 'absolutely everythings' is gifting away the charity shop stuff online because the charity shops are shut because of the plague. But she's also selling some stuff through social media too.

A lady wants to buy our wardrobe and bookcase combo.

According to her profile pics, she's a cuddly lady. Miriam Margolyes-esque. If she were a neighbour you'd happily leave your spare keys with her. Our stuff will be going to a good home. She wants to pay cash. But, hang on, she wants to post us the money, special delivery? An envelope of cash dropping through the door sounds exciting, if a little risky, but it's not yet our money, so...

She wants an email address? OK. Not sure why. Sarah, unbeknownst to me, has a second email address she uses for such purposes. (Should I be worried?) About eight seconds later we hear from UPS - via a Gmail address. O… K…

So, UPS, in a vaguely UPS-looking email, in terrible English we have to sift through with our nonsense detector, say they have money for us (hurrah) and in order to get it we simply have to pay them about £50 (boo). In gift cards. What?! The subject of the email is in German. The gift cards link is French…

It's all looking very much like the language of bullshit.

The seller claims this is normal - she always buys things this way. She will add the cost of this 'insurance' to the price of the furniture and was very friendly and sweet-ish.

On closer examination, this Miriam Margolyes look-a-(bit)-like turns out to be Irish… and her photos were added… yesterday. All of them.

I look for other people with her very unusual name. It seems it's a name more usually given to a man. And judging by the faces of the two Facebook men sharing her name, it's the sort of name you have if you kill people for a living. We pull out of the sale, block the profile. They have an email address, our address, a small reason to have a chip on their shoulder and, almost certainly, a wardrobe of their own, filled with sawn-off shotguns. However, Sarah and I have two pieces of furniture we don't want, and our dignity! We showed them.

Again, though, it screams how important first impressions are. And how important it is not to be a psychotic wardrobe-buying fraudster.

As if that's not enough excitement for one day, we also lovingly send Russell's letter overseas - to Canada.

Monday 18th January 2021

More post! A white envelope containing one of our envelopes and a simple 'sorry, address not known' written on the back. The expected dead end for Sally and Emma.

I discover the nuns at the convent school came, and they went. The school, as I already knew, had been razed to the ground. We don't know exactly how old the girls were in 1985, but the guys they were looking for were 13-15. So probably 14ish? Yep, let's say 14.

The rules of The RSVPeople Project dictate that once we reach a dead end, we're allowed to seek out other avenues in the search for a new address to use. And although I'd love to exchange letters with an entire convent of nuns, I'm fairly sure, with the school no longer in existence, finding a teacher from 35 years ago who remembers two girls without surnames from the hundreds they taught, is slim. In the olden days, the only course of action would have been to pray. By 'olden days' I mean pre-social media.

With the new religion beckoning, I poke around a bit and find an Old Girls Facebook group. It feels a little odd perusing dozens of photos of schoolgirls, looking for one tagged with an Emma or a Sally, but when I was their age it wasn't creepy. But I'm no longer their age… I stop looking at photos of schoolgirls. Instead I find another post, sharing the name of a second group of Old Girls from the same school - maybe both groups are followed by the same Old Girls, or could there be some sort of competition between the two groups? I look, find nothing, questions remain unanswered.

One of the groups has a website that no longer exists. I never understand why people close down their sites but still leave the links lying around. A little like the convent itself! There's a pattern forming. Both groups can be messaged and emailed. So I message and email them both.

The email to one address returns immediately - clearly related to the dead website link. But the Messenger messages disappear into the ether so I remain hopeful.

In other news, Coleen Hargarden still hasn't seen my message, so I check in with the Gisburn Chat admins again and they tell me Coleen knows about my query but is 'completely estranged from Fran' for reasons she isn't going to go into.

Oh. Dead End. What could be going on there?

Wednesday 20th January 2021

Stuff's been happening. Sally and Emma, Custard and Roobarb, Fran. It's kept me busy. But not as busy as trying to determine which books need to come to the new place and which need to go into storage. Downsizing to a much nicer place (hurrah!) while having to leave stuff in a lock-up facility at the same time (boo!) I'm literally surrounded by half-filled boxes - from where I'm sitting right now I count 38. Granted, many of them are pretty small (should theatre plays and screenplays be packed together or separately?) but hopefully their number will help make sure that nothing gets lost.

Lost. A bit like Fran.

Fran.
I like Fran, I've seen her face several times - she has a Twitter account, a Pinterest page, a LinkedIn profile and even photos on a Myspace page. (I didn't even know that still existed.) She also has a blogging page where she's a bit of a hippy (her words not mine). But everything seems to stop around four years ago. In her photos she's smiley but for some reason that smiley face stopped using social media, without explanation. Can't criticise her for that - there are more days than not that I wonder what the price of social media

will be in another 20 years - but most people leave a trace. If, God forbid, she's no longer with us, I'd hope there would have been an outpouring of grief online, because that's something we all do now. No such outpouring exists, so I very much hope, Fran, wherever she is, is in smiley good health.

I'd also hope that Coleen would have at least heard through an estranged grapevine if Fran had passed. There's a bit of a rift in my own family but when my Mum died, we made sure everyone knew. It's the right thing to do. So, where does that leave us? How about prison? I'm not sure you're allowed to tweet from a cell. But again, a court case leaves a trail, and if there is one, Google doesn't know about it. But she's still disappeared. How does a person disappear? Her hippy side might have taken her into some sort of commune? Or into some foreign land where she's doing 'good work'. Although, jobs leave trails too. Her LinkedIn has her still working in retail, but any job description you put on that platform remains until you change it - so although it suggests she's still there, there's no reason to believe she is.

What if she's changed her name? Or maybe she's transgender and we're chasing a dead name no longer in use? Now, as possible as that seems, why leave all your old profiles gathering dust in all corners of the Internet? It doesn't make sense to me, but then I probably make little sense to most other people, which cancels the other out. I think.

There was a singer I discovered online a couple of years ago. One of her songs became part of a listening soundtrack while I was writing a screenplay. She was brilliant. I wanted to tell her about the influence her music had on my creativity. But although, like Fran, she had pages all over the place, her actual self was nowhere to be found.

Her Facebook page and Twitter et al were still there, like signs creaking above a saloon door in the Wild West. But inside, I found the saloon deserted. Half-drunk whiskey glasses, cards still lying on a table, coins strewn around, a piano in the corner, sheet music wafting in the warm breeze. Something happened here, but with no one to ask, no one to speak to, there was only one course of action to employ - I found a beermat (they may not have had beermats in the Wild West, but this is my analogy, so they do now) I wrote a note and left it on the bar, just in case she returned.

Back in the real world that means I sent a direct message to her and moved on. Sadly, I never heard a thing from her.

It's against the rules, I know, but Fran is one of The RSVPeople and I'd really like to welcome her into the fold. The RSVPeople started as a means to explore communication. Fran deserves a beermat left on an analogous Wild West bar. It's the least we can do.

Sally & Emma.

Those teenage crazy convent kids! Well, not any more, obviously, but if I'd been a 14 year old writing to them 35 years ago, I might have opened my letter with something like that. I may not have got a reply, but that's the chance you take when you decide to go 'cool' rather than 'predictable'.

Cool? Would that have been a cool thing to say as a 14 year old? Now that I'm an adult (adult: yes, grown-up: meh) it's impossible to think like I would have done as a teenager. Parents say to their kids, as a means of trying to connect with them, help them, that they were once their age. It's what their parents said to them at some point, and their parents' parents before them. And everyone rolls their internal eyes, or external eyes, depending on the discipline levels of said parents. But the eye rolling always happens somewhere, because parents know nothing of what their kids are going through!

I used to work backstage in theatre wardrobe departments in the West End. It's mostly a young person's game. I did it for 20 years. I started off as a youngish person. I moved from show to show and new young people joined every year as I got older. I remained the same, no I really did (see 'grown-up' comment above). I was silly and irreverent, most everybody was, it was fun! Then one day, the gap between me and these young people suddenly became a ravine (I was already being referred to as 'Dad' by some, which I blindly accepted as ironic). Someone laughed at something I said and then caveated it as being 'like your Dad trying to be cool'.

Mic drop.

Somewhere across the years, the right to be a certain way is taken away and the 'kids' grab the cool/trendy/hip/fashionable batons from us and we're expected to begin a life of shopping in M&S for easy care trousers and comfy cardigans.

But I digress. Again.

While I'm lost in my own thoughts, Sarah pops in for a spot of late lunch. She's been in the front room, also surrounded by half-full boxes, working via zoom on something else. I know - lazy!

I receive a message from a lady called George. I'm assuming she's a lady because she's Admin for the Convent School Old Girls group - a collection of people who went to an all-girls school run by nuns. I don't want to be presumptuous, but were I a betting man, I'd stick a few quid on George not having a handle-bar moustache.

George: Do you have their surname? If so I can check our database and maybe forward an email for you. Thanks

No doubt, George is very busy. And mine is a strange request - wondering if a letter might be forwarded to two teenagers from 35 years ago, without me knowing anything about them other than their first names - but still I feel a little deflated that she's not more effusive at the intriguing journey Sarah and I are inviting her on. I don't think the fact she doesn't have the faintest idea what I'm talking about yet is any excuse. Plus, I've a smidge of irritation that I've already covered the fact there were no surnames.

Sarah points out that I haven't.

Sarah: *You haven't.*
Me: *What are you talking about?*
Sarah: *You say you know their names are Emma and Sally.*
Me: *Yes!*
Sarah: *But you don't say you don't have their surnames.*
Me: *What?* (reads my message again) *Oh. Well, it's implicit, isn't it?*
Sarah shrugs and pulls a face that says *'clearly not'* and walks out. Then she comes back.
Sarah: *George doesn't have the faintest idea who we are or what we're doing. Us being some old boyfriend from the past with a vendetta is just as likely as us being two idiots from South London with a romantic notion about old pen pals.*

She walks out. And stays out.

Sarah's so often right, I walk a thin line between adoration and irritation. I place my 'lemon lips' back in the reaction fruit bowl and pen a response with thanks and a smile.

> **Me**: Hi, thanks for getting back to me. Unfortunately, I don't have their surnames, or any other information at all. I shall try a post on the page, see if these scant details can shake anyone's memory. Thanks again.

Smooth.

That shows her and her handle-bar moustache. Ha! Busy-schmizzy! We're all busy, George, I can tell you, but a little less of your efficient/snipperty-ness wouldn't go amiss..!

Sarah shouts from the other room.

Sarah: *She said 'Thanks!'*
(I didn't know I was talking out loud.)

Reluctantly, I check George's message. And she did say thanks. I check again. She still did. I'd sort of missed that. That's nice, I guess.

Smugness doesn't suit Sarah, so I spare her by muttering to myself, really quietly.

Me: *She missed off the full stop, though*! (As if that somehow negates the word.)

I can literally hear Sarah's eyebrow raise at me from the other room. I wonder if she prefers that part of the flat because it has fewer grumpy, irrational people in it?

Next, I write a 'cool' message for both of the Old Girls groups.

Me: Hi, I wonder if anyone can help me. I'm trying to forward a letter to two girls who attended the school in 1985. The only information I have is that they are called Sally & Emma, were 13/14 at the time and were friends at school. I realise this is very little to go on, but if this rings a bell with anyone, please let me know. Many thanks.

No one can complain about my 'niceness' there. All the full stops are present and correct and exactly where they should be too.

Just saying.

Ping!

George: I'm happy to share your request on the page but could do with a bit more information. Why are you looking for them? How you know them, what's the story etc. We just need to be careful with regards to sharing personal information online - I don't expect anyone to give you an address on here. We hold a database of student emails but would need you to forward the letter to us for forwarding, asking the girls to get back in touch with you. I hope that makes sense? George

Bugger. No sooner have I messaged the page, than George shows this very honest, friendly side that I had entirely refused to anticipate behind her entirely fictitious facial hairs. And she's showing the very interest I'd chided her for originally. I hate to say it, but I've completely misread George. Double bugger. And now it looks like I've read her friendly reply and then ignored her by writing straight on the page. Thrice bugger. There's nothing for it but to come clean, save face and the day both at the same time.

Me: Hi George, I completely understand your privacy concerns, so if we manage to locate them, I'd be more than happy to pass the letter on to you, for you to forward, that would be great.

The story behind the request might seem a little odd, but as you asked…

And I proceed to tell George everything. The Smash Hits magazine, the quest, the letters and how we don't want to email Sally and Emma because that would deprive them of the joy of a 35 year old reply to their teenage pen pal ad.

The message is nice, presentable, friendly and passed thoroughly through Sarah's offence radar and found to be lacking anything even the most cynical recipient could find fault with.

Phew.

OK. So, for now, I'll leave George to her busy life and think well of her. I have spelled out the story. I hope she will play along.

I will not jump to conclusions. I will not jump to conclusions. I will not jump to conclusions. I will not jump to conclusions.

All worries evaporate though, with the arrival of the post… our SECOND actual reply!

It feels quite thick. Might be our first envelope returned to sender in the return envelope?

But it's no such thing. It's a letter and oh it's a beauty to behold.

Not one, not two, but three sides of paper, lovingly written by hand. But who is this new friend? Mandy!

Eh? Mandy?

The post stamp reveals a Bristol area posting… Hang on, Bristol means Mandy is… ROOBARB or CUSTARD!!

What are the chances? Two girls who didn't use their actual names, sent to an address 35 years old has produced a result! But more, much more than 'a result'. A story, an adventure, lovely people - it's what The RSVPeople Project was created for!

Are you sitting comfortably? Well hurry up, I need to get on...

So, Mandy's old neighbour, while no doubt having a chinwag over a garden fence about our letter, remembered Mandy was one of the R&C duo and found her on Facebook! This resulted in Mandy having a gaze at her old home for the first time in 15 years! And meeting the old neighbours too!

If 'us' is a thing, then I believe wholeheartedly that Mandy is, indeed, 'one of us'. She says she used to phone chat lines simply to talk to people! Magnificently weird. Although not so weird 35 years ago, as that was literally what chat lines were for.

And because of our letter and her ad and the passage of 35 years, Mandy may have made a new friend - her neighbour's daughter. That would not have happened but for The RSVPeople Project. We are bringing people together in a world desperate to keep us apart.

Mandy is Custard, not so close with Roobarb anymore, but then friendships between cats and dogs are seldom simple. However, the fact Custard's Mum now lives with Roobarb's Dad was a surprise and a half. But you know what, doesn't it say something about the intimacy of letters? Mandy doesn't know us, I can't imagine her volunteering that information if we'd just got chatting in a pub, but with a proper letter it seems there's something of the confessional about it.

Sarah and I think Mandy Custard is great!

She tells us that back in 1985 she and Roobarb got oodles of replies. Mostly from geeks claiming to be rich! (Not a 'cool' way to approach things if you ask me.) In fact there were so many of them they couldn't reply to them all.

It makes me very proud that Custard replied to the very last reply to their ad. But the piece of information that hits the home run is that Mandy's favourite band is still Wham! She then apologises for being no good at writing letters. How utterly wrong she is, she's brilliant and we'll tell her so.

Later in the day, like five numbers and the bonus ball, 'Reader Services and Lyrics' Sue is back in touch. When that bloke Mike lay on his back, drawing naked blokes almost touching fingers, he was trying to capture something similar to the excitement running through me right now. It's like being right there in the Smash Hits News Room, amidst the chatter and the chocolate biscuits. Everyone unconsciously tapping their feet to whatever Neil Tennant's singing to himself. This is proper 1985 Smash Hits Royalty! Maybe not King or Queen royalty, but certainly one of the ones at either end of the balcony during fly-pasts and the like. Smash Hits Sue! Wow!!

She didn't deal with the pen pals. Oh.

But she's going to chase up a friend to see if she remembers anything. Brilliant people are everywhere! Efficient people too - it's only a matter of hours before her friend replies to Sue and Sue replies to us…

Sue's friend lives in Australia now and she says everyone pitched in, it was no one in particular's job. Damn. Oh well.

But you know what? The RSVPeople Project has now spread its tendrils all the way to the other side of the world. All because Sarah and I had an idea. And too much time on our lockdown hands.

Thursday 21th January 2021

This is the first day since Sarah and I grinned at each other holding our copy of Smash Hits exactly three weeks ago, I sort of hope we get no messages. Our flat move on Monday is galloping at such apace and the packing elves have been rubbish - we go to bed, get up and the little shits haven't packed a thing. In fact, sometimes it looks quite the opposite!

Sarah and I are made of very different stuff. She's all things nice and I'm slugs and snails and puppy dog tails - or something. She's been working with her writing partner, making websites, composing songs, often making dinner too and sorting out the majority of the stuff needed for a smooth transition to our new place - which is why I need elves way more than she does.

The problem is I've been carrying round my history forever. My stuff. A lifetime of collected detritus. I move, it all comes with me. I acquire more stuff, I move, even more now comes with me. I share similar DNA with my Dad in this regard - throwing stuff away can be a very complicated process for us. I'm not as bad as I used to be, but I was always the person who kept the bus ticket, the cinema stub and the receipt for both the popcorn and the hotdogs - then I'd get home and write a page of diary about the occasion. There was something very important about holding on to the memory, therefore the triggers to that memory needed to be revered. If the bus ticket disappeared, so might the memory: the occasion, the trip, or possibly even the person. It's logical, but it places a lot of extra strain on you.

And as I've moved around over the past 25 years or so, somehow I've managed to have enough room for all the stuff. And if there's enough room for 'stuff' there's no need to make decisions about it, right? Just collect it, box it, store it and forget about it. Couldn't be simpler. Until the box reappears while trying to find the Christmas decorations or when a move is on the horizon.

I keep things I call 'softie boxes'. 'Nostalgia black holes' might be a better description. Whether it's the first, illegible felt-tip scratch on a piece of paper from one of my kids, or the cake decoration from an almost forgotten, unforgettable party, in it all goes. And in it stays. And once it's in there, it feels saved. There's a finger on the pause button of time. Until it reappears at some point in the future, like when you're trying to find a pre-digital photo, or when a home move is on the horizon.

I appear to have six softie boxes. I have one for Sarah. I have one for family, one for friends, one for each of the kids and one for both the kids together - clearly from when I had new nostalgia to hurl into a black hole, but couldn't find the black hole, so created yet another one. (Note to self: call scientists, I may have a skill useful to black hole fanciers.)

Now, the one thing I've told myself is that under no circumstances should I engage with the nostalgic/sentimental contents of these boxes. If I climb into those black holes Sarah will have to move without me. Or, worse, all this stuff I've been lugging round, will be thrown into storage, paid storage, until the next move.

The simple solution is to decant all six black holes into the Daddy of all black holes - or 'a large box' as astronomers might call it. Being me, I can't simply put all the files and boxes into the bigger box, no, no, no. Another sliver of DNA Dad and I share is that packing is not seen as a 'putting things in boxes or similar' task. Instead it requires the forensic activity of doing a mammoth jigsaw.

For instance, I've packed a few boxes of books (no applause please, but thank you). It took me about two days, not only because I used to write the purchase and completion dates on the first inside page, which has to be glanced at, just in case it wakes a memory, but also because until every square inch of the container is full, its innards may be yet better arranged. So everything comes out and goes back in until I'm certain that the jigsaw cannot be completed more efficiently in any other way.

Yes, yes, I'm exhausting. As we said to Andy, our first responder, while quoting from a Brat Pack film from the '80s: 'Me, oh, you know, it isn't easy being me.'

So here I am, digging through my stuff. I come across three letters from when I was twenty. From blonde twins. I'd forgotten all about them until this very moment…

Sometime in the 1980s, I'd seen two gorgeous twins in The Venue club in Manchester and then, entirely randomly, saw the very same twins in a photo in the Manchester Evening News a couple of days later. They were models. A local story about local twins, with decent PR people, doing well. Some might simply have thought what a coincidence it was, maybe even thought it spooky, then lined the cat's litter tray with the pages and thought no more about it.

Not me. I wrote to them care of their agent. No idea what I said, but it clearly worked as they wrote back three times. Then, I guess life got in the way and that was that. Three letters each and then we moved on. I can't remember the last time they crossed my mind. But the instant I saw a little studio photo they sent, the teenage me remembered that night in The Venue and the grand gesture of sending a letter to strangers. I haven't changed that much.

But the twins do not need to accompany me for the rest of my life, so into the recycling they go. I guess writing about them here means the memory is saved and will wake up again whenever I read these words. I told Sarah about the twins. Or the 'hot twins' as she called them. She was astonished - that these two 'hot twins' had replied! To me. Bloody cheek. I sense jealousy. What else could it be?

Remember I said I hoped I wouldn't get a letter today, because sans elves there just isn't the time? Well I got one. But not from today. It's from March 2000. From my Mum…

My Mum died just over a year ago. The lady who passed away was a shell of her former self. One of the things that's been tricky has been reminding myself of who she was before physical and mental frailty came to call in those last five or six years. But this letter is the perfect reminder. I've been filing lots of old letters into the black holes, but the words 'your Nana's ashes' jump off this one particular page. So I read it - this isn't twins spied in a club, this is important, this is my lovely Mum…

I have no recollection of reading the letter before. Mum is telling me my Nana had her ashes laid to rest in a little cemetery in North Wales. It is the very same cemetery where we laid Mum's ashes a year ago. I know Nana is there too, of course, but this letter from 21 years ago has made a perfect circle - Mum standing in a cemetery bereft without her Mum, instantly earthquakes my more recent memories of being bereft on the very same spot.

Then Mum's beautiful swirling handwriting tells me she had a dream about me 'last night'. She tells me I'd been a lovely child, both in the dream and in reality. (And my Mum would never lie.) She said I was emotional like her but 'so sincere'. In her dream she had her arms round me while I explained something was unfair but it could be righted. In the dream my Mum said it sounded right to her.

It's a very short, simple letter. It doesn't go in a softie box. It stays out so I can read it to Sarah. When I do, I cry. Mum's letter is going to come with me, unboxed, to the new place. I will read it often, I'll share it with my Dad. We may have a little cry then too.

Letters are very powerful things. Receipts for hot dogs rarely so. Keep your letters, ditch most of the rest.

It's late evening. Sarah's finally finished whatever it is she does in the front room that she passes off as 'work'. Now she's going to 'pack a few books'. I smother a scoff at her ambition. Good luck, lady friend - I've been packing for weeks, I know what's involved and how long it takes. I'll throw a supportive arm round her when the task reveals how daunting it is.

45 minutes later she's packed 9 and a half boxes. About 500 books. We have a lot of books. Hers are mostly packed now. Mine, not so much.

If I see those bloody elves I'm going to literally punch them in the face!

Sunday 24th January 2021

It's snowing!

Where did January go? Chances are it's been packed in one of the three million cardboard boxes in the lounge. I've been very careful to label them. Paul's Books. And, Paul's Books and also Paul's Books. Sarah, on the other hand, I noticed, has written things like Sarah's: plays, psychology, brain surgery, alchemy and angle-grinding books etc. The contents of each box as clear as a summer's day. Her boxes will no doubt float perfectly to their new location, while mine will try to unpack themselves in the street. This is why Sarah's sleeping and I'm awake at 5.45am, my mind whirring.

There are no new letters to report, but Old Girls George has been back in touch. She's nothing short of marvellous. Every other thought on earth has been pushed to the side by me and shame and self-chastisement sit in their place. George was busy - I mean, not 'moving-house' busy, but she has a life and stuff to do. The RSVPeople is probably only the second or third, probably second, most important thing she has to do at the moment, but still she's onboard to help! First this.

> **George**: Hi Paul, what a great story and would love to help. I will have a think as how to reach out to that year group without giving anything away and meanwhile I will check our database for a Sally and Emma in the same year who would have left around 1986-90 depending if they stayed for A-Levels. I'm also guessing that if they gave the school address then they would have been boarders? Let me see if I can find anything out.

Then a few minutes later - this.

> **George**: Hi Paul, I'm going to try a post on the main page. I have a picture from 1990 and will try and pop your request on. I also plan to write to all the Sally and Emmas we have on our database, asking them to contact me if they had a best friend called Sally or Emma! We have about 7-10 possibilities. Thanks George.

Wow. George isn't a lady who simply offers a suggestion, doesn't simply shrug and forget. George is a lady who rolls up her sleeves, makes a plan and blummin' well carries it out. I'm looking into the criteria for having a blue plaque put up somewhere in her honour.

My original post to the Old Girls site met with absolute disinterest. Fingers crossed for better engagement this time with George's post:

George: Can you help?
We are trying to get in touch with two ex-pupils, probably boarders, who were at the school in 1985. They would have been approximately 14/15 years old in that year and we only have first names of Sally and Emma but they were definitely close friends. It's nothing to worry about but we would love to forward something on to them. Please get in contact. Anyone else with an idea of who they may be then please also comment below. Thanks

It's almost as though complete strangers are less likely to engage with other complete strangers who go poking around on Facebook asking mysterious questions, than they are when a group they follow and trust asks a mysterious question...

But George is awe-inspiring, there's a magnificence to her request that makes me feel inadequate.

'Can you help?' - instantly putting all the Old Girls at ease. And I bet these girls were brought up wanting to help and wanting to solve problems and make their old nun-teachers proud. I had nun-teachers myself at school, I know what I'm talking about.

'We' are trying. Those Old Girls don't know it, but Sarah and I are part of that 'we'. We're hiding behind George's skirt tails, or in a broom cupboard nearby, peering through the keyhole, trying to hold our breath and stop giggling at the same time.

'It's nothing to worry about'. Blimey, if I'd written that I'd have had the police at my door. But George wields an inquisitive pen like a convent-educated Zorro.

Beneath her post is a row of dancers, in what looks like a school show. I'm not entirely sure why the post contains a chorus line in front of a lazily painted back-cloth, but I suspect George has imbued the photo with subliminal messaging about The RSVPeople Project. No one reading or glancing at that post will have any control over their actions, such is George's skill. Depending on her powers, viewers of the post might start impersonating farm animals, which, frankly, would be a little irresponsible of George to use her mind-control with such gay abandon. Let's hope they simply see it and go 'I think that's me…'

Eh? What? No! I've barely had time to put the kettle on before there's the equivalent of a good-natured, ex-privately educated convent school riot!

Emma: Hello, I am Emma…
George: Did you have a friend called Sally?
Emma: I had a friend called Sally and a friend called Salina…
Alba: Emma - I was just going to tag you x
Helen: Emma - bit late but I was going to tag you x
Dulcie: Emma - me too!

I don't believe it. I simply don't believe it. How many seconds did that take? Literally none. Also, there's no evidence anyone's been quacking or mooing under George's misused super-powers, which is a relief.

Just a group of nice, helpful people checking in.

But as you can see, once again, George keeps her eye on specificity, - compared to Sarah and me hopping with excitement - she doesn't see Emma's arrival as a victory. Oh no, she needs clarity:

George: DID YOU HAVE A FRIEND CALLED SALLY?

(Capitals my own, obviously, George is way too classy for an all caps sentence.)

And quite right. Emma, might have found The RSVPeople Club, but she's not coming in without the right ID. You tell her, George.

Emma has two pieces of ID. Difficult to tell right now whether they're authentic or the sort of identification made at home on the kitchen table. Only George will know. She's become the bouncer for this particular door of the club. We're happy to be led by her.

What a lot of stuff going on - and it's only 8.30am!

Tuesday 26th January 2021

Don't even talk to me about January being nearly over! And heaven help us when we kick through into February - it's about 10% shorter than your standard January!

Anyway, having moved yesterday (hurrah/my poor back) it occurs to me how easy it is to lose touch with people. We popped our new address in a few Christmas cards, but most people won't know. And for most it won't matter - I mean who sends things through the front door these days apart from Amazon, eBay and people wanting to clean out your guttering?

But it might explain why well over half our original envelopes haven't found their home yet. I mean, Sarah and I have paid for six months' redirection, but after that there will be no way for any guttering specialist to know exactly where we are. To be fair, we have a neighbour upstairs at our old place who would forward something on to us, but you get the idea.

You've probably gathered - no new mail has arrived. But it doesn't mean nothing's been happening. George has been happening. I'd even go so far as to say there's been a 'George Happening'.

George: Hi Paul, so we have a strong contender from an Emma who was a boarder and had a best friend Sally. I am assuming that as you originally wrote to the school address, they had given that in the magazine? If you could confirm that would be great, as only a boarder would do that. I also have her email address, so if you would like to scan & send or write your letter then please do forward it to me here and I will send on.

That's all we needed to know really, but George senses kinship. She can feel the quiver through the ether that we are surely kindred spirits. She tells us more…

George: The Old Girls group doesn't usually take up much time and I only look at the email account sporadically. Most girls loved their school years, and so the Facebook page helps to keep their memories alive. We have a few Old Girls who have really made a name for themselves and some "old boys" from the '60s!! We encourage photos and stories / memories and these usually go out in the newsletters, the group also allows old students to get back in touch with friends they lost touch with. I am only an "old girl" myself, not an old teacher.

I also saw we have a mutual friend, well more of an acquaintance for me really. Small world ☺
Anyway, please send through what you want and I will pass on. Thanks, George

There are many questions here, a mutual friend, many thoughts and much information that has made The RSVPeople World a better place. Sarah and I confer. We'll send our original letter, in its original envelope, inside a new envelope, with a stamp but no address. We'll ask George to pop the address on and send the letter out into the world once more.

It won't be long before we think of time merely in relation to pre George (a dark and miserable age where winters lasted an eternity, birds didn't sing and letters never arrived) and a post George future - a unicorn-filled rainbow land of glitter and starlight. They shall, henceforth, be known as PG and PG… oh. Damn.

Monday 1st February 2021

February! A twelfth of the year evaporated already. Just like that. Out of nowhere. Gone.

One day you're promising to drink less, lose weight and take up crotchet, the next you're wondering if a drop of Pinot would complement a breakfast crumpet while scratching your crotch-et. February. The month for lovers, romantics and those who can just about smell Spring on the distant horizon.

It's also the first day of being in our new place - without any remaining 'moving house' things still left to do! We've unpacked what needs unpacking, stored what needs storing and rubbed tiger balm on everything that aches like hell, which is everything. A reminder we are no longer as young as we once were.

The new house is beautiful. The family we're lodging with are lovely and welcoming. The two cats, Frank and Lily, still prefer their actual owners but we're working on it - a little bit of dropped chicken here, an inconspicuous ear tickle there, all it takes is time.

But it also means The RSVPeople Project has been on pause for the best part of a week. No letters written, no letters received, nothing, nada, zilch. However, because we've changed address, it's a reminder of what a big ask we set ourselves. As I said, we've set up a postal redirection for 6 months. That should be enough. But if I'd been one of The RSVPeople, and just before my ad was published my parents decided to move elsewhere, I'd have been distraught at the thought of all those potential pen pals slipping through the net. My parents, no doubt feeling really awkward about literally ruining my entire life, would hopefully have set up a redirection especially for me - just to shut me up and stop me crying.

So, Dad probably, would have filled out a form or whatever people did in pre-Internet history, and that would have been that.

Except, of course, redirections run out! Gah! Based on what's available today, a redirection can last 3, 6 or 12 months. So, let's assume nothing's changed since 1985 in that regard. Based on the fact it's been 422 months since that ad appeared, a redirection renewal followed by renewal followed by renewal, would most certainly rack up a few quid. In fact, if you renewed your redirection every three months for 422 months, at today's prices you'd be looking at a whopping £4,781. Naturally, a more savvy pen pal seeker might repeatedly renew the 6 months option (£3,376) or the much more financially acceptable 12 month plan (£2,426.50). Less than two and a half grand! Over 35 years, could that BE any more reasonable? Pah!

However, if we'd moved abroad, had a rolling 3 month redirection, and never checked a bank statement, the cost would have been £17,019 - and my Dad would have reported me to the authorities long before that wallet-watering sum was reached.

But, as the half-life of a pen pal advert is probably in the region of a couple of weeks, all the above maths is probably overkill. Probably.

What it all adds up to is - when people move it's very tricky to locate them without the aid of sniffer dogs, which Frank and Lily would never agree to.

Sarah and I have begun to wonder if our original mailout has now gone as far as it can go? All those coloured envelopes sitting in piles of undeliverable mail on the ledges above meter cupboards in blocks of flats. Or slightly (no let's call them out for what they are) *massively* miserable gits saw the envelope and decided popping it back in a postbox was too much trouble. We would never have behaved in such a way. Sarah and I are made of better stuff. Well, different stuff - mostly coffee, wine and chocolate biscuits actually.

Anyway, stop distracting me, on with the quest.

So, a strange thing has happened. Old Girls George and I have been sharing emails. I'm not suggesting we're pen pals or anything - but as well as touching base about The RSVPeople Project, we've been sharing a little bit of personal information, asking questions, a written chat if you will. And, in 2021 we have taken the very natural step of becoming Facebook friends! I mean if nothing else were to happen ever, our new friendship exists solely because of a 1985 copy of a pop magazine! How good is that?

George and I have decided her Emma is our Emma and an envelope will today be on its way to George, for her to add Emma's address and then everything is in the sweaty hands of fate.

And it turns out that friend we have in common is an actor I worked with on Les Misérables a million years ago. He was, and I'm sure still is, a lovely chap. George and her husband were shown around backstage by him after seeing Phantom of the Opera. Nice people doing nice things.

Oh, and a couple of famous people went to the convent school too. Sally and Emma are clearly from very good stock and education. I think I was at school with a couple of the younger members of a Manchester crime family. Oh, and Matthew Williamson, the designer - although his folks and mine were the best of friends so I've known him forever.

So, Sally and Emma are today back in the game.

Nothing so far from Andy. Or William. Or Matt. Or Russ.

And of course, we still need to write to Mandy Roobarb. She'll think we've forgotten her. We haven't, we're writing to her next, in a minute, over coffee.

Wednesday 3rd February 2021

We post Mandy's letter.

We post Emma's letter - inside an envelope, stamped but with no address, inside another envelope stamped and addressed to George. Everyone got that?

As we've yet to hear from Andy, we send a change of address note as a sort postal nudge. We lick those envelopes and walk, in the rain, to the postbox…

Do you remember Christmas? I realise it's now February, but if you cast your mind back a mere 40 days, there you'll find Christmas - a little dusty now, but easily recognisable as Christmas, what with the twinkly lights and the smell of Christmas Pud. If you have kids, that might be the end of the 'Finding Christmas' journey you need to go on. But without kids you may have to head much, much further back to one of your very own childhood Christmas mornings. Heaven knows where you'll find that - behind old piles of The Beano or Jackie or maybe even Smash Hits? Shoved down behind old clothes where the fashion has completely rubbed off and you can't help asking yourself what on earth you were thinking. But somewhere back there is an old Christmas morning - remember running down the stairs and shrieking, 'Has he been? Has he been?' And he always had. Every year without fail. Every single time.

Unlike our postman.

Like a child of days gone by I rush through the house at around 12.30pm (whatever happened to getting post first thing?) and check for what morsels of excitement have been squeezed through the letterbox, 'Has he been? Has he been..?'

No, no he bloody well hasn't. I'm fairly sure the good boy/naughty boy criteria don't count in the same way as they do with Santa, but I still feel like I'm on a naughty list for reasons I don't understand.

Post has gone quiet. I get disappointed much quicker than Sarah, which is a constant relief to me romantically. Sarah reminds me that things take time. And they do. This is much more true than it is helpful.

Let's take a look at where The RSVPeople Project is at...

1. R & C (Mandy) - tick.
2. Andy - tick.
3. Sally & Emma - looking very, very good.
4. Matt (and possibly Dave) - looking less good!
5. Russ - no reply but international post takes forever.
6. William - letter sent to head office.
7. Oli - letter to Oli's Mum's old address.
8. Everyone else - nothing or dead end.

The response so far has been amazing. It's been fun and very real people who haven't thought about their adverts for more than 30 years have been in touch. It's fantastic. But it's been raining all week and we'd really like to hear some good news.

If you head out to where the haystacks are, every now and then you need to actually find a needle to keep it fun. Otherwise you're just crawling around in spiky dry grass - which is fun for a bit, then it just isn't.

A glint of a needle, that's all we need, just a glint…

Thursday 4th February 2021

A glint! A glint! From George, who else!

George: Hi Paul & Sarah, I believe you would both like to see the email response I got from your letter, which I posted straight on the day I got it:

……………………

Emma: Omg! I have just received the letter you forwarded! You have definitely found the right Emma! And I've sent Sally, who I wrote to Smash Hits with, a message with a copy of the letter. I have no words at the moment as I am so stunned and amazed about getting a response 35 years later!! Thankyou soooo much for bothering to find us!! It means a lot. I am going to reply to them.

……………………

George: What a lovely idea to brighten people's lives with your letters and I believe it means more this year/ last year due to the tough times we find ourselves in.

Emma is one of us! A woman who knows a good thing when it knocks on her door. A woman who will play, and most importantly - 'I AM GOING TO REPLY TO THEM!'

Oh, all the scratches on the knees in the hay are worth it. Not only for Emma being game, but for George getting to bask in the joy too. She believes we are brightening people's lives at a time when there is not as much brightness around as there once was. I hope she's right. (See, it's official - we're not creepy, we're brighty!) If Sally is half as excited as Emma then we might find two new pen pal letters winging their way to us soon. Can't wait.

The discovery of George - as a beacon of good old fashioned values and 'can do' spirit has been a marvel. She's been so brilliant that I want to tweak the rules. Although I'm not 100% sure this was a rule, but maybe slightly against the original spirit of the project. I want to spread the wings of The RSVPeople to all the social media groups that represent the areas where our Smash Hitters lived. In a way, what I think I want to do is find more Georges. More people who will think making friends and writing letters is a wonderful thing. The RSVPeople are the goal, but if we can pick up like-minded friends along the way, then I'm all for it.

This will allow us a second chance to try and find most of the missing letters. Because, by now, every original letter must have found a home. They must be somewhere. The Post Office would have returned any that simply didn't have buildings any more - like the convent school. So the ones that haven't returned - all 12 of them, have been pushed through doors to people who either sent them on somewhere, or weren't interested enough to return them to us, or just forgot.

Sarah wonders whether at least one has reached its intended person, but has triggered in that person something dark from their youth. Memories of a particularly unpleasant Bucks Fizz concert or a Simple Minds disaster. It's possible of course. But I find it difficult to believe anyone wouldn't be at least a little bit excited to be contacted by the past. And Sarah and I are utterly adorable, so if there's a need for a handhold within an envelope, we are the people to do it. All they need is a gentle kick in the shins to get back to us.

We're hoping approaching social media groups will be that kick in the shins. It'll sting a bit, but it's all in the name of a greater good.

Now we have some successes, some leads, some new friends and new addresses, there's quite the plethora of mental post-it notes all over the place. Sarah loves an actual post-it note. Sometimes her Dad sends post-it notes to her randomly simply because they have come into his possession. When she makes a theatre show, her planning always reaches the 'post-it note' stage and a wall or table becomes a patchwork of square, sticky thoughts. Did I mention she's also partial to a multi-coloured biro? No? Well, she is. This is why her thoughts are well organised. My thoughts are like a bucket of spaghetti or a shed of wire hangers - it's all in there but an absolute bugger to get it out.

With this in mind, Sarah's very keen to find a wall, some pins and bits of string and make a sort of Incident Room noticeboard. You know the sort of thing - mug shots and crime scene photos that the lead detective knows hold the answer to the killer's identity if he/she only stares at it for long enough (usually after hours, without enough ceiling lights turned on).

It's a good idea, but the walls in our new place are all pretty well utilised. And, as Sarah points out, if we were to connect people geographically, Kirdford and Malaysia are not close. The map would have to be so big, or the post-it notes so small...

It's not the best idea she's had so far.

However, if we simply made a map for the First Responder Andy chapter of the search it would be very small. He still lives close to his childhood address, where his Mum still lives and, would you believe it, that's just down the road from where Sarah's brother Steve lives! Two pieces of short string, like the world's simplest knitting project. Sarah wouldn't like this, though. She wants a multi-coloured patchwork quilt of a knitted wall. But I've put my foot down, I've said no and that that's the end of it! (Sarah wasn't in earshot when I said it, but I was truly fierce and immovable. The sound of my foot being 'put down' was heard from, well, inches away.)

Friday 5th February 2021

This is ridiculous - it's nearly Valentine's Day!

It can be confusing to keep up with special card-giving dates in the calendar. Easter stuff arrived in Sainsbury's in the first week of January, while the unsold Christmas stuff was still on 'Sale' shelves - very confusing. Valentine's stuff appeared when the Sale stuff disappeared. Valentine's Day is very much about sending cards.

Easter, commercially at least, is about stuffing your face with chocolate - no one wants a card at Easter unless it's been dipped in sugar. But the 14th of February is still obsessed with cards.

They used to be about mystery - a question mark sent to someone you 'loved' as a sign of your romantic feelings. Obviously you didn't want the person to actually know who you were - in case they laughed at you and your tiny question mark. Worse still would be if they mistook your intentions as coming from a love rival - a love rival they'd sent a card to, and your card had indirectly brought them together and ruined your chances.

Another beauty of Valentine's cards is that they can be speculative...

Aged about 14, a friend and I got up at stupid o'clock one morning and walked Valentine's cards round to three girls in our class. It was quite the adventure. However, we sent cards to the same girls. If we were actually going to attain the affections of any of these girls, we would instantly become love rivals and never speak to each other again. I've no idea what we hoped would happen. But what did happen was the girls knew exactly who had sent the cards and said thank you. Thank you! We were young and it had felt important to us. To the girls it had just been nice.

I remember the empty Manchester streets being almost as exciting as the posting of adolescent hearts and hopes.

The main thing is not to remain bitter about romantic failure from your school days, Paul. Grr.

Looking through the pen pal ads it seems that romance may have been a bigger factor than I first thought. Like MC Hammer, from within trousers that defied all logic, let me break it down:

Of the 24 names in the magazine 11 were girls, 13 boys (or females and males as quite a few preferred to be labelled). 15 people were specifically looking for members of the opposite sex to write to (8 boys, 7 girls). 5 of the boys asked for photos, whilst none of the girls were so inclined. Faheen was the only one who expressed no gender preference but still wanted photos. Photos is a strange one...

The person we send a letter to is not made a better communicator by the good fortune of being attractive, are they? So these face-hounds were definitely after prettier pen pals, regardless of how interesting they were. Having been a teenage boy once myself, I remember the raging hormones (and the getting up stupid early to walk the deserted streets in search of... something). Romance aside, maybe we just like to know what the person on the end of a conversation looks like? Of course we do - Sarah smiling at Murphy the dog was a first step on the path to our chemistry, after all.

So did these boys and girls, males and females, lads and lasses (or whatever) want to write to people in the hope of something more? Maybe. We must ask them. At first it seemed music was the thread holding them all together. But maybe it was hormones? Jane, Sally

& Emma made mention of being lonely. So, are we saying a pen pal makes loneliness go away? Maybe. Meeting someone definitely does. If they're nice, obviously. Maybe most of our RSVPeople simply had that gnawing inside them that they didn't want to be on their own. It's part of the human condition after all. So even if not looking for romance, every single one of those 24 people wanted to invite newness into their lives. Newness to fill a void.

Of course the world was much smaller in 1985. You had your friends, neighbours, school chums and your family. Maybe you knew a few people at Cubs or Guides, or at your church or afterschool groups. But, not being old enough to wander around alone (apart from Valentine's Day, early morning, obviously) you couldn't connect with anyone different, outside those community circles. Unless you got a pen friend.

Different now, obviously. For instance, I've just learned about Clubhouse. (Yep, what I really need is yet another platform to interact with, learn from, waste time on.) I'd never heard of it before. Live podcasts that aren't archived is the only way to describe it (I may not be approached to write their marketing brief). I don't know if it's for me, so I file it in a mental 'odds and ends' drawer. Hang on, apparently you can only partake in Clubhouse if you've been invited. Invited? I've been invited. By Sophie (whose house we've moved into). Invited. And, after a quick check, I learn only a handful of my contacts have been similarly blessed, I mean 'invited'. That means, even though I don't quite understand what it is, how I would use it or whether I even need it - I want in! Sign. Me. Up.

Oh yeah, I'm on Clubhouse, don't you know? I'm *in* The Clubhouse with all the special people. Are you not? I could invite you, but I can only invite two people and well, once I've invited you and one other, the elite-ness will be a bit diluted, so I'll just hang back, thanks. Maybe be really nice to me and I'll bear you in mind. Elon

Musk was on it, you know? Richest man on earth apparently - yep, Elon and I are both in the same club, so, yeah, better get going. Ciao.

(I thought Elon Musk was a perfume…)

But whether you're on Clubhouse, in a WhatsApp group or following every new photo of your idol on Instagram, there's a massive belief that interacting with all this stuff on our social medias means we're not alone. I don't think that's true. Because mostly we watch. Each platform is a window to watch other people doing things, sharing things, griping and complaining about things. Then we stop watching, put our devices on to charge and stare out a window. Alone.

Compared to an individual writing a letter, actually focussing on you, answering your questions, asking you things, these incredibly important, hugely financially-driven, Internet-based arenas, are nothing. Aren't they? I mean I'd much prefer to get a letter, say from Elon Musk, preferably containing a cheque. Wouldn't you?

One of the sweetest RSVP ads was Andy, and the fact he was our first success therefore comes as no surprise. Only three of the 24 actually started with a 'Hi'. Most were, understandably, screwing as much self-interest out of their word count as possible. But Andy wanted to put readers at ease. Friendly, polite, a credit to his Mum, no doubt. And his main, non-music request? 'A nice personality'. How astute. All the pop similarities and pretty faces don't hack it if inside you're an axe-wielding maniac! No sir. A nice personality is essential. Not quite sure whether nice personalities are up to the owner of the personality to decide - like many things, nice personalities are surely in the eye of the beholder? Even axe-wielding maniacs appeal to other axe-wielding maniacs. Until one hacks off the other's head, obviously.

Clearly Andy was mature beyond his years in 1985. Oh, hang on, he also, in the small print at the end, requests photos - Andy may be a nice chap, but he's also no fool.

There's another reason Andy is no fool. He's replied again!

Andy: Dear Sarah and Paul,
So nice to hear from you again. Sorry I didn't write earlier but I had a lot going on. It is so sad to hear about Captain Tom Moore...

First, it's nice to hear from us again - that wasn't a given. And an apology for not replying sooner. We feel a bit guilty for allowing doubt in when we didn't hear back at once. We forgot Andy (and everyone else on Earth) has a life beyond the mail dropping through his letterbox. He's got lots going on, he's a busy man.

Very touching that Andy's first thought is for the passing of the amazing Captain Tom Moore. A man who was the sole competitor in the world's most successful sponsored walk. He made upwards of £30 million (and counting) for the NHS. I clapped on my doorstep for the NHS, it's not really a comparable act. Andy's right, Sir Tom was one of a kind. It is sad he's no longer with us.

Andy goes on to check how our move went (what a nice fella) and tells us to take care of each other, while we all wait for our vaccines. We will, Andy, we most certainly will.

However, I wonder if Andy lost our second letter? Or burnt it? Or ate it? Because he didn't reply to a single one of the questions we asked. There's 'caring' and 'kind' and 'nice personalities', but there's got to be a bit of back and forth, eh? Maybe our letter was a little overwhelming? Not to worry, when we reply next, we'll be a little more specific.

Oh, and Andy would like to meet up when that's allowed. So too, Old Girls George. Who knows, maybe in the future we'll hire a little church hall and invite all The RSVPeople and the heroes we meet along the way, to come and have a slice of Battenberg to a playlist of Duran Duran and Spear of Destiny! I can't wait!

Monday 8th February 2021

Oli(ver) Stone is one of the world's most famous film directors . Olis Platt, Hardy and Reed are some very familiar faces on our film and TV screens.. No doubt great guys. Oli Cromwell… not so much, but with Jamie Oliver in the world, I think that sort of evens things out, yeah? But none of these are the Oli who eludes us. No. Oli is The RSVPeople Person whose old address produced a forwarding address for Oli's mum, but at that address our letter disappeared and the trail went cold.

A postal trail, when cold, is a dead end - like the graveyard, just outside the town in the Wild West, where we leave notes on beermats. There's nothing we can do about the letters that have vanished - short of knocking on doors and demanding to know why our beautifully coloured envelopes didn't bring about joy and a need to play - there's nothing to be done. Like Estragon said to Vladimir while they waited for Godot.

Now, Beckett was a literary genius, but he left those two characters wandering round like that, without a single thing to do for, well, forever! And that was mean. It's not exactly the same, but we're not going to elevate those people at those addresses who didn't send our envelopes back, to the role of Beckett and allow them to leave us waiting forever. Beckett didn't allow (#spoiler) Godot to turn up, for whatever mad reasons, but our 24 Godots deserve to be found. So, now the trail is cold, there's nothing for it - let's fire up the laptop and pop on an internet deer-stalker.

'Oli', as he was in Smash Hits, would be impossible to locate without dedicating several months and risking restraining orders. But our Lovely Person gave us his surname. There are quite a few Oli Nansons, but most of them live in America. Like Oli the American guitarist, but he's only 41 and ours must be more like 50. Our Oli might have travelled and settled abroad, of course, but it makes sense to stay close to home until we've exhausted all local possibilities.

There are no Oli Nansons on Facebook who are friends of friends of mine, which is a shame, but not at all surprising. A couple of Olis were born and raised up North. Another, similarly geographically challenged, also looks a little older than our Oli. One has a photo and not a single friend. Sad.

Which leaves only one Oli Nanson…

There is of course the possibility that Oli is not on social media. I mean, he's probably way too busy listening to old Sister Sledge records to bother posting pics of sunsets. In an age of Duran Duran, Wham! and Billy Idol, our Oli was into Soul. I'm impressed. At 15, having been raised a Catholic, the only soul I had any relationship with was the one that was going straight to hell if I didn't get my act together.

To me, this paints a picture of an Oli who stands out from the crowd. An Oli who leads and others follow. And if they don't follow, Oli doesn't care. He's Oli and he's not bothered who knows it. You go, Oli.

But, final Facebook Oli, are you also RSVPeople Oli?

Damn, this Oli was born and bred in London. RSVPeople Oli was a Kent boy. Mottingham. I don't really know where that is. Wait a minute, according to the Internet Mottingham is in London! Did 1985 Oli not really know where he lived? Or maybe he wasn't in

Mottingham for long and made a mistake? OK, so I've just had a lesson in reading more than the first 13 words of a website. It seems Mottingham is in London *and* Kent. Greedy.

So this could be our Oli? Geographically confused, but it could be.

I've just seen that Oli doesn't have friends, he has followers. Does that mean he has friends I can't see, or is he is a modern day Christ and these are his flock? Maybe the soul he was interested in 1985 was not the Five Star kind after all? Sarah and I never pondered the possibility of any of The RSVPeople being a modern day Saviour Of All Mankind, but that's not a problem - we'll write to anyone, on a stone tablet if necessary, so long as it will still post as a first class large letter.

I mustn't get sidetracked, because currently this is still just a standard-issue Oli, not necessarily our God-given RSVPeople Messiah Oli. How does one identify a particular kind of Oli? Well, his Facebook account tells of his Soul & Funk Show. That sounds like the sort of thing 1985 Oli might do 35 years later. Is that enough? Let's find out…

> **Me**: Hi, I wonder if you can help me?
> I'm trying to forward a letter to the Oli Nanson who lived on Alexandra Parkway in the '80s. I have very little to go on other than the name and a 35 year old address. So, if you happen to be the right Oli, could you let me know and I'll send the letter on to you. If it's not you, apologies for the intrusion. Cheers. Paul.

That's a pretty non-threatening message. And I even signed off 'Cheers' which absolutely sets in stone that we are soon to be mates. So why am I nervous? Is it because all the 'no-surname' stuff gets thrown out because as soon as this Oli reads this message he can click through and know exactly who I am? And why does that matter? I just wandered around his profile without him knowing, so he has every right to wander round mine if he wants? Doesn't he? You show me your profile, I'll show you mine? That's got to be fair. It's not like I'm calling him at home or anything. Or maybe I'm just nervous because it speeds up the process.

First it was: post letter - wait - wait - wait - get reply or envelope back - wait - plan - act…

This is more like: post message - hear back immediately: *yes it's me, so what, what the hell do you want?* - run and hide under the stairs - stay there…

See the difference? The former probably contains a nice mug or two of coffee and maybe a biscuit, while the latter involves literally moving under the stairs and living there. Harry Potter did that, that's all I'm saying.

Or maybe it's simply excitement. Finding an Oli doesn't happen every day, I honestly can't remember the last time. And suddenly, today could be that day..!

This reply arrived half an hour after I messaged Oli. But I didn't know about it. I pressed send then signed off for the night. Even an internet detective needs some down time.

So it sat there, all night. Waiting…

Oli: Hi Paul, is this regarding Smash Hits?

Tuesday 9th February 2021

Imagine my surprise when I woke and discovered Oli's lonely and yawning message waiting for me! Less than half an hour, not even 30 minutes after I sent it, the 'not friends' Facebook inbox notwithstanding, he read my message and replied at once. Oli. The right Oli. Oli Nanson!

A-mazing! There were all those Northern Olis, nope not them, and all the American Olis and no-friend Oli. It was none of them. It was Oli who likes Soul (I've yet to enquire about Five Star). And he's already up to speed with the Smash Hits connection. He is on it!

Hang on. How does he know this is connected to Smash Hits? He was a guess, a haystack needle, and I'm a stranger, a haystack crawler? How could he..? Ah…

He's seen the letter? So brilliant. Which means the 'Oli's Mum' route has borne fruit? So good. Oh. Which means he got the letter and thought: so what? Oh no, he hates us. Maybe hates is too strong, but he doesn't care - or he'd have replied, right?

My fingers hover over my phone. Sarah and Sophie are looking at me. They know this is the edge of a precipice. Mount Oli had been found but how best to climb him? I'm at base camp. There could be many routes to the summit. And many leading to certain death. Sarah and Sophie are like my Sherpas, awaiting my decision…

An anagram of Sarah (and) Sophie is *Oh, Sherpas. Ai.* The 'Ai' not referring to Artificial Intelligence, but rather to the three toed sloth, so named for its plaintive cry.

(You knew that, yeah?)

An 'Ai', easily mistaken as a sibling of both Sophie and Sarah.

Spooky.

And scary.

The Sherpas are encouraging me essentially to run up Mount Oli in nothing other than shorts and flip-flips. 'Don't think it through', their combined cries, cry. 'Type, send, throw caution to the Mount Oli wind.' (The sloth is napping, so his opinion hasn't made it onto this page.) But this is why I'm leading this expedition, the pressures, the planning, the frostbite, are all mine to bear…

No, I'm not ready for such foolhardiness. Simply replying as if Oli is a friend from the off feels way too much like trekking across a snow-filled ravine. My gut is rumbling at me that the fresh snow ahead might be covering huge holes and a wrong foot here or there will lead to disaster. The Sherpas haven't thought this through, (the sloth remains silent).

Sarah Sherpa asks to see the message - as if I've missed something from the five words. It's not about 'missing' something, it's about staring at them, becoming one with them, learning from them. It's so difficult to judge tone and nuance. Is Oli annoyed? Is he suspicious? Is he irritated? Stop looking over my shoulder, Sherpa Sarah!

Sherpa Sarah: *It says 'Hi Paul'…*

I check. Sherpa Sarah is right, just as RSVPeople Sarah would have been right, if she'd bothered to get out of bed and come to base camp this morning! That isn't an irritated greeting, it's friendly and hints at a nice chat by a mountainside fire. I don't know how I missed it. I'm trying to get us safely to the top of Mount Oli and I've got to do absolutely everything else myself, have I? (I suspect the sloth is in some way responsible, but he's still snoring gently.)

Like an avalanche, the suggestions come tumbling thick and cold and fast via the Sherpas. They're practically in running gear such is their desire to get going. They mean well but things are getting out of hand. In a desperate struggle where I fight to retain control of the expedition, I rattle off the following (the smiley suggests nothing of the mutiny afoot in our South London base camp).

> **Me**: Hi Oli, it most certainly is, does that mean the letter has already reached you? ☺

OK, so it's a statement of the obvious. The only reality in which he could not have seen it is if he's psychic, in which case I don't need to reply at all. But he's not psychic. He's Oli. And although Olis are many things, I'm pretty sure being psychic isn't one of them.

> **Oli**: Yes my mother passed it on as an email. I'm currently in America at the moment but if you wanna chat anytime let me know.

Wow. OK. So, technically he got the letter, from his Mum. He just didn't get the actual paper it's written on, and he didn't get the SAE. And a letter from America is probably quite a price. This makes perfect sense why we've not heard from him.

His suggestion to 'chat' is problematic. Not that a chat with an RSVPeople Oli wouldn't be close to the top of everyone's optimistic to-do list, but rather it flies in the face of the pulsating pen pal heartbeat of this project. We know writing isn't everyone's idea of fun - especially to strangers when it's hard enough to find the time to stay in touch with people you've actually, you know, met.

Might it equate to a jolly and dedicated religious individual knocking on your front door? They know in their hearts they're bringing joy, devout belief and certainty that if you'd only drag yourself away from Corrie for five minutes you'll have the most amazing experience? They don't quite understand what it is the door-slammers don't get? Then they close the garden gate and try next door, despite the growling of a dog the size of an antelope.

So the invitation: 'write to us, it'll be fun', and 'you wanted to 35 years ago!' may excite some but make others think it's just daft, maybe even puerile (insert sound effect of whoopee cushion). And others might just have spent so long connecting only via the Internet, that any other sort of contact is now slow and archaic?

We hadn't planned for this.

Sherpa Sophie has gone to cuddle the sloth in front of the TV while Sherpa Sarah and I mull over the increasingly anthropological experience of The RSVPeople. The thought of consensually bending these 24 individuals to our will is gone. Not everyone is going to be an Andy or Mandy - and not just because their names don't rhyme. But we want to stay on track with the original idea, the previously mentioned 'purity' of connecting in the same way with The RSVPeople. By letter.

We have to accept that us simply getting in touch, doesn't necessarily make a person want to play along. We must cement the original idea and expand it.

After lengthy discussions we decide that, in a perfect world, we'd like a reaction to the letter, first. Then, we're going to ask them all for another pen pal ad, as they might write it today. And not just the 24, but also anyone else we come across, who joins in. No addresses, obviously, but rather than just a name, age, location, an actual profile of themselves written in pen pal ad style.

But the manner of getting that needs to be more direct. We mustn't let it look as though we're just grinning sponges waiting to soak up whatever words they offer. They're not in the driving seat after all, we are. Sort of. So once contact is made we will present them with a number of definite questions, let's say five - and everyone gets the same questions. This allows the door opener, to stay on the step no longer than they absolutely want to:

Us: *Hello.*
Them: *Hello.*
Us: *Five questions, please.*
Them: *There you go, five answers.*
Us: *Thanks, bye.*
Them: *Bye.*
Us: *No, you close the door first.*
Them: *No, you.*
Us: *No, you!*
Slam! (Rude. But done.)

The RSVPeople Questions

1. Can you remember roughly how many replies you got?
2. Did any of them become a friend and are you still in touch?
3. Did you get what you hoped for from the experience?
4. What music do you listen to now?
5. Most importantly, if you were to write a pen pal ad today, what would it be?

Those questions came relatively easily, followed by this lot, not for them, for us.

The RSVProject Questions For Us

1. How long do we wait before simplifying things for Oli and making him the first recipient of the above questions?
2. How do we get Andy to answer the questions he has side-stepped twice?
3. Is it worth emailing the Canadian hairdressing salon where Russ works to ask about our letter?
4. Should we be concerned we've yet to hear from Sally and Emma after their initial excitement?
5. Shall we initiate 'last ditch protocol' on Fran Hargarden? That is, contact her via all her social media? (Although it really isn't last ditch any more, as we contacted Oli that way.)
6. William and Matt have not responded to the letters forwarded to their workplaces. Should we contact the workplaces directly or go down the 'Oli' route via social media?
7. Who next to try and find via a social media group? (Maybe find a new 'George'.)
8. Talking of George, why haven't we heard back from our last email?

Thursday 11th February 2021

Trying to make strangers do your bidding, is exhausting. So yesterday I made the decision to leave The RSVPeople to their own devices, let them have a good hard think about what they've done, or not done. You can't spread fun and jollity if the people you want to spread it to don't do exactly what they're told in a timely manner! That's not the way enforced jollity works.

Today, across the world, there's a great pressure to be forward-looking, to be autonomous, to be powerful - sell, sell, sell! Become anyone you want to be. Be your best self.

People say things like: 'Everything you can imagine is real'. Which is absolute nonsense - I just imagined an enormous bacon sandwich and it hasn't walked up to my door wearing an 'eat me' t-shirt.

Pablo Picasso said that (the imagine bit, not the bacon bit).

As I said about Samuel Beckett a few days ago, Picasso is clearly a genius. But he imagined this Weeping Woman, and I'm pretty sure she's not real.

(Actually, this version was created by my 10 year old son, and I prefer it to Picasso's, so, well, sorry Pablo.)

And, if this is how much she was crying when Pablo started to paint her, I wonder how much more there was after he showed her the result? Even if this Weeping Woman was looking at a dog, I might have thought twice if this were Sarah's GSM dating profile picture.

All that looking forward is well and good, but I have such a thick vein of nostalgia running through me I can't help casting an eye over my shoulder every now and then (and not just to check The Weeping Woman isn't following me around the aisles in Tesco).

I think the past is where the lessons are learnt. We never really learn them in the Mindfulness playground called 'The Moment'. Because we're too busy stressing, being monstrous and wondering where Mr. Mindfulness lives so we can go round and scream, 'Can you hear me concentrating on my breathing?!' through his letterbox.

It's only later, when we're sitting with ourselves, and shame has crept in smiling her knowing smile, that we take a good hard look at our behaviour. It's when we hang our heads and mutter variations on 'oh dear'. It isn't about looking forward to try and be a 'better person'. Firstly, it's about looking back and trying to fathom why we were such an arse.

Of course, the past isn't just for lessons - and thank heavens for that. Imagine if every time we looked backwards we saw Shame, Regret and Brené Brown, arms folded, shaking their heads at us. We'd all have faces like The Weeping Woman in no time. The past is also where every single nice, decent, kind, wonderful thing that ever happened to us or that we ever did, lives. In a row of perfect cottages with pristine gardens and blindingly white picket fences. You can certainly look forward to being a better you, but there's no harm glancing over your shoulder to remember you're not a complete disaster.

This is why Sarah and I have a row of Annual Reviews on our bookshelves. Essentially, they're 100 page photo books, compiled by me, celebrating the year just gone. Throughout the year Sarah makes sure any memorable photos are sent to me for consideration. Then I collate the best photos of the best events and construct a 12 month narrative.

I have more than 20,000 photos on my phone (I know, I know, I know: 'Spring Clean Your Bloody Phone' has been on my Not Yet Done To-do list for many years). And do you know how often I look through those photos? Almost never. But the Annual Reviews all get looked at a couple of times a year. It takes about half an hour, with coffee. And it's wonderful. The past is a place to be revisited often. Well, the good bits anyway - who wants to be reminded of the time you got dumped, got piles or broke a leg? Especially if they all happened on the same day.

Today I am starting the Annual Review for 2020.

January has 184 photos to sift through. February has 236. March, 245. I mentioned earlier we take a lot of photos. At the moment I've no idea what they all are, I'm simply putting them in folders to make it a bit more manageable. April and May have 238 and 241 respectively, all fairly similar numbers. Then, for reasons I don't remember, June has a whopping 519! And July, with 419, is no slouch either. And just so we're clear, these numbers are after all the blurred and finger-over-the-lens shots have been deleted. I don't know what happened mid-summer, but we took a hell of a lot of photos of it. August comes in at a respectably high 323 but September almost couldn't be bothered with its miserly 194. October contains both our birthdays so 269 is entirely understandable. Then November and December lost their minds: November 1188 and December 899.

4955 photos to sift through. I'm already shattered at the thought.

Considering how often we were locked down last year, only going to the shops and out for 'exercise', I'm a little worried about what we took photos of.

I check. Stand down. November was when I started selling things on eBay before we moved. Loads and loads of those photos are objects and things taken from every conceivable angle. A small number of those might be included to commemorate all the selling, but most won't make it into the final book. Phew.

Some of the photos are a little more important than boxed jigsaw puzzles and unwanted CDs though…

In January last year we cremated my Mum. I hadn't forgotten, of course, but I hadn't wandered through so many memories all at the same time for a while. Photos reminding me about decisions we made about wordings and hymns and commemorative stones and menus et al. It was a little overwhelming. I had a little cry.

There are no photos of the day itself. That's not very surprising I suppose, but the day will have to rely on my memory for all the moments I want to keep.

Even in the midst of grief, life keeps soldiering on: straight after the funeral planning photos, there's one of me about to collapse on my new exercise bike and another of Sarah, in a big black wig, meeting Sir Ian McKellen.

All this looking backwards has me wondering about 1985. 35 years. So long ago, does it even matter anymore? In the overall scheme of things, probably not. But in the specific scheme of things, it most certainly does. Had I written to Smash Hits back then and if Annual Reviews were more than just a twinkle in my nostalgic eye, I would have dedicated some space to it. Both the ad and the replies and the people behind the replies. I might have given over several pages to it. I suppose back then it would have been a scrapbook. Next year this project will definitely make its way into the 2021 Annual Review. Not one of The 24 RSVPeople could have known that 35 years ago.

After the week's successful discovery and contact with Oli, my thoughts move to Jane (no surname) in position two on the Smash Hits ad page. Back in the day she lived in Scunthorpe and had some very eclectic musical tastes: Paul Young, Billy Idol, Siouxsie and The Banshees and The Thompson Twins. She was lonely in 1985. Her envelope was sent to Scunthorpe and so far, nothing. I wander around Google Maps to see if, maybe, like the convent school, her old house is no longer there. It would mean a dead end, but at least everything that could be done had been tried.

Turns out her address is no longer a house, it's now a Wellbeing Centre or even The Wellbeing Centre. Ah, it's in a row of shops, so maybe her address was a flat above, rather than a domestic house converted to this current 'wellbeing' purpose? I'm not sure I even know what a Wellbeing Centre is. It sounds great though. I mean if

I'd found out it was now a Misery Centre or a Really Poorly Centre, I might have been less inclined to dig further.

Sarah: *A 'really poorly' centre is a doctor's surgery!*

She laughs more than is polite. I don't get involved. She smiles the smile of the eternally correct.

Wow, the place is run by The Well-Community Collective. I like them immediately. In a nutshell they're good people who both need support and give support. That sounds like humankind working properly.

People helping people. So simple. Brilliant.

Their website is filled with happy, colourfully dressed folk, posing for photos with genuine warmth and joy. There's even a green wig and a sombrero! In a small nutshell they're about connection. The RSVPeople is about connection. It's like we're cousins. (Maybe we should get sombreros?) They're doing great community work and we're playing an elongated Christmas game of 'find the pen pal' - the similarities are astounding!

I don't believe it - during the pandemic they started a new initiative: The WCC pen pal project. Pen pal project! The address Jane lived in, looking for Paul Young connections is now home to a pen pal project!

That is too weird for words.

A lady called Olivia seems to be in charge of the whole shebang. And she has an email address.

I contact her immediately.

Me: Subject: I wonder if you can help me…?
Hi Olivia, at the start of January my partner and I sent a letter to your address optimistically/naively hoping it might reach a 'Jane' who lived there in 1985. First name and an address is all we had. We're wondering if you remember getting such an envelope? It was bright yellow. After not hearing anything, I Googled the address and found The Wellbeing Centre. I realise the great work you do trumps uninvited and undeliverable letters, but do you know anything about it, whether it had an onward journey? Or maybe you know anything about Jane?
Thanks in advance.

Now I've stretched this tentacle out into the world, I can't help wondering how many of The RSVPeople we might never find. The only person we've almost given up on is Fran. The fact she seemed hugely engaged in all sorts of social media until 2015/16 and then disappeared entirely from any online presence has made us feel both a little sad and a lot curious.

And if you remember, Fran's letter was returned by Lady Luck herself who checked the house deeds, mentioned the lady who bought the house and then suggested we contact the local group on Facebook? And if you don't remember, you should be ashamed of yourself.

Like I mentioned before, we're not going to allow this dead end with Fran to be an actual dead end. I equated it to one of those roads that only looks like a dead end if you're in a car - in fact it is a dead end to cars, but there's an alleyway at the end leading you through to another road. You know the sort of thing - a mugger's paradise. A channel for putting your head down, walking fast and marvelling at how bad most graffiti is. A home for broken bottles and hanging around. I hope the alleyway leading to Fran is not fraught with such things, but who knows?

I dropped a message to her LinkedIn and Instagram accounts. I don't really bother too much with Twattering on Twitter, and I'm not sure if you can DM someone if you don't follow each other. Anyway, if she still uses the email address she used to set up the accounts, she'll get a notification that a weirdo is trying to find her.

And we're back to that trepidation about strangers. Even digital ones give us cause for pause. The notion of Stranger Danger is to protect us from the minuscule number of strangers who mean us actual harm. We teach our kids to be suspicious from a very early age. And it's only really an insurance policy:

Parents: *Kids, avoid strangers, just in case.*

When we're older we make decisions based entirely on the deranged look in a stranger's eyes and whether he's dragging a rusty axe along the floor behind him, dribbling and staring out from behind a full face tattoo of Satan. Me, I'd think at least twice before engaging, but that might be your sort of thing, and I'm not here to judge anyone. But online we're surrounded by strangers. They're literally everywhere. Every day the social medias even suggest strangers that we might know, or want to 'follow' or something. I've seen some people suggested as a 'friend' so many times, I honestly think I know them because their face is now so familiar.

And don't get me started on how many absolutely gorgeous, scantily clad young ladies have chosen to add me as a friend, or follow me or whatever. Even though I've never met them. Magnetism like mine loses none of its pull, even down a fibre optic cable. I guess I'm just lucky to still have it. I wonder if they're related to that Nigerian Prince trying to make me rich?

There's now a chance Fran will see this stranger, me, trying to make contact and will think it's interesting and reply. Or she'll block me for not being scantily clad enough, or, I can't help thinking, most likely - she won't read them at all because her social media days are behind her. And waiting for no reply is not a good place to be. What else can I try?

I could search for her name in general on Facebook, in case someone else has mentioned her? Nothing to lose.

Blimey. There are all sorts of photos. I don't understand why some of them are here. A young couple on a night out seems to have come up because she's called Fran. That's it. Useless. Another one is simply a photo filled with cheese. And another one selling an old record of a singer called Sergio Franchi, imaginatively titled: The Exciting Voice of Sergio Franchi. Facebook is being so unbelievably half-arsed, I think the fact Sergio has 'Fran' in his name is the only reason the photo's being suggested. There's even a photographer in California who is having a special offer and Facebook thinks I might care because there are several people surnamed 'Fran klin' tagged in the photo (Franklins with a typo, surely?) This is ridiculous.

But, hang on, what's this?

A darkish photo. Hands, close up, holding something. Maybe a piece of paper? Let's have a closer look.

Oh my goodness...

There's a condition called Apophenia. It's defined as:

The tendency to perceive a connection or meaningful pattern between unrelated or random things.

Generally this applies to the face you see in your wallpaper or the way the cornflakes sort of resemble a rabbit on a bicycle. We all do it. It's only when we apply huge importance to the illusion that life goes down a strange rabbit hole, on a bicycle.

This isn't that...

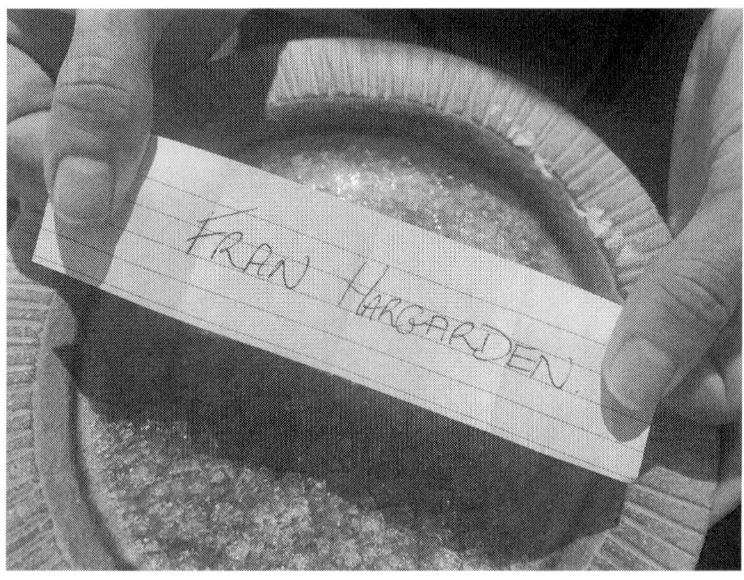

Finding a photo of someone holding a piece of paper with the exact name of the Cure fan you've been hoping to find isn't apophenia.

And Fran isn't tagged and hasn't commentated on the photo so this can't be put down to 'searching', can it?

I'll tell you what it is, it's actually proof that all the angels, probably on bicycles, are smiling down on the alleyway at the end of the dead end and are urging us to keep looking. Yes, oh Angels of Smash Hits pen pals, we see your sign and we will not stop, we will venture onwards until we find either Fran or your next signpost (probably her face in a piece of toast).

Sarah's got a thought. I can't wait to hear her excitement and acceptance that a higher power is at work in our search and that The RSVPeople will undoubtedly become a religion with a billion followers and probably the solitary difference between good and evil in the eternal battle with all the legions of…

Sarah: *Maybe Fran had a Facebook account, was tagged in the photo, sometime later closed her account, and the ghost of the tag has somehow remained attached to the photo?*
Me: *Eh, what? Is that even a thing?* (I'm literally aghast.) *But what about angels?*
Sarah: *No angels.*
Her cold certainty is an ice-pick through the stained glass windows of the new Church of The RSVPeople.
Me: *No angels?*
Sarah: *Nope.*

To think, this revelation and epic-scale balloon-popping comes from the same lips that only yesterday compared The RSVPeople Project to the Tom Hanks movie Cast Away and our letter being like (#spoiler) the FedEx parcel Tom delivers at the end of the film. She said it with almost religious fervour if I'm honest. And, if memory serves, she also referred to us as the 4th Emergency Service. And now she says this isn't evidence of angels?! Fickle, oh ye of little faith!

Me: *A couple of days ago we're Tom Hanks and today angels are not sending us messages? Which is it Sarah? You can't have it both ways. Ha!*

She's no answer to that… mostly because she's left the room and I was speaking quite quietly. But still, '*Ha!*', eh?

Tell you what though, Hanks and angels aside, it's still pretty spooky. Here we are celebrating putting pen to paper and there, clear as day is Fran's name, on paper, written in pen. Even if it's not by way of angels it's definitely worth investigating.

The photo is from a page advertising rather brilliant handmade upcycled women's clothes. A lady called Abigail runs the page. We have a brief online chat. She can't remember what the photo was about or who Fran might have been. Sigh. I imagine if Abigail was drawing the name of the next person to be pushed into a volcano, or to be shot at dawn, she might remember, so it's probably not that. Another false start. Back to the Facebook photo suggestions for one more look…

And as if the Facebook Angels have been teasing me, there she is. Fran. A proper post from Fran. I recognise her from all her socials. Again, there's no tag or mention. (Sarah might be right about the tagging ghosts we leave behind.) Fran is with a lady called Carrie. A comment underneath states, simply, 'Cousins'. I send Carrie a message laying out the path that's led me here and I wave the, 'It's about Smash Hits' white flag so, hopefully, fears will be allayed.

Evidently they are…

Carrie: Hi. Fran is my cousin. If you try contacting her mum, she's on FB, her name is Erin Kennedy. I can't give out addresses etc. please don't take offence but I'm sure her mum can help you. Hope this helps.
Me: Hi Carrie, absolutely no offence at all. I'll contact her mum. Thanks very much for the pointer in the right direction, much appreciated.
Carrie: No problem, hope you get it sorted.

Carrie sends a screen grab of a lady called Erin. And it's the lady who made the 'Cousins' comment. Fran's Mum, Erin. (I might have to add all these helpful ladies to next year's Christmas card list.)

It's surprising how easily both Carrie and Abigail today, and Oli earlier in the week, found the Messenger messages even though we're not connected on FB. I thought they usually disappeared into the darker edges of our profiles. Brilliant that they found them, but I can't say I understand why.

Sarah: *You get notifications for messages not from friends.*

Oh. That'll be it. I guess I didn't know because no one is sending me messages from 35 years ago? Anyway, I pen a similar message to Erin, again laying out the journey that led us here. Maybe we'll have a bead on Fran before the night's out.

Friday 12th February 2021

It's the middle of the afternoon. A gorgeously big purring cat, Frank, is keeping me company while I accept the reality that Erin hasn't seen my message. Frank thinks that if he just gets another tickle under the chin, or is allowed to lie prostrate on the keyboard, a whole world of answers will open up.

Cats know stuff, but Frank can't help me here. If my 82 year old Dad was sent a Messenger message by someone he wasn't friends with (which is pretty much everyone on earth but my sister, because Dad doesn't like to be bothered by people who will only want him to write back) he'd never find it. Not ever. Never, never, never. In a billion years or with a gun to his head. It simply couldn't happen. However, I can see from the simple fact Erin left a comment on the photo: 'Cousins'. Her use of social media is in a different stratosphere to that of my Dad. But it still doesn't mean she'll see it.

Frank is disgusted. Whether at Erin or me remains to be seen, but he's gone to sit on another chair, pretending I don't exist.

Nothing from Erin on Messenger. Nothing from Olivia at The Wellbeing Centre. Nothing from Oli in America. Nothing from Emma from the non-existent convent school. Nothing from Sally either and nothing even from Mandy. Christ, we're in the middle of a global pandemic - there is literally nothing better a person could be doing right now than getting back to us.

Sarah: *People might be saving lives or being frontline workers or…*
Me: *Fine, yes, right, right, yes, OK, fine.*
I can hear Sarah grinning, she loves a petty victory - almost as much as I would if I ever experienced one.

Who's next in the RSVP bit of Smash Hits? Russ. Well, we managed to find Russ - in Canada. We sent the original letter to his place of work. I've no idea if he's been able to work or not. But what he might not be prepared to do is buy an international stamp. That's fair enough. But we cannot let the simple fact of stamplessness cause stagnation in our pursuit. Let's chase the shop.

> **Me**: Hi there. Mid-January we sent a letter (from the UK) to Russell Daniels at your salon. I don't know what the Covid situation is like in Canada or whether you've been able to open up at all, but I'm wondering if you remember getting such an envelope and whether it was possible to pass it on to Russell, please?

Another gentle kick in some faraway shins.

Another message comes in, just as I was kicking Canadian shins. Erin. Fran's Mum Erin. She knows what she's doing on Messenger. What a fool I was to think she wouldn't know how to access the 'other inbox' thingy. Even if most contacts in there are probably weirdos. Erin has viewed, read and regarded me not a weirdo…

> **Erin**: Hi Paul - Fran is happy for you to forward a letter to me and I can make sure she gets it. Hope that helps. Thanks.

And she happily gives us her address. Fran Hargarden will now definitely get her 35 year old reply to her RSVP ad. I don't know who is more excited, me or Fran (probably me).

I screen-grab the message and send it to Sarah who is doing the sort of work that pays bills - as opposed to the kind of work that's really, really, really, really exciting!

I think we need a recap:

1. Custard & Andy - tick tickerty tick.
3. Sally & Emma - Emma has said she's going to write but nothing's arrived yet. Emma has told Sally.
4. Oli - made contact from America, but no RSVP response yet.
5. Fran - reached her via a photo ghost anomaly, a cousin and her Mum! Letter going off tomorrow.
6. Russ - directly chasing up the hairdressing salon in Canada.
7. Matt (and Dave) - no reply to his work-sent envelope.
8. William - just like Matt, nothing from his work - these people with 'proper' jobs!
9. Jane - contacted The Wellbeing Centre to ask about the letter.
10. Johnny, Delilah, Louise, Brian, Monika - all need a Plan B.
15. Donald & Richard - I have a feeling they are going to be a very tricky find…
16. Nayumi Eklund - should have been easy. Not easy.
17. Lars, Adam, Faheen, Becki - sighs and groans, groans and sighs.

Saturday 13th February 2021

How do you solve a problem like Nayumi, I hear you hum from within your wimple?

First off, Nayumi is not a problem. She, I'm sure, is a wonderful human being. Her Swedish-Japanese heritage is not the problem - in fact, such a relatively unusual mix of names suggested she might be easier to find - as opposed to a John Smith in England or a Dai Jones in Wales. The problem with Nayumi is Nayumi's name appears to be a name almost no one has. And her first and second name together produce no search hits whatsoever. Strange.

Eklund produces nearly 20 million hits. Nayumi, 287,000 hits. But together, nothing. Google is most insistent on Nayumi being a Manga character or a treatment for literally whitening the skin. Nayomi (with an o) brings up a lot of ladies' pants.

Is it possible we've been seeking a spelling mistake? And if so, who is to blame? Was it an over-caffeinated Smash Hits staffer, so agog that Neil Tennant, only a couple of months ago a journalistic colleague, was now a Pet Shop Boy racing towards super-stardom, that he took his eye off the keyboard? Or was it the 18 year old Swedish/Japanese Duran Duran fan, so overjoyed by expectation that she let her handwriting clog dance, rather than glide across the page, creating letters that a jealous staffer could never decipher?

Or is it possibly a question of translation? Swedish has all sorts of umlauts and circles that have names I don't know. Maybe these were lost in translation onto the shiny Smash Hits' page? Language can be a very complicated business.

When I studied languages at school I was terrible. I chose German in the end, because I was so far behind in French (and Latin was the other ridiculous choice). But I was still rubbish. I sort of knew what the exam essay questions were going to be about and if I'd learned an outline answer (as I was advised to do) I should have been fine. I was not fine. My mind went blank and the only word I could remember with any certainty was glücklich. Happy. So all my essays were about my happy experience when I went to the happy school, had happy lessons, happy dinner and happy homework. It was all drivel. Happy but drivel. This is reason enough why I am not the person to investigate either the Swedish language or the Japanese language, let alone the two combined!

ALSO - Nayumi's ad has her living in Stehaig. I've never heard of it, but no matter - because nobody has ever heard of it! Because it isn't a place in Sweden! It's not a place anywhere! This is descending into typo hell! And exclamation mark hell too!!

Sarah says I need to cut down on my exclamation mark use. Yes they're a sign of both excitement and frustration, but I'm in danger of dislodging the key from my laptop, then when I really need one, I'll have nowhere to go. A man without an exclamation mark is only half a man, so I will try and take her advice on board!

Sorry.

Happily, I have a Swedish friend here in London, who might be able to help me with the Swedish part of the name and address. He's called Fred. He's very tall. This is not essential in regards to my request for help, but it's still true.

Fred is also a performer, and as there is precisely no performing going on right now, what with the lockdown, I know he has absolutely nothing better to do with his time.

That last bit was tongue in cheek (he's always busy) but he got back in touch so quickly, maybe I was right. He suggests that the address in Smash Hits is an anglicised version of the address, and he agrees there's a typo. I knew it. Stehaig is actually Stehag. It's not a dramatic mistake, a single letter, but to an appalling, but happy, student of foreign languages like myself, it's the difference between happiness and hipponess. And no one wants to go round telling people that today they're feeling like a 4000lb semiaquatic mammal responsible for 500 deaths per year - when what they really meant was that they feel 'nice'.

For goodness sake - Fred's worked out the postcode is also incorrect! It should be 24168 NOT 24200. This might be a recent change though, as opposed to a Smash Hits change - like when I was a kid and phone numbers kept getting longer to allow for all the new numbers needed as more and more houses got landlines.

Oh you couldn't make it up - the area's spelled wrong too!!!

I don't care what Sarah says about the overuse, that realisation requires an exasperated half page of exclamation marks at least!!!!!!!

Smash Hits have Nayumi living in Mareiholm and Fred tells me it should be Marieholm. So potentially wrong town and postcode and wrong district. Maybe she never really liked Duran Duran either! Maybe she really liked Iron Maiden and things got lost in translation there too?

But you know what it could mean? It could mean that, through no fault of our own we may have sent an undeliverable letter. And if our letter was undeliverable, could that mean no letters were deliverable and Nayumi never received a single pen pal reply? Surely not. Maybe, a few issues later there was an apology and a repeat of her ad, with all the mistakes corrected? Either way, if I were Nayumi, I would not be very glücklich!

Let's see what a search for the correct spelling of Stehag brings us online. It looks lovely. Not very big, but still it manages to be home to a very old church, which is something.

Marieholm itself seems to be more of a road leading to dwellings. Lots or trees and grass around too. Fred translated the placename as roughly 'garden field' and with beautiful eloquence added it's 'an area where they've put a bunch of houses'. Ah, the poetry of his Swedish tones.

So we are looking at a Swedish/Japanese Duran Duran fan from a very small area of a quite small area of Sweden. Surely that means Nayumi is a needle the size of a happy hippo in a haystack?

With shaking hands I search for Eklands in Marieholm in Stehag fully expecting to see at least a member of her family staring back at me...

Oh. Five hits. None interesting. All the words but not related to each other. Then I see my error. Google sees my error. An error so glaring it almost qualifies me to be in charge of the RSVP section of Smash Hits in 1985. I've spelled her name wrong. She wasn't an Ekland (like Britt). She was an Eklund (like, er, Nayumi). I make the correction and hit return...

It takes Google less than a second to find a mere nine hits. Nine? Is that all? Maybe if search engines took just a little more time I'd have hundreds? But, no - nine. That's it.

I widen the circle to just Stehag - geographically the place has fewer than 20,000 people, they can't all be called Eklund...

165,000! 165,000 hits? That's more than 80 hits per head in Stehag! Where do you even start when the majority of those hits are, not unsurprisingly, in Swedish? Gah!

I click photos, just in case there's someone holding Nayumi's name, handwritten on a piece of paper. Fred, going over and beyond the call of duty, has informed us Stehag is a town in the county of Skåne? The county has around 700,000 people in it. That's a lot. But a Japanese lady, potentially wearing a Duran Duran t-shirt can't be that hard to find, can she?

Woah!

I'm looking at a photo of a lady who speaks Japanese and is some sort of guide for the area. It's not a guaranteed sighting of Nayumi, especially as I can't see if she's wearing a Duran Duran T-shirt or not, but I must confess I'm nervous now...

Let's click her photo. Click...

...Mayumi Eklund...

Oh, for the love of God, Smash Hits got her bloody *name* wrong too!!!!!!!

Not Nayumi Eklund at Mareiholm 12, 24200, Stehaig, Sweden but - Mayumi Eklund at Marieholm 12, 24135, Stehag, Sweden.

This is how much of Mayumi's ad that was correct: Eklund, 12, Sweden. That's it! It's a wonder Smash Hits didn't have her living on the moon.

I'm reminded of a night about twenty years ago, when I was working backstage at Les Mis in the West End. I was in the bar under the Phoenix Theatre. Back then we called it Shuttleworth's. It was supposed to be a private member's bar, but if you worked on any of the big shows you were in. And a bunch of us were there so often it felt like a second home. And home is the relevant thing here...

A friend. Caroline, was out with us. She worked in the theatre too. It was very late and we were all deciding whether it was actually worth going home or just hanging round until it was time to go back to work. Oh those heady days. We were doing that final check of all our friends who had lasted till now. Was anyone asleep under a table, that kind of thing. Caroline appeared from the loo in a state of drunken undress. She'd managed to pull her jeans up before emerging but her zipper and button were a step too far for her drunken brain.

She was very smiley and rather amazed at her surroundings. The lights were all on now, so maybe she'd popped to the loo when it was still quite dark and she felt like Dorothy leaving the black and white world of home behind and finding herself in Oz?

Anyway, Oz or not, she wasn't dressed properly and she didn't care. I told her of her unsuitability for the night bus and she flung her arms round me like I was an old friend she hadn't seen for a couple of years, rather than a mate she'd spent all evening working with and all night drinking alongside. I ended up having to do up her jeans for her. It was all very proper and she was terribly pleased to find there was one less job for her to do - on top of standing and breathing.

I asked how she was getting home and she thought long and hard and came back with 'bus?' I said maybe she should get a taxi, and she thought this was the very best idea she had ever heard. I asked if she could travel with anyone. She thought this was the stupidest thing she'd ever heard. And laughed. A lot. I wasn't sure why. Then she said, yes, Ellen was coming home with her. Great, I said and offered to call them a cab. I asked where she lived. She thought about this long and hard too.

Caroline: *26.*
Me: *26? We're going to need a bit more information than that.*
Caroline: (grinning) *London.*

26, London?

Ellen, not as wasted as Caroline, but still a little bit like a new born foal on roller skates, had never stayed with Caroline before. Brilliant. There was nothing for it, my girlfriend and I bundled them both into our taxi and took them home to our place to kip on the couch. Caroline and Ellen slept all the way home.

When we got to my flat, Ellen was sick in the wheelie bin.

Good times.

Caroline's attempt at her address was as useless as poor Mayumi's in Smash Hits. That's where the comparisons end - I'm sure

Mayumi is way too classy to throw up in someone else's bin - but hang on, never mind her nocturnal chunderings, we don't yet know if in fact Mayumi *is* Nayumi?

Only one way to find out: ask her. The link on her 'guide page' is broken but LinkedIn provides an email address. Hurrah!
Another dead end bites the dust - no thanks to Smash Hits!

Things are a little different in Sweden. Their equivalent of Google Maps shows me, right now, from above, where she lives. I'm looking at the roof of her house! And also looking at her full postal address. A sort of aerial, digital yellow pages. Never mind emailing, let's send a letter right to her front door.

I sit back in my chair. What a day. I have literally been to the ends of Sweden and back, and detected in a way that would impress even Sherlock Holmes. However, is sneakily finding an onward address in a sort of yellow pages online allowed? I'm not sure. I'm exhausted. I'll consult with Sarah when she gets back from buying brownies - the sugary treats, not miniature Girl Guides.

Sunday 14th February 2021

Happy Valentine's Day!

Apparently somewhere in the region of 25,000,000 Valentine's cards are sent annually in the UK. I cannot vouch for the accuracy of that. However, Sarah and I definitely sent two of them. Additionally, Sophie gave cards to both her kids. And she gave a present to us, and we sent her handmade cookies. Obviously, Sarah and I swapped presents too. It's reckoned about half a BILLION pounds is spent on Valentine's Day gifts, which I can well believe as almost half that was spent in this house alone.

Sarah and I bought each other poetry books.

Last year we got into the habit of reading poems to each other over morning coffee, while waiting for the first lockdown to end. Luckily we bought different books.

I bought a mixed collection of over a hundred poems all entered for a poetry award. Sarah bought one very long poem about the experience of some very brave people under terrible hardship. (I haven't read it yet so I'm paraphrasing badly.) I'm sure it's grimly fantastic, but I'm also sure there aren't too many laughs in it. Or hearts. Or flowers. But it's the thought that counts, eh?

We dip into the collection, expecting something a little more appropriate for the day, saving the long poem for a later date.

The first poem is about a colossal woman being fed by a 'feeder'. It's remarkable. She ended up (#spoiler) rolling over and intentionally smothering him. It's great. But it couldn't be less romantic - not any fault of the poem, rather a fault of our expectation.

I read the next one. A man battles pampas grass in his garden with a chainsaw. This is quite something too. The descriptions of the chainsaw are ominous, the descriptions of the battle, bloody and powerful. Its romantic undertones - utterly non-existent. The notion of giving poems as gifts because they're romantic isn't always the case.

Vaguely traumatised we open Sophie's present to us - a beautifully handmade bowl which will become an essential home for the mountain of fruit we've just bought - it's always nice to have a lovely background to watch fruit shrink and rot in.

It's a gorgeous present, and when we put Sunny D'Nonkey in it, finally, Valentine's Day is heading in the right direction.

We also decided to leave The RSVPeople alone today.

Cold turkey from The RSV-People? It's a wild, brazen and yet brave decision. We can't talk about teenagers from 1985 all the time, can we?

(Mentally I apologise to Fran and Oli and Russ and Mayumi and promise I'll return to them very soon - whilst nodding to Sarah and agreeing it's important to take a day off.)

A nice Valentine's Day walk is the perfect choice as a non-RSVPeople activity.

We go to the common, where The RSVPeople Project first came alive at the start of January. We can't help ourselves - we end up making a list of all the things we still need to attend to regarding a certain matter of pen pals and a certain copy of an old music mag.

Sigh. It's almost as unromantic as abusive feeders and demonic chainsaw gardeners, but at least we do it hand in hand, which is something. I do manage to make Sarah laugh out loud at least once, though - when I declare, with an air of exhaustion, that what I really need to do is 'make a list of all the lists I need to make'.

While taking our 'romantic' walk we see a couple on a bench with a small bottle of champagne and two glasses. A while ago we would have smiled and hugged each other, sharing the energy of love in the air. Today, however, we're more drawn to examining the 'mild obsession' of our undertaking. (Here, the word 'mild' is being used in its Ye Olde English context: meaning 'verging on unhealthy'.)

For a start, my detective work is clearly producing dopamine hits on a par with my first encounter with Candy Crush or Angry Birds, or like when my son goes on a murder rampage on his Play Station. Each new revelation about Mayumi yesterday gave me such a buzz that the desire to peel away the next layer of the mystery was very nearly unstoppable. Like Hercule Poirot - but without spats or ridiculous moustaches.

Naturally, the process we're undertaking today is not the same as those pen pal senders from the '80s. Anyone replying to an ad back then could be pretty certain the address supplied was the one where the person could be found - with the obvious exception of poor Mayumi. There was no guarantee of a reply though - Mandy Custard told us she got 'loads' of replies and couldn't write letters to them all, which is fair enough. However, Mandy and her cohort were at least primed and ready for potential correspondence suitors. They asked people to write to them, getting letters wasn't really something they could complain about. But 35 years on, Mandy et al would be forgiven for thinking the shelf-life of their ad had expired. The equivalent of that jar of something at the back of the fridge that's pretty much frozen to the cooling element and all the label has flaked off. You know the sort of thing?

Along with the ad, the desire to communicate might not be the same now. And patience definitely isn't what it once was. If you grew up in the '70s or '80s and you wanted to contact Blue Peter for written details on how to recreate the Sistine Chapel out of nothing but crisp bags and egg shells, you had to tape some coins to a piece of card, pop it in an envelope and post it with your request. Then you had to obey the rule, the law that was attached to every postal request for anything: 'Please allow 28 days for delivery'.

28 DAYS!?

Literally, today the only thing that I'll allow to take 28 days is February. And even that annoys the hell out of me when I'm waiting for spring to arrive.

28 days. Blimey.

Sarah: *Some of my gigs still insist on having 28 days, or longer, to pay an invoice.*
Me: *Why's that..?*

Sarah doesn't know, but I can hear her teeth grinding from across the room, so I quietly replace the lid on that box of furious frogs.

28 days. It made the post exciting though - you'd usually forgotten what you'd ordered so it was often a surprise. Of course, by the time it arrived, as a kid you were almost certainly no longer interested in whatever it was you'd taped money to a card for. And as an adult, those 'catalogue' clothes you ordered probably went out of fashion while you were waiting for them to turn up.

Now it's instant or nothing. Send a text/WhatsApp/Snapchat or whatever, and we'll give them about 28 seconds before checking if the message has been 'seen'. If it has, and there's no reply, we're immediately irritated. A couple of hours later we're scratching their name off the Christmas Card List that we no longer have - because who sends Christmas cards anymore? Apart from my Dad. And Sarah. OK, people still send cards but not as many and anyway that 28 second ex-friend is going to save you a stamp come December. Alternatively, if the message remains 'unseen' or the ticks haven't gone blue, you give them a couple of hours then assume they must be dead, what other explanation is there? We then unfriend them immediately.

I'm only joking, of course - no one unfriends someone just because they might be dead! We don't want other people to see our 'followers' going down, otherwise they might unfriend us, for being a Billy-no-mates loser. It's an absolute minefield.

28 days seems utterly ludicrous now. It's like having a rocket launch countdown starting from 23,000... 22,999... 22,998... 22,997... 22,996... ZZZ.

The main reason for the disintegration of our patience is surely just because tech has improved so much we've got used to not having to wait? Not so, the letter. The tech has remained exactly the same - get pen, get paper, write letter, put letter in envelope, write address, get stamp, discover you have no stamps (because you sent three Christmas cards last year, no doubt) take envelope to post office, buy stamp, declare 'HOW MUCH?' (silently, of course, because you don't like to make a fuss) lick stamp, realise it's already sticky, remind yourself that even stamp adhesion is now super-charged and stamp licking a thing of the past, post letter. Finally.

The temptation to wait by the postbox to see if you can hurry things along is huge - until you notice there's only one collection a day and that's not for another seven and a half hours. What is wrong with the world today!?

Rumour has it we Brits are supposed to be better than most at waiting. Not so - we're just better at internalising our annoyance for having to wait.

Sarah: *They've waited 35 years already, what difference does a week or two more make?*

Being in a pointy-out kind of mood, Sarah points out it's only 6 weeks since we sent our initial letters. And it was only the 3rd of February we last wrote to Mandy. She might not have received it until the 5th, that means, by 1985 standards we should be well into

March before the 28 day rule has been breached and we call in the postal cavalry. Mandy, (grits teeth) take your time, take your time…

Waiting brings us full circle to the notion of having a day off. The project, inanimate (yet organic) can wait a day, just a day. It'll do it good, stop it thinking it's important and everything's about it. Stop it getting a really big head. That's not going to happen.

For a start, there's a letter to write to Fran Hargarden. I didn't do it Saturday and it's weighing on me very heavily. The amazing process of finding Fran was like gathering the ingredients for the best cake in the world and writing to her will be the cherry on top. The cherries are just over there. And the cake's just over there. And all it takes is introducing one to the other. It's just a mechanical action. Compared to actually finding her, it's a piece of cake. Without a cherry. But it's not been done. Let's get it done…

Done. We pop Fran's letter in another envelope to Erin, her Mum.

Frank helps me write the envelope.

'Helps' might be bigging up Frank's part a little.

Actually, looking at him, I think something extra-terrestrial has just floated through the wall, outside my peripheral vision, naturally distracting him from Sarah's camera.

Fran Hargarden. Tick.

And did I mention we got another letter today?
On a Sunday? I hear you holler. *Oh no you didn't,* I hear you shriek!
Oh yes we did, I respond in full throttle panto mode.

You remember how I'm the impatient one? And Sarah, the laid back one? Yeah? Well the post that arrived today was this…

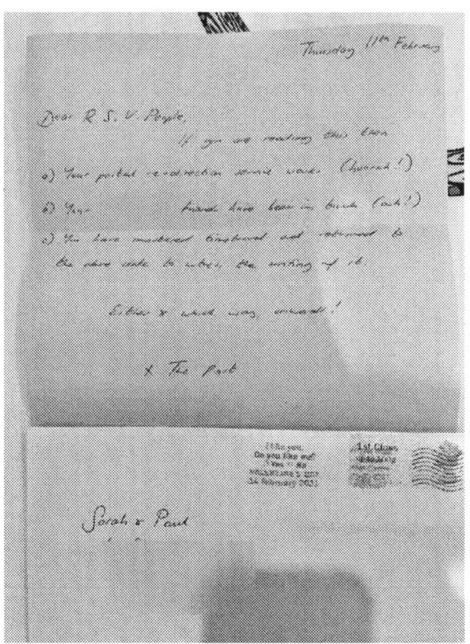
Thursday 11th February

Dear R.S.V.People,

x The Past

Sarah & Paul

A letter from 'The Past', or, to give it its full title: Sarah's Experiment To Check If Our Postal Re-Direction Service Is Working Or Not.

And it was a very good experiment because it seems the answer to the question is 'not', as this letter didn't come through our letterbox. Sarah was passing and popped to the old flat to see if any post was waiting for us. It shouldn't have been.

But it was.

The redirection can cope with both our individual names but together 'Sarah & Paul' is unfathomable, so post to us both ends up at the old address. This envelope and the journey it took was supposed to allay our fears. It hasn't. It's made us more paranoid than ever.

That's what you get for trying to take a day off.

Wednesday 17th February 2021

Sarah sends me an article about a love letter finally finding its recipient after 72 years. A fascinating story but hopefully not an indication that my unborn grandchildren will still be pursuing the long dead remains of The RSVPeople. 72 years of waiting makes 28 days feel like a momentary pause. It's all relative, I suppose, but 72 years will not hack it here. Sarah and I have 'crisis talks'. Well, maybe not quite crisis talks, but definitely talkie-talks. We ponder some ponderables:

* Is the day of the letter, no matter how awful the thought, actually over?

* Is the joy of the letter the receiving, rather than the replying? Like when as kids, we loved getting presents but we'd have to be threatened with a cancelled Christmas next year before writing a thank you letter to Granny sometime in mid-March?

* Not that the letter has become extinct exactly, but has it been reinvented for the different world we now all live in? My kids can't see the point of emails. My 15 year old doesn't even really understand how they work. (He can probably hack the Kremlin from his smartphone but emails elude him?) A message/text (although they're virtually obsolete now)/WhatsApp takes away the need to find an address, write a subject etc. It's like getting the car out of your garage to go to your own front gate…

This is what communication looks like to my 15 year old:

Teen 1: *Hey*
Teen 2: *Yeah?*
Teen 1: *K?*
Teen 2: Thumbs up emoji
Teen 1: *Later?*

Teen 2: Thumbs down emoji
Teen 1: *K*

There's never going to be another Shakespeare unless he finds a way to be on Instagram and can somehow post photos in iambic pentameter.

* If replying to letters is too much of a pain, in a time of instant gratification, then shouldn't we be evolving too? No good having a series of dead ends because we're not willing to bend to the possibilities of new rules, is there?

* Our letters have created mysteries. When the original ones were returned to us we knew they had arrived at the right place. When we sent them back out on a second journey and heard nothing, we cannot be sure they were seen by anyone...

That's a lot to ponder.

Take William and Matt (of Matt & Dave). Their letters went to their places of work. But who knows what happened to them on arrival? Big, proper-job type people with big, proper-job work addresses probably have, not necessarily 'big', but certainly 'proper', job secretaries or security who pick up mail, take it somewhere for someone to sort and filter out all the crap the big proper-job people haven't the time for.

Maybe a bright orange envelope to a 15 year old music fan, now a big proper-job person making millions or running the NHS doesn't make the cut. Maybe there's no pile for it, maybe there's just two piles:

1. Official Stuff: bills, lawyer's letters, gilt-edged envelopes written in fountain pen, the occasional pizza delivery leaflet for when the chaps are working late.

2. Crap: (non-pizza) circulars, double glazing ads, free newspapers pushed through by the teenage delivery kid who doesn't care where his wares end up, so long as the delivery bag is empty when he finishes the round (I didn't last long when I did this job aged 14).

That's pretty much it. Where does an orange, hand-written envelope get filed? No one at a big proper-job office knows. A meeting will have to be called, remotely, obviously. But who should be invited to join the Zoom?

The individual who doesn't know what to do with our envelope needs to be there, but it's also their job to make these decisions. But if a new box or in-tray needs to be bought, a form will have to filled out because there's no such thing as petty cash in a cashless pandemic society. They're not going to spend their own money - remembering very clearly what happened when they bought that party pack of chocolate digestives and were never reimbursed. No one goes through that and forgets. And it's just this one letter.

There's never been a need for 'pile 3' before, probably never will again, and there's nothing but personal financial loss at the end of this road anyway. What to do?

Three choices:

1. Open it, deal with contents.
(But with the level of work, trying to do the jobs of two people already and after biscuit-gate, no thank you. The job is to distribute it, not deal with it. Nope, no chance.)

2. Return it to sender.
(What with no one in the office and everyone working remotely, there are no internal postal employees around at the moment - just me and that security chap whose feet don't make a sound when he walks. First I'd have to find a pen, then Google the nearest postbox, walk there… all unpaid! Nope, no chance.)

3. Pop it 'over there' till the pandemic passes.
(Then someone else makes it their responsibility. And if it should drop down the back of a filing cabinet and not be found for another 72 years, like that lost love letter, so be it, it's not my problem. Now, where's the key for my locked drawer of choccie biccies?)

Yet more ponderables.

It's not that we're in a contactless existence, Sarah and I, but we're not getting the contacts we're hoping for.

After the redirection problem, Sarah decides she's had enough and really sticks it to those bully boys at the redirection place.

Add an attachment

Choose a file

You can upload up to 3 attachments, each not exceeding no more than 3 Mb in size. Valid file types are JPEG/GIF/PNG/TIFF/PDF/DOC

Test letter .jpg Remove

Enter your message *

A letter addressed to my partner and me did not reach us at our new house. We are both named on the redirection and 'Sarah' is part of 'Sarah-Louise'.
We are expecting some more letters sent to either Sarah and Paul or Paul and Sarah soon.

Let us know you're human *

I'm not a robot

reCAPTCHA
Privacy - Terms

Submit

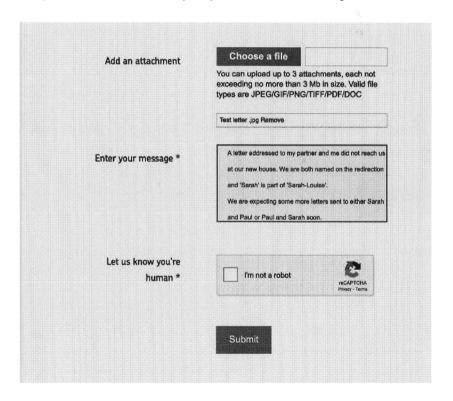

It's a good complaint. It's pithy and it's capable of being screen grabbed all within the same little window. Clever.

I particularly like the, 'we are expecting some more letters…' bit. Because we are and hopefully soon.

'Let us know you're human'. That's odd.

If we weren't human we probably wouldn't have set up a redirection service in the first place, would we? And even if we are an evil 'robot', since we've managed to write a coherent message into the box, surely an additional tick won't pose any sort of problem?

Oh, although the tick won't be the end of it, will it? There'll be some strange photo of a street or a grid of photos and an invitation to 'click crosswalks' and, as everyone knows, this task is impossible to a mere robot.

However, if it had been me asked to click crosswalks I would have clicked nothing - it's not a crosswalk, it's a Zebra Crossing! Always has been, always will be. Crosswalk? Pah. (A crosswalk is what you have after arriving at your friend's house and discovering they forgot they were meeting you and have gone out without you.)

This is why Sarah is in charge of such things.

I'm very much in charge of wondering. Wondering things like - of all the thousands of teenagers who reached out in Smash Hits, how different might things have been if a different edition of the magazine had dropped into our laps?

Different pages, different bands, different hair, different RSVP pen pals! A different world, a different universe!

I mean, what if had been this one, randomly found online…

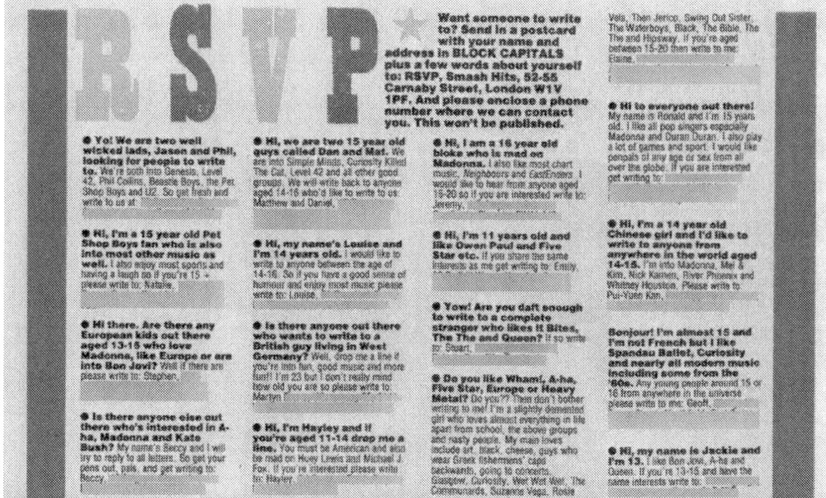

RSVP

Want someone to write to? Send in a postcard with your name and address in BLOCK CAPITALS plus a few words about yourself to: RSVP, Smash Hits, 52-55 Carnaby Street, London W1V 1PF. And please enclose a phone number where we can contact you. This won't be published.

● **Yo! We are two well wicked lads, Jason and Phil, looking for people to write to.** We're both into Genesis, Level 42, Phil Collins, Beastie Boys, the Pet Shop Boys and U2. So get fresh and write to us at

● **Hi, I'm a 15 year old Pet Shop Boys fan who is also into most other music as well.** I also enjoy most sports and having a laugh so if you're 15 + please write to: Natalie,

● **Hi there. Are there any European kids out there aged 13-15 who love Madonna, like Europe or are into Bon Jovi?** Well if there are please write to: Stephen,

● **Is there anyone else out there who's interested in A-ha, Madonna and Kate Bush?** My name's Beccy and I will try to reply to all letters. So get your pens out, pals, and get writing to: Beccy,

● **Hi, we are two 15 year old guys called Dan and Mat.** We are into Simple Minds, Curiosity Killed The Cat, Level 42 and all other good groups. We will write back to anyone aged 14-16 who'd like to write to us: Matthew and Daniel,

● **Hi, my name's Louise and I'm 14 years old.** I would like to write to anyone between the age of 14-16. So if you have a good sense of humour and enjoy most music please write to: Louise,

● **Is there anyone out there who wants to write to a British guy living in West Germany?** Well, drop me a line if you're into fun, good music and more fun!! I'm 23 but I don't really mind how old you are so please write to: Martyn

● **Hi, I'm Hayley and if you're aged 11-14 drop me a line.** You must be American and also be mad on Huey Lewis and Michael J. Fox. If you're interested please write to: Hayley,

● **Hi, I am a 16 year old bloke who is mad on Madonna.** I also like most chart music, Neighbours and EastEnders. I would like to hear from anyone aged 15-20 so if you are interested write to: Jeremy,

● **Hi, I'm 11 years old and like Owen Paul and Five Star etc.** If you share the same interests as me get writing to: Emily,

● **Yow! Are you daft enough to write to a complete stranger who likes It Bites, The The and Queen?** If so write to: Stuart,

● **Do you like Wham!, A-ha, Five Star, Europe or Heavy Metal?** Do you?? Then don't bother writing to me! I'm a slightly demented girl who loves almost everything in life apart from school, the above groups and nasty people. My main loves include art, black, cheese, guys who wear Greek fishermens' caps backwards, going to concerts, Glasgow, Curiosity, Wet Wet Wet, The Communards, Suzanne Vega, Rosie Vela, Then Jerico, Swing Out Sister, The Waterboys, Black, The Bible, The The and Hipsway. If you're aged between 15-20 then write to me: Elaine,

● **Hi to everyone out there!** My name is Ronald and I'm 15 years old. I like all pop singers especially Madonna and Duran Duran. I also play a lot of games and sport. I would like penpals of any age or sex from all over the globe. If you are interested get writing to:

● **Hi, I'm a 14 year old Chinese girl and I'd like to write to anyone from anywhere in the world aged 14-15.** I'm into Madonna, Mel & Kim, Nick Kamen, River Phoenix and Whitney Houston. Please write to: Pui-Yuen Kan,

Bonjour! I'm almost 15 and I'm not French but I like Spandau Ballet, Curiosity and nearly all modern music including some from the '60s. Any young people around 15 or 16 from anywhere in the universe please write to me: Geoff,

● **Hi, my name is Jackie and I'm 13.** I like Bon Jovi, A-ha and Queen. If you're 13-15 and have the same interests write to:

Imagine a world without an Oli, but instead - a Ronald? A world where Bon Jovi have arrived and one where it's now OK to declare programmes and actors as part of your wants/power-hungry demands. Neighbours? EastEnders? What did they sing?

A world where Wham! are still despised, naturally, but where a Greek Fisherman's cap, worn backwards, is seen as common ground for getting to know someone. Are we 'daft enough to write to a complete stranger who likes It Bites?' No Stuart, no we're not. What circle of hell is this? Oh, and just for a second I thought Beccy was from a rather less innocent teenage future, until I realised I'd misread her request for pals to get their 'pens' out.

Sarah finds this alternative collection of RSVPeople intriguing, but there's repulsion too - as if this new Louise, Mat (with only one 't'!) and their friends are imposters. And of course she's right. We now live in a world with a Fran Hargarden, a Custard called Mandy and an Emma who went to a now demolished convent school. These are our RSVPeople. They would not have come into our lives unless they mattered more than all the others.

Sarah suggests her 'repulsion' was a bit strong and what she was actually feeling was exhaustion at the idea of starting again and approaching these new clones of actual real people. These are the people the Post Office is trying to weed out!

I mean, Hayley only wants to write to Americans, Jason & Phil are asking their RSVPers to 'get fresh' whereas if you wanted to write to Stephen but lived outside Europe - you can bloody well forget it! Interesting there's another Malaysian address. Regarding Elaine from Scotland, we both agree she would have been fun to write to - because she's clearly insane.

We're pretty sure, with the slight change in musical tastes, that this bunch appeared in 1986. A single year but a million miles apart from The Real RSVPeople. So similar but these are not our people. We're sticking with our gang. Don't worry gang, we're on our way, we're coming to get you.

And still not in a weird way.

Thursday 18th February 2021

I'm very busy today. Sarah's very busy too. But the manners in which we deal with 'busy' are barely related - like third cousins several times removed on that side of the family that had all historical records burnt in a church fire. Distant relatives at best.

Sarah wakes slowly and calmly as if she may rise from beneath the duvet or she may not, the world is her oyster, the day her friend. I wake like the House Of Commons during a particularly impertinent question by an opposition backbencher during PM's questions: dozens of voices all jeering their objections, comments and allowable expletives. Everyone trying to be heard over everyone else, so ultimately no one gets heard - it's just a stir fry of noise going round and round in the wok of my head.

Then Sarah mentions coffee and whether I'd like any. It's an unnecessary question. The times I've turned down coffee I can count on the fingers of a handless thing that doesn't exist and I've never even thought about. Never. Coffee's always a welcome addition to the Right Honourable Dervishes in the brain wok. It doesn't bring things to 'Order!', but it does stop me disappearing down the plughole of my own messy thinking.

When I get up I usually head straight for the shower. Today I'm not feeling great. I've run all the plague symptoms through my head - thankfully I have none of them. No need to self-isolate everyone in South London. Hurrah!

During that one thought Sarah has risen, made the bed, got dressed, dealt with a fresh email deluge and reminded me twice that she's working from ten.

She kisses me on the cheek, and with the promise of a bacon bagel if I get a move on, I gather all the snarling MPs and as a writhing mass of man-sized eels, we head downstairs.

Half way down, I realise that the Member for East Forgetfulness has left my phone upstairs. With the Right Honourable Ladies and Gentlemen of Oh-For-God's-Sake, I head back up. On the way, a Junior Minister from the Department of Remember-You're-Not-Feeling-Great points out I'm a little breathless and the phone will still be there, no matter how long I take. I get my phone.

As I head out to the garden office, I have a gander at the notifications on the home screen. Blah, blah, blah. Facebook suggests I have a million things to read that will make life unbearably better. Then. Oh my goodness.

I am immediately reminded by The Speaker of The House of Chronnell (who will always have the perfect tones of John Bercow) that an email arrived late last night, and I'd completely forgotten, what with all the other cawing noises in my head…

Lovely Ron, from Canada, he who runs the hairdressing salon where Russell works, checking in, letting us know our letter has arrived.

Ron: RE: A letter for Russell Daniels

Hi Paul, we are still under lockdown here in Ontario but I go to the salon regularly to get the mail etc. Your letter was in the mail today. I have left it at the salon for Russell and texted him to let him know it's there. It may still be a few weeks before the salon's open and he gets it.

I bet you get a brilliant haircut when you're in the capable hands of Ron's salon.

The reason the email has just Bercowed into my head is this…

Notifications

New

Russell Daniels commented on your post.
6h - 'Is it you that has written to me..?'

Russell Daniels likes your post: Hypothetical dilemma/social experiment…

Not only have we heard from a certain Mr. Russell Daniels, he's also liked the original post too - the one where we asked Sarah's honest friends and my criminal-leaning associates, what they'd do if one of our envelopes appeared through their door?

One of our RSVPeople is now actually responsible for a comment on the very first post about this project!

No, you're missing the point - it's much more important and mind-blowing than however you're thinking about it.

The realisation that's come with Facebook's notifications is that Russell is game. Ron must have told him of my email contact. Russ must have used that to find me online, found a spookily relevant post only a few weeks ago and immediately connected and asked if I'm the person sending him letters. On one level I'm absolutely thrilled to see Russell make contact. On another, I'm a little jealous that his search for me appears to have taken around eight seconds - if only finding the rest of his fellow pen pal seekers was even a hundredth as easy! 'Order!' says The Speaker and I sit back in my seat and cease heckling the more important joy of a new connection. Literally, right now, a man is standing on the roof where I'm writing. He's wielding a chainsaw at a tree that's gotten on the wrong side of him. Sophie, who owns this garden office where I'm working, came down the path to tell me. Maybe he's the guy who wrote the Valentine's chainsaw-garden-battle poem? She said the chap came to the door to ask if he could wield his chainsaw from the office roof and when she asked if the roof would support him he laughed. He laughed.

So if this is my last entry, I would like it known I want as many of The RSVPeople as possible to be at my wake…

I tell Russ I'll message him directly and I do. I reassure him our search for him is nothing horrible and await his response.

This also means that today, Sarah, Russell and I are all together in the same place! Our names and faces all in a row as people who have liked our dilemma post (you have to like your own posts, obviously, to make it look like there's more engagement with them than there actually is, no?) The three of us, RSVPeople. Together on Facebook. Nice.

It's the middle of the night in Canada, so we won't expect a reply right away. And just as well, do you remember me mentioning I'm really busy today? If you've forgotten, go back a few pages and check. I'll wait. See? Well that hasn't changed amidst all this Canadian excitement. I have a monologue to write for an actress and some notes to reply to from a Hungarian actor/pilot who I'm writing a short film for. These things don't write themselves, you know. And all this before a bacon bagel.

I'm also considering running for the safety of the house if this chainsaw business carries on above me much longer - I've seen the Texas Chainsaw Massacre, it's garbage, but I've seen it!

Several hours later chainsaw wrangling is finished and I still remain in possession of all my limbs. But even better than that - who remembers Matt and William? Feels like about four years ago but it was only yesterday we last mentioned their Springsteen and Madonna-loving selves. Remember we had letters returned from them? Yes you do, you've just had a lot going on. Exactly, right, good. Well you'll now remember their letters were sent back out into the world via their work addresses?

Well today we heard from neither of them.

Which is pretty much the way things have been with those two for more than a month. I mean, who has the time to not be in touch every single day? Occasionally one or other of them will fail to be touch two or three times a day. Those guys! Well today I had enough of it. I chased William at his place of work, where we sent his letter and Matt I contacted directly through a work email address. That'll show 'em. I'm not messing around!

Friday 19th February 2021

No time for an intro. Lots to say. Lots of information. Lots of detectives in my head jumping up and down, causing a lot of noise and mayhem. I call them to order.

Sherlock's pretending he's not excited, like he's only three coughs away from needing opium and someone to shout at. Poirot's hand is up. Not now Hercule, you'll have to wait your turn - I know Agatha always gave you the limelight, but those days are gone. And there's way too many of you here to make it about any single one of you.

Anyway, I want to start in Wales.

The scruffy looking bloke from Hinterland looks up, I think he's been napping. He pats all his pockets. He's either got a lot of pockets or he's patting areas that don't have any, as though, maybe he has other clothes that have pockets there and he's forgotten what he's wearing. Come on Hinterland Man! He has notes. He tells of the search for Brian 'Hi world!' Evans. Brian is in Wales. Hinterland Man is in a Welsh detective series. It's perfect.

He mutters that a search for 'Brian Evans' produces more than half a million hits. A search for 'Brian Evans' and 'Wales' is a mouth-drying 75,000. (Damn you Wales for loving your surnames so much you only have about eight of them.) Hinterland Man shrugs his shoulders. Brian's a Welsh man, with a Welsh name, who lived in Wales. He's right, what did I expect?

Hercule's hand raises again, a single glare from Hinterland Man and it's back in his Belgian lap. More Welsh tones inform the room that things are nowhere near as impossible as they seem. Because Brian lived on a road called Minffrwd Lane (thank you Wales for your unusual use of letters).

Minffrwd? Apparently this translates as 'edge of a stream'. My application for a doctorate in the Welsh language is still under consideration, for which I am extremely glücklich. Minffrwd Lane still has around 4000 hits, which is a surprise. I thought there'd be about three. But if we add the house number we get: D Evans & Sons and a photo of a house in a little row of shops. An Evans in Wales is like finding a needle in a needlestack but to find an Evans still living at the same address? Surely it's too much of a coincidence?

Sherlock yawns. He doesn't 'do' coincidences. He wants to talk about William. I tell him no, and Hercule to not even think of raising his hand again.

D Evans & Sons has no other mentions anywhere. Hinterland Man considers approaching the post office a couple of doors down, but it seems there's a discrepancy about where the actual P.O. is. It was over a decade since Google drove down Minffrwd Lane and the Post Office has its building listed across the road now. Typical. Maybe, I wonder, could this be one of those mythical Welsh villages where the shops move around every week or so, by magic? Hinterland Man's stare is almost painful, so I let him continue. He produces a screen grab from one of his pockets.

> D Evans & Sons, 38 Minffrwd Lane, Trerhyngyll, Cowbridge, is at a height of 186 meters above sea level. There are 19 more properties in the postcode.
>
> Mail information: Postcode of this property receives 25 or fewer mails per day.
>
> Mail delivery to this address is a slow.

Knowing the building's height above sea level is all well and good.

And the fact there are 20 addresses within the postcode is interesting - everyone gets approximately a letter a day.

But when they're delivered, that delivery is 'a slow'. Not 'a bit slow', just 'a slow'.

Before I can ask the question, Hinterland Man says the letter should have got there, no matter how 'a slow' the delivery.

It isn't a lead. But this group might be…

Memories Of Trerhyngyll. Public group - 4.5k members

Memories of the area are what we want. Especially memories of number 38 Minffrwd Lane and Brian, who'll write to boys and girls, he doesn't mind.

I message the admin, Paula, that name's surely a good sign? She approves my membership and I pose this question to the good people who have joined this group to do nothing more than simply remember Trerhyngyll.

* New Member *

Me: Hi, I wonder if anyone remembers a Brian Evans who lived on Minffrwd Lane in the mid '80s? I have a letter I'm trying to forward to him and was wondering if anyone on the group knows him, or maybe his family, or knows where I might be able to contact him. Many thanks.

The splendid folk of South Wales chip in with all sorts of messages. It's a completely different experience to our time with the Gisburn town folk…

Lesley R Alders: If it's who I think, his mam lives in Minffrwd Lane.

Simon Flowers: His mother still at 38 Minffrwd Lane.

Barry Shaun: Maureen the shops son. Don't think on FB.

Lesley thinks his Mam still lives on the street. I've never met a Lesley who lies. Simon goes further, he confirms both street and number. Thanks Simon. Barry offers a strange titbit: 'Maureen the shops son'. Is 'Maureen The Shop' a Welsh moniker like 'Jones The Steam' at the station or 'Dai The Fish' at the anglers or 'Jill The Embezzler' who's appearing in court next week?

Neil Connor: Maureen, his mum, still lives at no. 38.

Barry Shaun: *Ron Brown* your old butty.

Lisa Styles Pack: Post it to his mother and it will get to him.

Mira Heath Donaldson: Would ***Christine Johnson*** be able to help? X

Andrea Folds: Auntie ***Christine Johnson***.

Me: Thanks everyone for the suggestion. I will try his mum. Thanks again.

Certainly seems Maureen might be Brian's Mum's name. Neil, clarifies. Maureen, indeed his Mum, lives at No. 38. All summed up nicely. Barry's back though, he's had a thought and wonders whether a chap named Ron might have been Brian's old sandwich. Or possibly a typo for 'buddy', or simply a playful word for 'friend' in Trerhyngyll? Either way, Barry, your help is invaluable, I salute you. Lisa, clearly busy and wanting to move things along, is certain that posting it to his Mum will guarantee its safe arrival with Brian.

Little does Lisa know, we've already tried this and whether it didn't arrive because of the 'a slow' postal service or because Maureen hasn't acted on the letter yet or even because she has sent it to Brian and he's not impressed, remains to be seen. But Andrea and Mira aren't finished. They think Christine Johnson might be able to help. Whether Christine is Brian's auntie, or Andrea's, is not completely clear.

Hinterland Man is finished. Even Sherlock is a little impressed. So many helpful chaps and chapesses. Poirot's staring out the window, offended at being made to wait his turn. Not my problem.

Here at The RSVPeople we are polite and grateful for all help and assistance, so I click the blue thumbs-up button of 'like' on the replies. But I wasn't the only one. A lady, Julie, without joining the conversation is simply glad and thumbs-uppy that something as exciting as the (not weird) Hunt For Brian is afoot.

Facebook suggests we might like to add Julie as a friend, and no wonder, she's clearly enamoured with The RSVPeople search. What a nice lady. Strangely, I now feel the search for Brian is as much for Julie as it is for us. Never fear, Julie, we won't let you down.

The brilliant helpfulness of the Welsh comes as no surprise to me. Having spent more than a decade living there myself - my Dad still lives there too - I have nothing but good things to say about The Welsh. Although, if I should find myself in Wales on a day Wales are playing at home to England in the Six Nations, I'll be sensibly keeping my head down.

Without invitation, Sherlock swans to the front and tells us Matt, contacted through a work email address, has yet to reply. End of. He looks around. He's not carrying on until we… oh right. We all clap politely. He carries on. William, similarly contacted through a work address, has borne rather more fruit. But not the right fruit. Like bananas appearing on your Granny Smith tree.

A chap called Nick (currently Head of Regional Sales, but you mark my words destined for a large corner office in the future) was back in touch in less than an hour and a half. But the news wasn't good…

Me: *Poirot, put that damn hand down or I swear I'll put it down for you! Sherlock, carry on.*

William doesn't work there anymore. Seems he didn't work there when we sent the original letter. Damn, damn, damn. Nick also states that no letters for William have been forwarded in his direction either. I sense a hand reaching for a locked drawer full of chocolate biscuits. Mustn't jump to conclusions, Nick sounds like the sort of man with an aversion to crumbs, so I'm sure he's telling the truth. He kindly offers to help, but he means in a big proper-job way. I explain it's a letter of a more personal than business nature. You can almost sense Nick's disappointment that he won't be getting a new client, but he's sorry he doesn't know where William went after leaving the office with a cardboard box containing a framed photo and a pot plant, but why don't we try LinkedIn? Sherlock sits. He rises. We clap. He sits.

Out in the corridor there's a commotion. The door bursts open and the Canadian Mountie from Due North and the waistcoated chap from Murdoch Mysteries tumble in, still wrestling on the floor in Canadian accents. They have news. Each wants to speak first. They kind of speak simultaneously.

Canadian Detectives: *Russell's been in touch!*

> **Russell**: Hi, just walked to the salon and back in a snow storm (1hr 10mins each way) as I was too nosey to wait until March when we might open again lol. How did you track me down to the salon? I will write back the old fashioned way though and not on Facebook ☺
> It was very funny and a blast from the past!

Pandemics don't stop Russell 'Thompson Twins' Daniels. Snow storms are mere piffle to his Wham!-loving feet, so too walking 6 miles or so to fetch a letter, the contents of which could have been anything. He refers to himself as 'nosey' Russell, but we call him Brilliant and Wonderful Russell. (And possibly 'a little bit chilly and tired' Russell.) And bless every inch of his nostalgic frame but he's already planning to write to us the 'old fashioned' way. Brilliant, quite simply, brilliant.

The Canadian Detective Duo have one final piece of information - Russell is the only contact we've made so far who has asked how we found them. He's thinking like a true RSVPeople Person. Astute and brilliant!

Me: *Right, Poirot, what is it?*

Hercule shrugs, it doesn't matter now. Oh, he's wet himself. Sigh.

Saturday 20th February 2021

Sometimes we make mistakes. Hopefully not all that often, but occasionally. We're only human after all. We'd asked to join the Ashworth Memories Facebook page, in the hope of finding clues to

Becki. But the request was turned down. Not because the people who run it thought us not good enough, but rather because it's the wrong Ashworth.

A jolly chap explained, very nicely, that geographically our hopes and dreams of finding Becki were at odds with the fact his Ashworth is 60 miles away from Becki's Ashworth. I nearly pointed out that The RSVPeople Project doesn't let a thing like 'distance' get in the way - Russell and Oli are thousands of miles away from where Smash Hits listed them. But that doesn't change the fact we're looking for Bradford in Derbyshire.

What's that? Why haven't we heard anything about Johnny 'Simon Le Bon lookalike' Carter? Well, come on, there's been a heck of a lot of Fran and Andy and Custard and Mayumi and Matt and Oli and William and Brian and Russell going on, hasn't there? Never mind the George-Sally-Emma triangle from the old Convent school. It's just taken a little while to get to Johnny. But, settle down, Johnny Time is here.

His letter didn't come back. And although it may have been forwarded elsewhere, we've no way of knowing - it might just as easily have ended up in the bin. Either way, it's time to use other means.

The Trerhyngyll group proved so amazing guiding us towards Brian, let's see if the Appleton Community Noticeboard is populated with equally helpful folk.

The gatekeeper/admin has no problem letting me post my request. Ta very much. Replies come quickly.

Matt Logan: I'm pretty sure his Mum & Dad still live there, might be wrong.

Matt Logan's first up with a reply. He reckons Johnny's Mum might still be at the address. Good for Matt, but bad for us. If Mum of Johnny is still there, she already has the letter and we have to awkwardly tell her we've already been in touch. But at least Johnny is remembered. It's a positive start.

Greg Lovitz: Mother lives in Anglesey. I have her address somewhere. DM me.

However, Greg can't bear the uncertainty for another second. He can't even face mentioning Matt's attempt at helpfulness. He knows Johnny's Mum, knows where she is and has her address. Get in touch and it's ours.

Wow, Greg takes no prisoners. Weird how Greg doesn't want to share the address with just anyone - especially none of his neighbours or community, but he's less concerned sharing with total strangers like us. Must be my profile pic, makes me look very safe and un-murdery.

Marie Styles: *Alison De Niro*

As I'm telling Sarah how the whole of Cheshire has cancelled the rest of their evening and are on the case, Marie's appeared. Silently, saying nothing, commenting on nothing, just whispering the name *Alison De Niro*. For the briefest of moments I can't help wonder if Alison is actually Robert De Niro in disguise. I mean, stranger things have happened.

Sarah: *They haven't.*

But Marie's dragged Alison into our world. Could she be his sister? Johnny's or Robert's? Maybe Johnny's optician? Or his heart-broken teenage girlfriend who still thinks he looks like Simon Le Bon?

Ping! Blimey. There's literally nothing else going on in Appleton right now. Nothing.

Neil's next. He also knows Johnny's Mum. She's in Anglesey. He could find the address but he's being a tease.

Neil Lowe: Yes, I know his mother. I could find her address for you. She is still in Anglesey.

Llio Tidd: I'm on the big Anglesey FB group as we have a caravan there - happy to share on here if I can help?

Ping! Now here's Llio, probably quite the celebrity in Anglesey because she's on another group, a 'big' group, and is more than happy to help. I bet people always turn to Llio in a crisis.

I once went to that neck of the woods with a friend called Mark. There were a million huge caravans there. The static ones - bigger than some London flats. Much bigger actually. I remember getting kicked out of the grounds of a pub there. Mark and I didn't have the money to buy the cans the pub was selling, so we bought them at a supermarket and set about being smug, saving money and discovering we were hopeless at chatting up girls. For about 20 minutes until a bouncer told us to leave because we were drinking cans they didn't sell. That walk, past all the other teenagers who'd done their lager research, still smarts. Oh those dark North Wales memories.

Ping!

Alison's all over Matt's earlier message.

> **Matt Logan**: I'm pretty sure his Mum & Dad still live there, might be wrong.
>
> **Alison De Niro**: Not for 8 year now ☺

Matt's doubt is trumped by Alison's certainty. And her certainty is funny. What could that mean..?

Ping!

> **Alison De Niro**: PM sent x

The Deer Hunter, the Raging Bull herself, sorry - *Alison*, has messaged me, with a kiss. Well, this is exciting…

Crikey. It's not a PM, it's practically a short story that begins…

> **Alison De Niro**: Hi Paul, my apologies as I'm in receipt of a letter from you I think…

I read it to Sarah immediately.

Alison lives in Johnny's old house! She has our letter. Johnny's letter. And she wants to help, she really does, but has not yet located Johnny's Mum's address to send it on.

There's lots of news. Her move in date, the sad passing of Johnny's Dad and the fact all the fault lies at the feet of her neighbours who were asked for a forwarding address but haven't come through yet. Well, come on Alison, without an actual pen pal letter in their hands they don't have the same excitement coursing through their veins that you have, you lucky thing.

Sarah and I glance at each other when Alison writes: *I should have returned your letter…*

Yeah, well, maybe, I mean it has been six weeks, some might mumble the word 'tardy'. Not us! Other people. We forgive you Alison, because you wanted to help. You saw a colourful envelope and knew colourful envelopes mean only one thing - they're full of fun! Alison, you are brilliant. Welcome to The RSVPeople!

Sarah suggests maybe Alison has suffered enough and if we take Greg Lovitz's earlier kind offer we can pass on Johnny's Mum's address to Alison and if she's ok with it, she could forward it for us. Great plan. Greg is as good as his word and we get the address to Alison immediately. What fantastic teamwork.

Ping! Alison's not finished…

Alison De Niro: Fab… I'm glad to have it now too in case I need to forward on other post so thank you too ☺ I'll get that posted off tomorrow for you. x

Excellent, the address will be useful to her should further misguided post arrive on her mat, a mere eight years late. And she promises to get the letter in the post tomorrow.

No doubt, for Alison, having had the letter all these weeks, it'll be quite a wrench letting it go. Like a foster mum, protecting her charge but always realising it was never hers to keep.

That trip to Cheshire was intense, but even before the fireworks have disappeared from the sky, a different type of intensity arrives…

Maris: Hi, Brian is my cousin why are you trying to contact him or what is this letter about?

Brian's cousin. I'm sensing hostility. Maybe even a hand on a hip. Then again, why not? She's his cousin, Trerhyngyll has been going crazy trying to find him. I message her and say it's nothing bad, it's about Smash Hits!

How could anything about Smash Hits be bad?

Maris: Awh right okay sorry was just a bit worried haha

Worried? We never meant to worry anyone, but, still, I sense a large exhalation from her. We're going to be fine, probably pen pals. I reply saying I'm happy to tell her all about it but we don't want Brian to find out because it's a big surprise. She'll probably be as excited as George. A new George! Isn't it amazing how everyone this project touches gets so excited, it gives them, almost, a new lease of life..?

Maris: That's fine just didn't want it to be anything bad that's all

No matter how many times I read it, I can't turn 'that's fine' into: *Yes, please, absolutely, tell me all about it, I'm stopping making tea, holding my breath actually, until I have every last morsel of the details!*

She may have no knowledge of punctuation, but she may have knowledge of Brian. I ask if she knows how I can get hold of him.

Maris: I'm not sure I'm not passing on address as it's nothing to do with me just wanted to double check it was nothing bad that's all

She's still polite, and I completely understand she's not sharing an address with me, but let's look at her message again. Yep, I can see it, can you? Look closely. See? That's it - underneath the typed words is the very clear message: *Go away now, please.*

Consider it done, Brian's cousin, Maris, away we go.

One day though, after we've made proper contact with Brian, we'll buy Welsh cakes from the local post office on Minffrwd Lane, now also a corner shop, and they will be appropriately happy for our sugary custom. For the time being we bid a fond farewell to Wales.

And just when you think The RSVPeople day is over, it isn't. Because, out of nowhere, the wonderful George returns with apologies for delays, offers of her personal email address, which she checks much more frequently than the convent Old Girls' one, and is sorry that neither Sally nor Emma have yet deigned to reply. I can sense that she's a little disappointed with them. And, as we all know, disappointment is the most crushing of criticisms.

Come on Sally and Emma. Even if you don't get in touch for yourselves, get in touch for George!

Sunday 21st February 2021

A day off. That's what a Sunday is. But, if last Sunday proved anything, it's that Sunday itself is not capable of doing all the 'day off' stuff unaided. You have to take responsibility yourself. Otherwise it becomes a day on and you find Sunday shaking its head disappointedly at you.

But it's so hard to do nothing, not to think about all the stuff you think about the rest of the week. The thing is, when you try not to think about a thing, it makes you think about it.

You know elephants?

Here's one. Fairly standard. Huge, big ears, trample you to death if he saw a mouse coming. Elephants. Now don't think about elephants.

How's that going? Not so well, my elephant-obsessed friend. I call this The Elephant Syndrome. Or possibly the Elephant Paradox?

What about The Elephant Thingy? I'll give it more thought when Christopher Nolan wants to use it as the central feature of a future sci-fi blockbuster.

So: The Elephant Thingy © (See that, I've copyrighted it - or at least I looked up how to insert the copyright symbol on my laptop - and I'm not going to tell you how, or you'll all be doing it.)

So: TET © (It's getting so well known, people now recognise the Thingy as an acronym alone.) proves that being told not to think of a thing makes it impossible not to actually think of it. It's similar to TDTTIBPF © (may have to work on that acronym, not as catchy as I'd hoped) or The Don't Touch That, It's Bird Poo Fallacy that all parents with small children come across when having a lovely picnic at a wooden table in the countryside. No sooner has the parent used the phrase, 'Don't Touch That, It's Bird Poo', than the child is consumed with the need to focus on said poo and eventually almost (or actually?) dip a rice cake in it before taking a big bite. This leaves the panicked parent split between examining the poo for signs of dippage, whilst also trying to get a phone signal to Google CANMYCHILDDIEFROMEATINGBIRDSHIT? As we know, all children are made from slugs and snails and puppy dog tails (it's not just boys) so they're already in close biological harmony with every foul and disgusting thing and will somehow, mostly be OK no matter where those fingers have been.

Because believe me, they've been everywhere.

DISCLAIMER:
The above should not be taken as necessarily complete and accurate medical advice, and if your child does actually eat bird poo it might be sensible to actually consult an actual medical doctor.

By all means quote the above TDTTIBPF © if you think it helps.
Thank you.

In a similar way to T© (the term *Thingy* is now universally recognised so the acronym *T* is equally well recognised. *#T* is trending as we speak) when Sarah and I try not to think about The RSVPeople we fail. So we decide to action a small bit of the project - rather than blathering about the whole thing all day.

We look at things that needed posting.

Mayumi needs a letter at the new (photographic Yellow Pages) address. Hopefully she still lives there. That won't take long. We decide to send the exact same first letter. (Because heaven knows where her original is now?) And as she's absolutely not at the address in Smash Hits, we also explain how Lovely Fred, using his expertise of all things Swedish, helped us find this new one.

Tick, an obligatory record-keeping photo and a wander to the postbox, and Mayumi's letter is back out into the world, while Nayumi's will forever wander the earth looking for a woman who doesn't exist, in a place that's spelled wrong. One day it may return to us, who knows?

We're reminded of an unhappy list we made. The envelopes that are MIA, presumed recycled. It's a miserable list and one we never wanted to think about again. For want of a better term, we call it the Chase Original List: a last ditch attempt to wobble the letterboxes of the MIA letters to try and discover their fate.

However, because of the Alison De Niro from Appleton (wonderful Appleton!) experience we have a glimmer of hope - all might not be lost on the Chase Original List. Maybe mantlepieces across the world have envelopes, gathering dust and pining for their true homes. Like a thousand war films before us we make a decision - no envelope will be left behind: nemo resideo. Or in our case neenvelopeo reside..? Ish.

So, we order some 'will arrive by 10pm tonight' postcards and pen a brief explanation for whoever picks them up from various front door mats.

Obviously, on the individual postcards, we didn't write, 'X' and 'Y'. The example below is the template from which all the postcards were created. I know you knew that, but, well, if you didn't, it'd be confusing. And awkward. And no one wants that.

Us: Hello, hope this finds you well. A few weeks ago we sent a letter in an X coloured envelope addressed to Y who lived here 35 years ago. As it wasn't returned we wondered if it arrived or was forwarded on? We're sure you're very busy but if you'd be so kind as to let us know about its status we'd be grateful. Many thanks,
Paul & Sarah

That doesn't look like a lot of words, but most of us (and by 'us', I mean me) have forgotten how little space there is on a postcard.

After all, who sends them?

You go on holiday today and you've got 371 different ways to let people know you've arrived, what the weather's like and what you're eating, before you've even unpacked a suitcase. Postcards traditionally arrive when you've already returned home. You get phone messages saying 'your postcard came' which only reminds you how cold it is here compared with there and how quick the holiday passed and how much you want another one.

Using Social Media instead of a post card, at least gets a whole bunch of reactions and jealousy, which is what we're all really after.

Smug Holiday Person: *Hi everyone we're on holiday and you're not!!!!*

So there's not much space on a post card. We might have to look at that. But that's enough work for a no-work Sunday: one letter to Sweden, a pack of fun postcards ordered and a (potentially too-long) message constructed for the postcards when they arrive. Nice.

We go for a walk.

We talk about whether anyone under the age of 60 ever really went for 'a walk' before lockdown, before we learned of our God-given right to exercise outside once a day? I don't mean travelling out into the countryside for a walk and then six lovely hours in a country pub before catching the train home, that's different. A walk, close to home, going nowhere, just walking, and then coming home, I don't think that was even a thing before last March, was it? Unless you have a dog and enjoy carrying 'it's business' around the neighbourhood in a little black bag - in which case you've been doing it forever.

It's such a lovely day!

After walking, we sit in the garden and eat ice-creams. We consider other things like foxes, squirrels and cats - all of whom wander through the garden from time to time. We don't look at our phones. I have a deeply held belief that it's very important, when doing nothing, to remember that it might feel like 'nothing' but it's still living. It's not just a holding cell where we wait for the next thing to do or to happen. Life is not just about sitting by the front door waiting for envelopes to drop into our laps, it's about all the other things that make us happy. Foxes, cats, squirrels etc.

My eyes have glazed over a bit…

My eyes refocus and Sarah is smiling at me. She adds to my poetic discourse .

Sarah: *You have ice-cream running down your arm.*

In traditional Sunday style I cook a roast. Pork.

In the evening Sophie watches a piece of theatre downstairs, Sarah watches a solo piece of theatre at the top of the house, and half way up, in The Snug, I re-watch Leon.

Brilliant film. Jean Reno is superb, Gary Oldman is terrifying and Natalie Portman is utterly mesmerising. It was her first film for heaven's sake.

She was a similar age to most of our RSVPeople. While they were liking Duran Duran and not liking Wham! she was living with a professional hitman and having Gary Oldman almost kill her. The RSVPeople don't know how lucky they are, they really don't.

All in all, Sunday has been a classic mix of a bit of work, a bit of fresh air, a bit of ice-cream and a bit of classic film from the '90s. Great stuff.

But The RSVPeople Project is like a juggernaut that cannot be stopped. It's like a tectonic plate, quietly going about its business, undetected by mere mortals like me.

Because I've forgotten something. I've forgotten that on Saturday night as I climbed into bed, I popped a post on the Memories of Hemswell group page. Hemswell? Hemswell is home to the Wellbeing Centre who do great things for people much better than they reply to emails from us. They arrange pen pals as part of a project, but don't want to write to us. We mustn't grumble because they're all about supporting people in the community. So, yes, we mustn't grumble. But, well, grumble, grumble.

But grumbling and roasting and ice-cream dribbling can sometimes mean you take your eye off the ball and forget to check what's going on with a post you've sort of forgotten about. I'd taken the familiar, well-worn, and previously successful, route of a pleasant post asking for information about Jane. Bright, breezy, jolly.

It's also steeped with gauntlet - the like of which the good people of Hemswell can't ignore.

Let the games commence..!

Nadia Williamson: I think 183 Dalmorton is the shop (and flat) that used to be Gallagher's.

Me: It's now the address of the Wellbeing Centre. Was Gallagher the family name?

Nadia Williamson: Mr. Gallagher had left by the '80s but I think there is someone in the group who worked there during the '80s so she may remember the occupants of the shop/flat.

Anne Regan: Jane lived there probably in the '80s coz I was born in 1972 and I was Loretto at the time.

Me: Jane was definitely living there in 1985. She would have been 13ish…

Martin Kelly: Definitely there in '81 to '85 my parents owned the veg shop at 177.

Nadia is the lady who let me join the group and she leads by example. It seems the address may be both the shop and also a flat above. But she offers a wild-card suggestion: she thinks it used to be Gallagher's.

I don't know what that means, but I'm going to lock the doors and windows in case it's special Hemswell code for sending elite tactical forces to the home of anyone asking about residents called Jane.

GALLAGHER'S IS GO! GO! GO!!

No, false alarm, stand down everyone, it's a surname - but I'm not unlocking the doors and windows. She wonders if someone who worked with Mr. G might be able to help.

Help arrives in the shape of Anne. She offers her own birth date as evidence Jane was there in the mid '80s. I'm not sure why this is entirely helpful, but let's take it in The RSVPeople way it's meant. Thanks Anne, born in 1972.

Martin stamps his post with facts. Damn straight Jane was there till 1985. Know how he knows? His parents only owned the veg shop a couple of doors away. He was there, he was talking from experience - no question marks in his message at all!

With Martin's indisputable knowledge still resonating through the very fabric of Hemswell, other people up their game.

Anne Regan: I went to school with Jane her parents owned the shop not sure of her surname though. ***Clare Jones, Nancy Matthews, Mandy Sands, Diane Kemp*** you any idea x

Anne's back and this time she's not messing around, or using punctuation.

Bang! - she went to school with Jane. (Yes Anne, you go girl!)

Bang! - her parents owned the shop. (Fact, Anne! Fact!)

Bang! - she's not sure of Jane's surname. (Not to worry, Anne, I can't remember what I had for breakfast, memory loss happens to the best of us, and you, Anne, are right up there.)

Woah! Clare, Nancy, Mandy and Diane all get name-checked publicly. *Bang! Bang! Bang! Bang!* The sound of four more gauntlets crashing through the skies of Scunthorpe can be heard far and wide.

I'm wondering if maybe, just maybe, and this is like a spirit voice from another dimension, yeah, a seventh sense, pure intuition - I wonder if Jane isn't just Jane, I wonder if she might be Jane Burton..?

Angie Halter: Jane Burton
Martin Kelly: Jane Burton
Diane Kemp: Definitely Jane Burton

As if by magic, Angie (welcome), Martin (from the veg shop) and Diane (thanks to Anne) all arrive with Jane *Burton*. Smash Hits didn't have her surname, but 35 years later, the wonderful Hemswell people have shared it for the very first time. I bet even Jane will be thrilled to learn she's got a last name!

Hang on, new thoughts…

Sean Rees: Wasn't it the lady who run Gally's daughter if I remember rightly?

Blimey Sean, keep up - and that's *Mrs.* Gallagher's, if you don't mind. If he's suggesting Jane was a Gallagher, why is every single person in a nine mile radius whispering the name 'Burton'?

> **Anne Regan**: I've sent a message to who I think is the same Jane on fb but you might know ***Nancy Matthews*** as you're her friend on here x

Anne really doesn't like it when people know more things than she does. But it doesn't deter her in any way, quite the opposite, it spurs her on. They might have known Jane was a Burton, but do they know Nancy? Nancy who apparently is Jane's friend on Facebook? Nancy who she has already gauntleted, but is now seeking confirmation of her suspicions. And why does she need her suspicions confirming? Well Anne's only gone and messaged a Jane! Not necessarily the right Jane, she only thinks it's the right one, but she did it first, no one will ever be able to take that crown from her.

Things have moved so fast in Hemswell, that poor Mandy is late to the party. She was probably out getting milk or having a walk or working on the front line in aid of a better, safer world. But now she's here, she heard the call of the Anne and she wants in…

> **Mandy Sands**: Yep I think ***Nancy Matthews*** will still be friends hope the letter gets to her!!

She can see Anne has the whole situation under control, so her offer is a simple 'what Anne said' about Nancy, who is the keeper of the final piece of the puzzle.

But you know what, it's as if Mandy has just remembered a situation from their school days. Maybe a pigtail pulling episode, or a graffiti expletive that Anne never owned up to. Maybe it was just a selection issue for the netball team, we'll never know. But what we will always remember is that Mandy has confirmed the Jane Burton in person by posting an actual link to Jane Burton's profile. Amazing. I tell you what - Anne's going to be bloody furious!

Nancy, having been tagged three times already in this conversation, emerges, ethereal, stating simply…

Nancy Matthews: I've messaged her x

She's messaged her. Second to Anne on the message front, but the only person to contact Jane with certainty.

And now, another certainty, Jane knows a letter is trying to reach her. But will she reach out to us, or keep her head down to see if we contact her first? It's curiosity verses RSVPeople dedication. Let's see who blinks first.

What a day! It started with elephants and now has ended with finding Jane. How often does that happen? Not often.

Monday 22nd February 2021

Sarah's writing postcards. Eight of them. One to each house where a letter went and was never heard of again. They're nice postcards, designed to look a bit old and weathered. They're a fitting choice for a 35 year old project. And because they remind me how I feel most mornings, I've had a second mug of strong coffee.

As we thought, our original message is too big for the tiny space on the postcards, so Sarah did some very efficient editing and, satisfied, embarked on more handwriting than she's done since she was at school.

Meanwhile, using the photos we took back in January, I work out what colour envelope each RSVPeople Person received, in the hope the mention of a specific colour will jog the memory of someone at the address. Then I check the various addresses. By which I mean I wander around Google Maps, checking streets and house numbers. Like going for one of those walks we've learnt how to take, but much further afield, all over the country in fact and without actually standing up.

For Delilah (red envelope) and Brian (green envelope) we have the correct addresses, exactly as printed in 1985. Two down, six to go.

The mighty duo known as Donald and Richard (yellow) from Claverdon were never, ever at Maltden Lane, because no such address exists. A quick postcode check and Mallden Lane reveals itself. Easy, thanks post code checker at the Royal Mail. If only the people in charge of the post code checker were the ones in charge of our postal redirection, well the world would be a better place.

Adam (orange), the eclectic fan of Frankie, football and computers, (he's not been mentioned very much, I'll pop him on a list for investigation) didn't have a postcode. There was a time when postcodes were seen as the raised pinky finger of addresses. You can drink a cup of tea without raising your little finger, in the same way you'd always been able to send a letter without a postcode, putting one on seemed a little bit show-offy. Maybe that's what Adam thought in 1985, so he left it off? I return to the Royal Mail, and they provide a postcode in an instant.

Louise (green), her 1985 post code doesn't exist anymore: *No longer in use.* Who knew they retired postcodes?

Or maybe it wasn't a retirement - maybe this particular postcode failed a performance review? Maybe RS1 4DN was caught stealing stationary and let go? I hope this was the opportunity RS1 4DN had been waiting for and she can now be found bringing order to a postal district near a sun-kissed beach - rather than living in a skip under a viaduct in a place where letters are neither sent nor received. I hope not. I'm going with the beach - don't forget the suntan lotion, RS1 4DN! You wouldn't believe how easily a post code can burn.

However, her old address has a new postcode. One that has never so much as borrowed a post-it note without filling out a form, proper boy scout. Five down.

Faheen (red) I discover, has '55' printed in the magazine when it should be 'SS', a fairly easy mistake, especially if 15 year old Faheen's handwriting was fairly 15 year old-ish. And there's a space missing, but I've every faith those Ipoh postmen and women can decipher the spatial typos of the uninitiated. We won't make that mistake again - no point making life harder for the Malaysian postie who gets to deliver our postcard. Six down.

Monika (orange), I'm putting her on that list with Adam. Your time will come Monika, never fear. From her ad, Monika is notable for a couple of things. Firstly she's the oldest of The RSVPeople. She was 21. A quick look for her address online shows it's very close to the university. So there's a good chance she was in student accommodation, so roughly 38 billion students will have stayed at that address in the last 35 years? The chances of anyone knowing her are zero. Added to that, if German universities are locked down or closed then the students might have gone home and our first letter is still waiting with German pizza and double glazing leaflets on the Willkommen mat. As you know, we're not at home to dead ends, but a new and exciting way to get her letter to her needs to be found.

The second notable thing is that Monika is a language genius. I was already on the verge of hero worship with Mayumi - she speaks English, Swedish and Japanese. But Monika can write to us in English, Swedish, German or French! Or maybe all four languages at the same time? Wow - and I mean proper 'wow' - if I could speak four languages I would be sehr, sehr glücklich.

Sarah speaks almost fluent French and will have a stab at any language in any country. She loves spoken foreign languages. This means when we go abroad she tries her best to communicate in the mother tongue of wherever we are. She impresses the local waiters and waitresses, and they always appreciate her effort. I, on the other hand prefer not to starve to death, so I'm fluent in pointing and then having whatever I'm brought.

Obviously, because Monika's 1985 address was in Leipzig, Germany, and what with my affinity with all things German, I'm in my element, this should be a breeze...

Should be. It isn't. Let me explain.

Monika lived in Lertheauster 12. To a German language scholar like myself that translates as an address of someone at number 12 Lertheauster. Now, pay attention at the back. When you put Lertheauster into Google Translate it detects the word as French. OK. And it translates it as Lertheauster. So the English translation of Lertheauster is Lertheauster. Like the English translation of croissant is croissant.

But I insisted, I want the word to be German not French, which makes the translation people living in the Internet wonder if maybe I mean Lertheaustr? How on earth do I know what I mean? But OK, let's go with that...

And I tell you what, it was worth the wait, because when I translate Lertheaustr from the German into English...

German	☞	English
Lertheaustr	☞	Lertheaustr

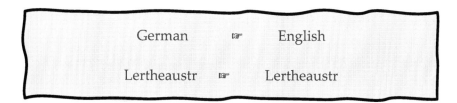

Lertheaustr is another croissant.

As utterly fascinating as all this croissant discovery is, it's not in the least bit helpful. I sense something is wrong with multi-lingual Monika's address.

And sure enough, I discover the 'str' is street (German PhD pending). Or Straße as we fluent German speakers say. So she lived on Lertheau, which also translates as Croissant Street. You know what, I'm wondering if maybe it isn't that impressive to say you speak four different languages when you live in a place where all words are universally accepted in every language! Martian for Lertheau, you ask? Well that would be Lertheau thanks for asking, safe travels back to the space ship.

Smash Hits mistakenly had 'ster' for street, not 'str'. Now, my research has discovered that in most languages 'ster' translates as 'ster'. Except for Bangla where it means 'star'. I have no idea what the RSVP section compilers at Smash Hits were drinking on the afternoon they typeset Monika's details, but is was clearly a very odd day at the office.

Sarah's tapping her foot. She wants addresses. I'm in charge of addresses. She's written all the words, she needs addresses, dammit! Being under pressure is no walk down Glücklich Straße I can tell you.

We almost fall out as I explain the peculiarities of German addresses - evidently a space before 'str' is optional and the Germans are cool with str or Straße. She in turn suggests that they don't mind and she doesn't care so can we just post the damn things already.

Judging by the look on Sarah's face, she has a splash of German DNA in her 'I need to get on, Paul' glare. I mumble something about the D-2600 bit maybe being a throwback to East and West Germany times, but she doesn't want explanations, she wants words, more precisely, words in the shape of addresses. I give her the words. A single foot tap, then she looks expectantly at me for Lars.

Oh, Christ, Lars (green). In a nutshell, because Sarah has to get on, I pass her two more errant umlauts for Hövägen and don't go into why the post code is now completely different. To me, discovering it's now 745 81 (not 741 77) was 35 minutes of research, cross-referencing and buttock-clenching worry. To Sarah it was nothing more than a five digit number for a missing Swede. But to others, via a Google search, that number is a problem about…

> Some flutter libraries have unnecessary import directives #74581

…er, something else?

And they're done. Sarah has worked miracles to get all the words in the tiny little postcard spaces. They look fab.

Sarah's not foot-tapped for a while now, in fact she's smiling at me. She says she has a surprise. What could it be?

Details of how German postcodes have evolved over the years?

No! Better than even that…

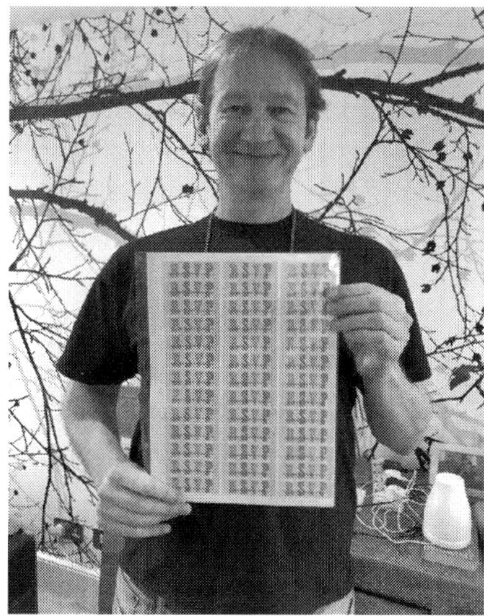

RSVP return labels!

With an actual RSVP logo from a copy of Smash Hits. Not our copy of Smash Hits, sadly, because that was the wrong size to work well with the order.

Sarah made them. They are brilliant! Sarah is brilliant.

Thank you, thank you, thank you!

Everything's turned out fabulously - I hope the chap with unnecessary import directives has had similar good fortune with his flutter libraries. (NB: There are people out there who know what a flutter library is. I am not one of them.)

The thing about days is they don't end when you zip up the laptop bag and decide it's time to unwind. Often, well usually, Sarah and I have dinner then retire to watch TV. We don't watch TV actually. TV is really the sum total of the five terrestrial channels plus all their catch-up channels. Though maybe that's not right either: catch-up is catch-up, not TV. Anyway, we watch Netflix or Amazon. Or catch-up. I can't remember the last time I saw an actual advert for cars or holidays or toilet rolls. Occasionally, when I'm not around, Sarah will watch Bake-Off and Strictly. I try not to hold this against her, as she tries not to hold the occasional live screened football match against me. It works, it just works.

But Sarah wants to read. I'm still in the land of The RSVPeople. My commitment is much greater than Sarah's, anyone can see that. Sorry, did I say commitment? I mean obsession.

So, Sarah's reading over there. I'm over here wondering how to pursue the likes of William and Matt when all previous avenues have failed. Then I remember Dave. Matt was not just a Madonna disliking individual, he was also half of the Queen and Springsteen loving duo known the world over as 'Matt & Dave'. The initial address was dead, Marwater school a vague memory, and in the same way we'd looked for a work address for Matt, maybe a work address can be found for his partner in crime?

Sarah turns a page, it's very loud and distracting. Tsk. I retort by tapping my keyboard just a little bit heavier than necessary. There's nothing passive about my aggression.

She doesn't look up. My finger stings. I hope the keyboard's OK.

I can't remember Dave's surname. I've seen it on that whole school photo of Marwater back at the start of January. But I can't find it now. There's always search history, but not knowing exactly which day I found it could mean a hell of a search. Search. Hang on, you can search your history. Who knew? No one knew.

So I search Matt, because I have his surname and my history throws up a Facebook account. I have absolutely no recollection of seeing this account. Maybe that was where I saw the school photo? I have a very quick scan of his photos.

Nope. There's a cake. Matt's recently turned 50! Happy Birthday for whenever that was Matt! No school photo at all, where the hell did I see it if not here?

Then an odd photo. It takes a second to register..!

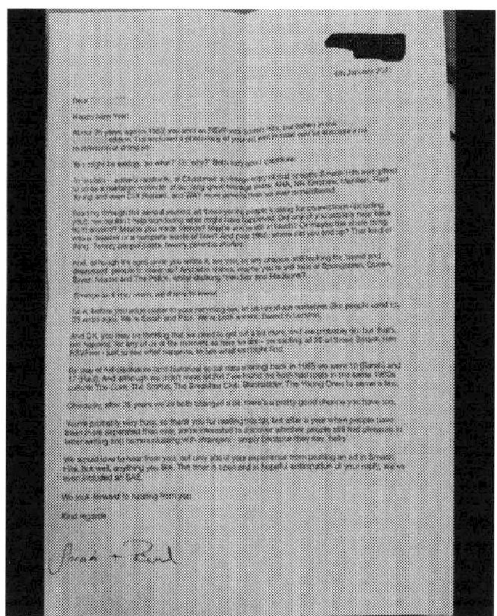

THAT'S OUR F*CKING LETTER!!!!!

Sarah falls off the bed, flocks of starlings on Brighton pier take flight and somewhere an angel gets its wings. That's our letter. On Facebook. On the 28th of January. A photo of our letter. On Facebook. Looking at me. Sarah very kindly passes me my jaw from the floor where it just fell.

We look at each other and bounce up and down on the bed making odd sounds. But good sounds. And no, stop it, not those sounds, this is a pure RSVPeople Moment. The photo doesn't have a single comment. That makes me nervous. The next photo is our equally familiar RSVP ad section, (as seen at the start of this book).

It's not like we need reminding what the letter means, but here in slightly wonky technicolour is The Whole RSVPeople Project for the world to see. This here is everything. I have the smallest of pangs that someone else has gone 'public' with all this before we have, but it's a tiny negative in an ocean of thrills.

But still no comments?! How could Matt post that on social media and absolutely none of his friends care or comment on it? I bet if it were a photo of Alphabetti spaghetti on toast he'd get a dozen clever types picking out words and giggling as they share it with the letters BUM highlighted. Some people.

Sarah suggests we look at the actual post, on his 'wall' not just the photo in 'photos'... and suddenly all the heavenly choirs burst into song in the golden firmament...

Matt Larkin is feeling embarrassed with ***David Bell***
January 28 at 9.22am.

Blast from the Past!

In 1985 David Bell and I put an advert in Smash Hits (look it up if that doesn't mean anything to you). We had literally 1000's of replies from all across the world; most nice but some bloody unpleasant ones (probably from trendies and Madonna fans!)

I'm ashamed to say that we didn't reply to a single one and in fact ended up passing carrier bags full of letters around the school.

The attached letter was sent to my work address this week - must have found me on LinkedIn. Your past will always catch up with you!

(44 likes/smiles/laughing emojis & 41 comments)

Look. At. That. Matt might be feeling 'Embarrassed' but I can see immediately that what he really means is that he's feeling 'utterly brilliant!' And he's tagged Dave, clearly still a friend.

The urge to click the like button over and over is almost too great to bear, but I hold back - especially as, Sarah points out, repeatedly pressing a like button doesn't add more likes, it just turns your own like on and off. How the hell can she think so sensibly at a time like this?

Look at that, 41 comments. And nothing but thumbs-ups and laughs and surprise/amazed emojis. Matt's Facebook friends recognise just how close they are to something monumental. Like

Moses approaching The Burning Bush, with a fire extinguisher, only to discover the bush wants to chat. Just like that.

Thousands of replies? Thousands? Really? People bandy the word 'literally' about all the time with utter contempt for the English language and its definitions, but he seems to mean it. It's a shock to read some respondents were unpleasant. Then again, kids are horrible and Sarah and I immediately feel defensive for teenage Matt & Dave, locked away at school, no doubt surviving on 'character building' gruel and daily beatings with a mortar board from 'Sir'. Hard times. And all they ever wanted was a little fun, a few friends...

They didn't reply to a single one!

What?! WTF?! I mean What The Actual F? 'Literally' thousands of hopeful, potential pen pals, probably still, to this day, checking the post, sighing, wondering how different their lives might have been with a Matt or Dave plopping through their letter box.

'Passing carrier bags full of letters around the school'.

Well, I guess this is a smidge better than burning them, but I'm still suffering pretty high levels of disappointment in the chaps. They may have thought they were spreading the love, but those respondents didn't want Johns or Stevens or Archibalds. They wanted Dave and they wanted Matt. And this was cruelly taken from them - by Dave and by Matt! I hope grown-up Dave and Matt know how much misery they're responsible for.

Sarah: *Maybe they had a good reason. Think of the stamp money they'd need. It's not our place to judge.*
Me: (muttering) *Much.*

Matt's dead right about finding him on LinkedIn, and thankfully he doesn't seem to mind.

It's too enticing not to sneak a peek at what Matt's friends think of it all…

Emma Smith: Brilliant! Not surprised you put that ad in, definitely something you would do!

Matt Larkin: I'm not sure that's a compliment, is it! ☺

It's unclear whether Emma thinks Matt's ad is 'brilliant' or Sarah and I are brilliant. Clarity, Emma, clarity.

Mm, and she seems to have made it all about Matt. As I recall Matt & Dave wrote fewer than 50 words whereas Sarah and I wrote twenty letters and posted and photocopied and waited and worked and checked for hours and hours and hours and never mind all the postcards and German post codes..!!

Sarah says I need to calm down. It's late. I'm probably just tired. And she's right. But there's no way I'm turning the light out yet…

Gary Ashworth: That's fab, I'm trying to remember how post was handed out but I'm sure your fan mail caused dismay with the management system!

See that 'fab', I'm taking that as a fab for us.

Sarah & Me. Team RSVPeople.

Yes I am.

See if I don't.

Matt Larkin: It did - remember there used to be ticks on the nominal role which was put up by the small gym. One tick per letter (or P for parcel) - eventually there would be 'See me' written, which meant a humiliating trip to see the Head's secretary to collect that day's carrier bag of post.

I didn't go to a school with a 'nominal role'. I didn't go to a school where anyone had ever heard the phrase 'nominal role'. Or a school with two gyms! I went to a school where battles between my school and a local rival had to be broken up by police in local parks!

Delpherine Blum Knott: Oh that's hilarious! 'Looking for girls'. Smash Hits brings back so many good memories. Hope that it cheered up your day as it has mine!! X

Matt Larkin: It really cheered me up - if mildly embarrassing! And has induced great guilt that we didn't reply to anyone. That opening line did haunt us both for many years!

Delpherine, thank you, not only do you have the most brilliant of names, you have been cheered up by The RSVPeople Project, suggesting we could make it something marketable, maybe a prescription drug? But that's for the future, right now it's all about spreading joy - becoming multi-millionaires is secondary at best.

We've cheered up Matt too. And having a little guilt for not replying to anyone seems about right. All is now well with the world.

Oh. But not with everyone.

Keith Norris: I dare you to reply back with just two words - 'Girls only'.

Alright Keith, wind your neck in, eyes to half, lips to lemon, jealousy's an ugly trait, my friend, an ugly trait.

Now Mary, a Madonna fan to this day, sees things as they truly are: amazing! Her words, not ours - but undeniably accurate.

Mary Weaver: Matt, this is amazing. How much did that cheer up your day? I was just saying the other day how kids having mobile phones so young and Facetime etc. miss out on the joy of being pen pals. I had loads of pen pals who are still my friends now. What an amazing memory to have sent to you. Thanks for sharing. And, by the way, Madonna ruled!!

Matt Larkin: It's a bit weird but I will reply. Might end up on one of those Channel 4 programmes you love like Embarrassing Pen Pals!

When we were trying to throw things away before our move, we kept saying how with some things, it was only because we still had the object that the memory remained. As if it were embedded in the thing. And if the thing's sold or lost, the memory, still clinging to it, disappears. We gave Matt & Dave a memory back. That's quite something.

However, Matt thinks it's a 'bit weird'. Well, maybe it is, Matt, but that's how we roll. Tell you what, though, weird or not, he's going to reply - music to our ears, Matt.

Charles Deaver: Reply to this one, Matt. Keep everyone posted too.

Matt Larkin: I will!

Georgina Bridge: This is superb.

Charlie's very insistent Matt reply. Maybe Matt once let Charles (whose initials suggest he invented the replacement of tape cassettes) down? Did he ask Matt something and never got a reply?

Charleses are like elephants, they never forget.

Georginas, on the other hand, are famous for their inability to tell a lie. Everyone knows that. Literally ask anyone.

Jess Gerrish: Loved Smash Hits for the lyrics when taping Top 40 off the radio, but you probably too cool for that ☺ This is a great story, keep us posted x

Matt Larkin: We did that as well. Still not sure what a 'trendie' was though - suspect it was anyone who wasn't us.

A desire is brewing. People want to be kept informed. They don't want our mysterious letter's arrival to be the end of the story.

Finding our letter to Matt like this is not dissimilar to when the original Smash Hits present arrived unannounced. The letter is the first step on a journey to who knows where? Hopefully back out to another postbox soon, eh Matt?

One of the questions I wanted to ask Matt from the start was what in fact a 'trendie' was? I sort of remember the phrase from my own teenage years but I can't recall exactly what it meant. Was it a New Romantic? Was it people with one of those 'flick' at the front and 'wedge' at the back haircuts? I only knew one person with that haircut - he threatened to throw me off a ferry to France when we were 12. I'm not sure exactly why but I think there might have been a stolen can of Stella involved.

The praise keeps coming.

Carol Archibald: What a fantastic letter.
Liz Hughes: Ha, this is awesome!
Pauline Billington: Brilliant stuff! That could turn into quite a story.
Christine Cheshire: Brilliant!
Rob Nugent: That's cheered me up no end Matt!

Guys, guys, stop it, we're blushing!

Kate Umar: Brilliant! Maybe this one deserves a reply!

Kate, yes. But it has been said already, proving no one, except us, reads all the comments on someone else's post.

Lisa Crowe: At least you didn't sell the replies to other 15 year old boys. Missed business opportunity though.
Matt Larkin: We literally got thousands (over a two year period) as the magazine went around the world. Could have been my pension!

Maybe Lisa's a financial advisor? She's got her eye on where cash could have been made. Matt laughs about it but beneath that laughter you can sense the horror of a sure thing missed.

Let it go, Matt, let it go.

Kiki Lake: This is brilliant!

Difficult to tell if Kiki of the Lake is getting involved or accidentally posting the comment here she meant for a video of a dog juggling bananas while riding a bike?

Declan Kirke: This is amazing!

Thanks Declan, and you're right, but we're covering the same ground here. However, you're the first 'amazing' which, for anyone who is interested, is defined as: *causing great surprise or wonder; astonishing*. Astonishing - just saying.

And finally, here's Dave - Matt's pen pal partner in crime.

David Bell: Oh no the past's coming out. I'm cringing with embarrassment, as we got thousands of letters, and I'm not exaggerating. From the UK to begin with, then later they started coming in from all over the world. Me and Matt, being poor students who couldn't even afford a stamp, replied to a grand total of 0! I didn't expect an ad in Smash Hits would get so many girls writing to us and I certainly didn't think anyone would bring it back up 35 years later.

Maybe this is the first Dave knows about it? Or did Matt contact him directly, all old feuds and grudges buried for the moment, to bask in The RSVPeople memory?

Well *of course,* schoolboys don't have money! That's what Sarah said. How were they going to reply to thousands of letters? It was an impossibility right from the start.

Bill Tate: I remember the letters, you and Matt used to leave them on the library table for people to read ☺

Vic Taylor: OMG I remember the bags of letters you guys got - you had so many you handed them out to others to read.

Clearly these Marwater boys stick together. 35 years on and there's a load of them who remember the letters being left around the place.

What's also clear - Matt hasn't changed a bit. 35 years ago he shared every single letter with anyone who wanted a look. In 2021 he's done exactly the same! But this time round we're thrilled to bits!

Una Gibson: How brilliant! Just think of all those girls sending off their letters and anxiously awaiting a reply! I hope you're going to reply to Sarah and Paul! And confess your guilt. Thank you for a great Smash Hits memory!

Finally someone acknowledges it isn't a couple of ex-15 year olds that are responsible for all this. It's a Sarah and a Paul - who can barely remember being 15. Thanks Una, you're a Bengali 'ster!' (In case you've forgotten, that's a 'star'. If you *have* forgotten, then see me after class.)

Mm, Dan's arrived late and has chosen fraud, identity theft and mild grooming as his party piece.

Daniel Palmer: That is SO funny! We did a similar thing at school - writing to lots of girls and sending fake photos of a good looking bloke, saying we had met them at a party and would like to get to know them better! Quite a few wrote back - some even claimed to remember us at the party!

Matt Larkin: That's taking it to a new level.

Anyone else get the feeling Matt's suggestion it's 'taking things to a new level' is in fact his awareness that this is a: Totes-Awky-Mo-Mo?

Sarah and I sit back. Wow. Matt's there, he's got the letter, his friends think it's great, and everyone except 'girls only' Keith, thinks a positive response is the way to go.

But Matt & Dave have a track record of broken good intentions; plans made and not acted on. Maybe our letter will end up in a shopping bag on a library table like thousands before it. They didn't reply to a single one. Sigh.

I can't help but notice that Matt's most recent post is telling his friends his account has been hacked. I posted a similar thing myself not 48 hours ago telling friends they'd been similarly infiltrated - Messenger was sending me videos, supposedly from friends, but actually intended to steal my log-in details and send out even more of these fake videos. I sympathised, I hadn't pegged Matt as someone who would fall for such a thing. But who knows what links a man devoid of pen pal replying scruples might click?

I wonder if someone might suggest that getting a weird letter and then getting hacked are connected? I take a peek...

Rowena Hall: I think it was an aggrieved Smash Hits reader! ☺

I knew it. Bloody cheek.

But the best is yet to come. And here it comes...

Matt Larkin: It could be! I've just sent off my reply today so will see what comes back.

Matt's replied! He's actually replied.

And Sarah's pointed out something truly beautiful - we are the *only* response that pen pal ad ever got!

We're honoured, Matt, truly honoured.

I'm so exhausted with all the excitement, maybe a little read to clear my head? Sarah asks if I got in touch with Jane. Wellbeing Centre Jane! That feels like weeks ago. But no, I haven't, for the time being at least, we're both still fixed in our staring competition, neither of us yet willing to blink. Our eyes have started to water though.

I add Jane's name to the one with Monika and Adam and turn off the light.

Wednesday 24th February 2021

Before the move, Sarah and I would start our mornings in a flat we shared with no one but each other and the slugs that appeared in our bathroom and under the back door - rarely seen themselves, but their silvery trails were undeniable. Oh yeah, and a solitary mouse too, seen only twice. Once by Sarah, so we knew we had 'mice'. And the second time, after the ethical trap snapped shut. The little fella was trapped inside for less than half an hour - the time it took me to walk him all the way to the far side of the common and release him into the undergrowth. I hope squirrels don't eat mice. The capture was ethical, I hope the release wasn't a ticket to certain death.

We also shared the flat with the cold. How the flat could remain in a state of winter for all but the hottest days of the year, I never understood. Apparently it was only a couple of years before we arrived that the place had double glazing put in. It's an actual miracle that we weren't also sharing space with the frozen corpses of previous tenants.

But Sarah and I, like Emily and her old, saggy cloth cat, Bagpuss (baggy, and a bit loose at the seams), loved our flat.

A couple of days ago, after a phone consultation with my doctor, I'm now suspected borderline asthmatic for the first time in my life. I'm not saying there's a direct correlation between living in a malfunctioning igloo for two years, but what with the mould under the dining room table, that we didn't see until we moved the table, it might be a factor.

Anyway, the point is now we wake in a lovely house. It's warm, light, airy, and although infested with cats and teenagers, a couple of well-placed ethical traps will have that sorted in no time. I get to make coffee and wander to the garden office a mere 10 second walk across stones, breathing fresh air and feeling glad to be alive, if a little more breathy than I was in 1985. I've had a garden office before, of course, but back then I used to call it a 'bench in the park'.

I potter the dozen steps to these words after a very lively 'project meeting' with Sarah. We had two strong coffees and a bowlful of something worthy and full of bran - like cardboard shavings, but good for us. We chatted and Sarah sent bullet-point messages to a WhatsApp group called *RSVPeople*. The idea was we'd have a chat in the kitchen for 40 minutes and then I'd try and make sense of her 23 messages in the shed for the next 17 hours.

It's such a lovely morning, I've left the door open while I get sorted - unpack laptop, plug it in, find headphones and music (I always write to a soundtrack, hand-picked for the project) flip the switch on the ethernet, pop my metal water bottle within reach and I'm almost ready to go. Before starting I always remove my shoes and put slipper socks on. Not the slipper socks I wear in the house, but the ones I only wear for writing. This entire project has been typed while wearing slipper socks - I don't know if that's a first for literary endeavour. I don't recall Shakespeare or Dickens referencing their particular footwear choice, so I'm going to say it is.

The open door has allowed the shed to fill with lovely garden air. I think it was my Mum who said you should change the air in every room every day. She had lots of good ideas. Last year I had the very great but very sad honour of writing and making her eulogy. I'm reminded of a single line now:

'She had beautiful handwriting that danced across the page.'

And she really did.

As you know, I have many of the letters she wrote to me over the years. There's no chance I could ever part with a single one of them, no matter how unremarkable their content. That's the power of writing, the power of the letter. I think about my Mum often anyway, but when writing here about the past and contact with lost friends and connecting and writing letters, I feel her close by even more. Mum would have approved of this project. And had she replied to any of the pen pal adverts in the magazine, those Wham! haters would have received proper letters, beautifully written, with a fountain pen. If you'd received one, you'd have kept it.

However, Mum could get really annoyed about the ever-increasing cost of a stamp. I don't think she considered how many people touched the letter, sorted the letter, distributed the letter to sacks, loaded the sacks, transported the sacks, re-sorted the sacks' contents for the postie, and then walked the letter to the front door and got their fingertips nipped by a rabid Yorkshire Terrier on the inside. All for a few pence. She'd have pulled her, 'I was a war baby' face if she read that - as if that excused everything. Maybe it does?

But what Mum would have lost her mind about was a missing letter. It may be a 'few pence' for a letter to get to its intended address, but it was the same few pence for a letter that didn't arrive at all.

Let me take you back to the 40 minute chat Sarah and I were having this morning, with coffee (and without slugs or mice). We were discussing the issue of disappearing letters…

You see we've heard from a very pleasant chap called Mark Gerrish. Mark lives where Donald (of Donald and Richard) used to live and he emailed us to say he's already passed the postcard on to Donald, but, unfortunately, beyond the fact Richard got married and moved to Australia, he has no more information for us there. Interesting.

So Donald knows we want to send him a letter. However, we've decided we don't want to tip-toe around an email enquiry from him (my email address was on the postcard) asking what this is about. We want him to have the same surprise Matt or Mandy or Russell got, but without the six mile walk in the snow. So I've messaged

Mark to see if it's OK to send the letter to him and whether he'd be kind enough to pass it on to Donald, as he did so efficiently with the postcard. Hopefully he'll respond with a resounding yes.

But the reason 'disappearing letters' is on the agenda is because Mr. Gerrish told us he hadn't received our original yellow envelope. If you recall from earlier in the week, the only Donald error in Smash Hits was his road name being Maltden, when it should have been Mallden. Could that be the entire reason for a yellow envelope being undeliverable? This is the sort of thing that gets my cogs whirring. And Google was invented for my whirring cogs.

So, do you know how many Maltden Lanes there are in Claverdon? None. Staffordshire? None. England? None. The World? Yep, none. There has never, ever been a Maltden Lane. There's a Maltden Street in The Anderson Township of Ohio, but I very much doubt our envelope has ended up there.

Could a 'T' being inserted where only an 'L' should go, really make all the difference?

Tove Me Do? Hetp!? Eteanor Rigby? Hetter Sketter? The Foot On The Hitt? (All by The Beattes.)

They're still fairly recognisable, aren't they? I don't know very much by Bittie Eitish but I'm sure the same holds true for her and other 'L' heavy artists.

So you have to wonder what happened.

Now, I've been subtly slipping it into the conversation, so you'd be forgiven if you didn't know our (not cheap) redirection service from the Post Office isn't working. The odd thing is arriving - credit card bills and the like - but we're also getting a number of things that our old neighbour and the new tenant are very kindly forwarding on to us themselves. This is not what we paid for - we did give our brilliant actress-upstairs-neighbour wine when we left, but it wasn't given as an advance payment for taking charge of our wrongly delivered mail. Nor did we expect the new tenant to have to look after our letters - she's probably got more than enough to deal with, what with the cold, slugs and long-distance travelling mice.

Sarah's already been in touch with the redirection service people twice. Their complaints system leaves a lot to be desired. Lots of new web pages, no actual help, new forms that return you to the same starting page. We're confused. And with so many eagerly anticipated letters coming from all over the world, this is no time for confusion.

The Post Office state it takes ten days for them to deal with the problem of why they can't send a 'Chronnell' addressed letter to a Chronnell and why a 'Sarah & Paul' letter is simply impossible to fathom. This 'ten day' revelation makes Sarah furious. Sarah's terrifying when she's furious. It doesn't happen often, but when it does, it's best to just stand in a corner, looking at the wall - like in (#spoiler) The Blair Witch Project.

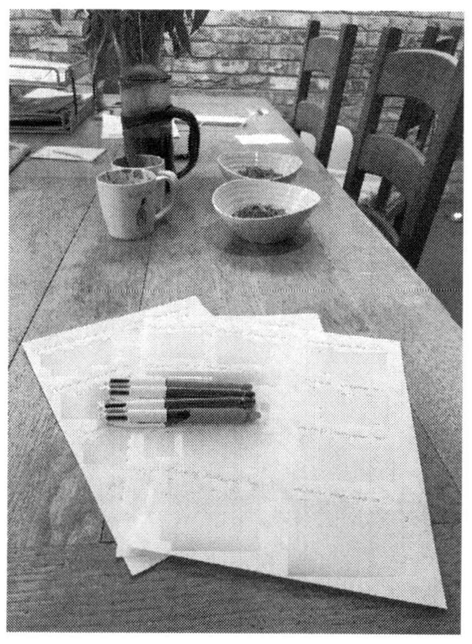

When I turn from the wall, open my eyes and stop repeating the mantra, 'There's no place like home, there's no place like home', I'm met with these bad boys.

Address labels for the old address. Brilliant. Saving the lovely people at the old address time and hopefully speeding up the process of bringing The RSVPeople post safely home to roost.

You're probably wondering why The Blair Witch needs four multicoloured pens to write address labels with only red and blue on them (which you can't tell from this black and white photo, but trust me: just red and blue). I know I certainly am. When she's finished dealing with those lost students who keep bloody filming everything, I'll ask her.

Apparently, in her day-to-day Witchiness, she doesn't ever use the blue on the four-coloured pens and so this is a good use for it. I was hoping for something more profound, but her face suggests this is all I'm getting. OK.

I'd always thought redirected letters were selected by machine, therefore there's no human to blame. Blair Witch Sarah, in a shriek of magic tinged with evil, cackles that the redirection new address labels don't stick themselves to the envelope. True.

Her labels will 'show' the Post Office, and who am I to argue?

Then, out of left field (why is it never right field?) something arrives...

Monika's (orange) envelope! All the way from Germany. Wow. It's not been returned to us via someone at the old address. It's come by those mega efficient postal chaps over there in Germany, and then via the new tenant at our old house, Anna.

The German Post Office rightly apply a sticker stating the address is unknown or insufficient to deliver.

Remember all those post code musings? Here's evidence what a lot of address nonsense poor Monika's Smash Hits details amount to today.

So, the Germans can facilitate a 1000 mile round trip for a letter with an address that doesn't exist, whereas over here we can't get a letter correctly forwarded from a house, a walking distance of 0.9 miles away - less if you cut through the back of Sainsbury's. This is definitely what Brexit was about. Wasn't it?

It takes Sarah and me just over 15 minutes to walk to the old flat, don masks and hand over the address labels. Anna's very happy to take them, if a little bemused as to why we might be expecting so many misdirected letters. We look up and down the street, to make sure no one's in earshot, and in hushed tones tell her we're engaged in a postal project. Her smile only wavers a tiny bit, but I'm certain she closes the door faster than is absolutely necessary.

This problematic postal situation has us thinking about our other MIA letters…

Jane, Becki, Mayumi, Lars, William, Faheen, Louise, Adam, Donald & Richard, Delilah, Brian - 11 letters. They're all somewhere. But where? The postcard experiment might give us a clue to one or two (like Ms. De Niro with Johnny's letter). Of course, of those 11 letters - we did get William's back, but the repost to his place of work has gone astray. And the three overseas ones might yet return courtesy of our friends at various international postal services. But that still leaves seven original letters that just vanished.

The Dead Letter Drop is the net for all undeliverable letters. But ours were literally covered in Return To Sender details. I doubt any have ended up there. Seems very unlikely.

It never occurred to us that an address might be wrong. We expected people to have moved away in the 35 years since they wrote their ads. But we expected them to at least have moved away from the address in their ad - not from places that never existed.

It also never occurred to us that a person might get the envelope and not want to reply.

It also-also never occurred to us that a redirection service could simply not work.

And it absolutely never, ever occurred to us that so many letters could disappear.

I had a friend at University, let's call him Paul, because that's his name. At University we were known as Paulie Pinky and Paulie Poo. I was Pinky, he was Poo. He called me 'Pink', I called him 'Paulie'.

He wanted to send a Christmas card to the 'Rees' family in Llanelli. Paulie was most definitely a 'path of least resistance' kind of guy and couldn't be bothered actually finding the address for the Rees household. Instead, he addressed the envelope: The Rees Family, The Green House, Llanelli. He had the town right, the family name right and the colour of the house right. He had nothing else.

As it happens, Alan Rees (of the Green House, Llanelli) was a postman and periodically would look through the box of undeliverable post, in case anything pinged a memory. Of course, he was the best placed postman in Llanelli to see his own name and the colour of his house on an envelope and, as if by magic, that Christmas card found its home. Probably sometime in March, but the point is the same - every piece of post is somewhere, and can get to where it's going, if the right person knows where to look.

When we started this in January, the letter was king. It still is. We still want each of The RSVPeople to hold in their hands an actual letter to their teenage selves. That's why we're trying so hard to leave as little trace as possible online. Like walking backwards in our own footsteps in the snow, making it look like we passed by and kept going. Obviously, on a town or village group we announce ourselves, but we don't publicly tell anyone why.

Letters bring fun and surprise - just glance back at the 40+ comments on Matt's page. Out in the world, we're like a gossamer ripple on a pond. But here on these pages you hold in your hands, we're as obvious as a rhinoceros stomping in puddles in hobnail boots. Maybe it's like a burglar who silently breaks into your house, then sits at your breakfast table, writing you a letter about how they did it. Only in these pages is what we're doing not a secret.

Mark Gerrish has no such qualms. He's already liked a post on my Facebook page about the vile vaccine scammers. I see this as acceptance that I am a decent chap, appalled by the behaviour of some of my fellow, so-called, humans. Sarah wonders if he's letting me know he's seen me. A sort of visual, 'I've got your number' or 'I know your Dad', from comics of old. I think I preferred Sarah before she got hooked on this dark Blair Witch state of mind.

While Sarah goes shopping (for toads, newts and broomsticks) I go on a speedy walk around the lovely quiet neighbourhood side streets to let this borderline asthma issue know that if it's at all possible, I'm going to get the border moved.

Along the way I pass a lady in overalls splattered with paint. She's half on a driveway, half on the pavement, with an easel - a proper artist. She's appraising her work. It's the wrong way round for me to see, and I have an attack of Englishness and don't want to be seen glancing at her private painting. But seeing another creative at work is lovely - getting on with her practice, no matter how many tall Mancunians try to sneak a peek. Painting appears a very calm way to express oneself creatively. If The RSVPeople Project were a painting, it would be a canvas being worked on by a family of octopuses, a brush in each and every tentacle balanced on a cement mixer on a trampoline in high winds.

I get home first. When Sarah comes in she says she's been chatting to the new postman. Jim. She told him about The RSVPeople and that our redirection doesn't work, but that it wasn't his fault and he could stop standing in the corner staring at the wall. She mentioned the many local communities who have helped us and discovered his parents live in Gisburn! (Where Fran Hargarden used to live.) Small world. He doesn't think they're terribly involved in social media, but his Dad, in his 80s still runs zoom wine tasting sessions with other members of his street.

He thinks the project sounds great (thanks Jim) and definitely remembers Smash Hits but would have been a little old to read it then, he thinks. Well Jim, Monika was still reading it at 21 and she speaks more languages than literally anyone, anywhere. If you'd been still reading it back in 1985, instead of that 'I think I'm a little old and grown up for that' attitude that's defined you all your life, you could have written to Monika. And if you had you might now share a wonderful brood of miniature multi-lingual, university-aged postal delivery wannabees who, half the time, can't wait to get to grips with a difficult postcode and the rest of the time can't be arsed. That could have been you, Jim. Just saying.

Imagine though, if Fran Hargarden writes, (oh, please write, Fran, please write) her letter, sent via Gisburn, twice, will be pushed through our door (well, possibly the old door) by, first a different postman, but eventually by Jim, the Gisburn connected Postman!

So many people must touch the letters, consider the letters and then do something about the letters. It's a many-linked chain that could fail in any number of places. I wonder if there's a pattern to the replies depending on the colour of the envelopes?

The MIA letters are in grey…

Orange	Yellow	Red	Green	Blue
Oli	Jane	Andy	Russell	Becki
Sally & Emma	Johnny	Mayumi	Lars	Matt & Dave
Monika	William	Faheen	Louise	Fran
Adam	Donald & Richard	Delilah	Brian	Custard & Roobarb

This scientific experiment gives clear and transparent evidence that Red and Green envelopes disappear most often, followed very closely by Yellow (William's 50% action rate, allows for a slightly fainter shade of grey). Blue and Orange are the way to go if you want someone to look at your letter and say 'I'm going to do something about that right now!'

Good, I'm very glad we've got that sorted. Sarah wonders again if I need to get more sleep?

But there's no time - I want to see where we're up to with everyone… and blimey we haven't had one of these for ages!

1. Mandy (sans Roobarb) - two letters!
2. Andy (sans nobody) - two letters!
3. Matt (and Dave) - he doesn't know we know he's replied!
4. Russ - he's got the letter and we await his reply.
5. Sally & Emma - nothing from either of them.
6. Fran Hargarden - letter has gone to her Mum.
7. Johnny Carter - Ms. De Niro had his letter but has forwarded it to his Mum.
8. Nayumi Eklund - is Mayumi and lives elsewhere and a new copy of the letter is off to Sweden.
9. Oli - got letter, made contact, no further reply.
10. Jane - Hemswell rallied and have messaged her directly.

11. Donald & Richard - first postcard success. Mark Gerrish has contacted Donald for us.
12. Brian Evans - the Trerhyngyll lot were a great help - we know his Mum still lives at 1985 address and have sent her a postcard enquiring after the initial letter.
13. William - letter lost at work, no reply from email address.
14. Delilah Fielding - have yet to initiate Plan B but have chased her 1985 address.
15. Louise Fairstone - likewise, no Plan B yet but have sent post card to 1985 address.
16. Monika Meyer - letter returned, have optimistically chased 1985, possibly student address, with a postcard.
17. Becki - Ashworth enquiries were fruitless and geographically challenged. Need to cast net wider?
18. Lars - postcard to 1985 address.
19. Adam - postcard to 1985 address.
20. Faheen - address was full of typos, have chased envelope at correct address.

11 certainties that we've located the right person. Not bad, if I do say so myself.

As I was compiling that version of our 1985 Hit Parade, this popped up on my screen.

Russell: Ok, letter in the mail today!

Short and sweet, like a strawberry. Kind of.

We've also had an email from Bryan (yes, with a 'y') Evans! (More of that in a minute.) Bryan's more of an Oli, than, say, a Matt or Russell. I doubt our letter will be posted online and a six mile walk through snow seems unlikely. But I'm being unfair. Sarah and I started this project because we wanted to. Our argument was that invitations to correspond were there in black and white (in Smash Hits) but we were stretching it a bit if we expected everyone to still be as open and excited to receive letters from strangers as they once were. So the fact Bryan's message doesn't smack of jumping up and down, should not be seen as a refusal to join us, but rather the response of a busy man who doesn't currently have time to 'correspond with two possible lunatics' on his to-do list.

He may also be utterly sick of people spelling his name wrong. Smash Hits, once again, played fast and loose with the spellings of things - like names. Bryan with a 'y' sent information to the magazine, but Brian with an 'i' was the one whose ad appeared. And it was Brian with an 'i' who was written to. And if Bryan with a 'y' wrote back to anyone, the first thing he'd have to say to them was, 'Actually, it's Bryan with a 'y', not Brian with an 'i'. He's probably had to explain that to people his whole life.

Bryan: *Hello, yes, my name is Bryan - with a 'y'.*
Idiot: *A 'y'?*
Bryan: *Yes, a 'y'. Bryan with a 'y', that's me.*
Idiot: *A 'y' where?*
Bryan: *I'm sorry?*
Idiot: *The 'y'? Where's the 'y'? Is it Ybrian? Or Briany? Or Byrian?*
Bryan: *Instead of the 'i'. B. R. Y. A. N.*
Idiot: *Instead of the 'i'?*
Bryan: *Yes.*
Idiot: *How do you pronounce that?*
Bryan: *The same. Bryan.*
Idiot: *You sure?*
Bryan: *Am I sure how to pronounce my own name?*
Idiot: *Yes.*
Bryan: *Positive.*
Idiot: *It's not what it says here.*
Bryan: *Oh for heaven's sake, can you just give me my takeaway before it goes cold?*

I sympathise. With a name like 'Chronnell', I too don't wait to be asked.

Me: *Hi, yeah, that's Chronnell - C.H.R.O double N...*
(And that's always enough. There are never any other names on the list beyond that.)
Everybody: *How do you pronounce that? Chron-elle?*
Me: *No, actually it's Chron-ull.*
Everyone: *Chron-ull?*
Me: *Yes.*
Everyone: *Not Chron-elle?*
Me: *No.*
Everyone: *You sure?*
Me: *Whatever, call me Tinkerbelle if you like, but can I please just pay for the damn haemorrhoid cream and go, I'm borderline asthmatic you know!*

Let's look at Bryan's email...

From: **Bryan Evans**
Subject: Smash Hits
Hi, I'm hoping this is the correct email address for the people trying to contact me. I have received your letter and have read it. It's very interesting. I guess you have questions for me. As I do for you. Kind regards, Brian.

On first reading, we have a whole bunch of thoughts about it:

* 'Hi' rather than mentioning either of us by name.
* Only 'hoping' it's the right email address.
* 'Interesting' is a lower bar than we hoped for.
* 'Guess you have questions' - we do, we put them in our letter.
* 'As I do for you' - does that sound ominous?

Crikey.

My first assumption was this is a response to the postcard, not the letter. It was the only way I could fathom why he'd made no mention of Smash Hits or pen pals or surprise or joy or fireworks of the soul going off as he read our letter. But sometimes my search for a logical explanation makes me miss the evidence right under my nose - the subject line says Smash Hits. There was no mention of Smash Hits on the postcard. He's read the letter - another of our letters has reached another actual RSVPeople Person! Which is great, but Sarah and I still went to bed a little confused and perturbed. And not just because of who we share a duvet with.

Thursday 25th February 2021

Being borderline asthmatic, today feels like being 'asthmatic'. I'm not actually sure whether the 'borderline' bit was actually said by my doctor or inserted by me as a form of denial that I'm getting older and things don't work in the same way they used to - like eyesight and hearing and postal services. Because I'll tell you what works better and quicker than the postal service - email. Mark Gerrish replied to our postcard. And he'll definitely pass on our letter to Donald! But let's rewind a moment…

This morning, we woke romantic and thinking of horses and a Welshman with a 'y'. The romance and horses are not a euphemism for gentlemanly prowess, but quite literally horses. One particular horse actually.

You see, throwing these 'message in a bottle' type letters into the world isn't new for me. Incidentally, are you still allowed to chuck messages in bottles into the sea in these eco-conscious times..?

A long time ago, on holiday at a hotel in Evesham, aged about 16, I fell in love with a waitress who served me and my family one evening. Being 16 I had absolutely no idea how to talk her like a human being and instead mumbled my monotone appreciation and assured her categorically that 'everything was alright, thanks'.

But I couldn't stop thinking about her. When I got home I wrote to her, care of the hotel, as The Blonde Waitress Who Was Working On Saturday.

And I waited. And she replied. And we sent a few letters and eventually met and even conspired to something romantic for a while. We're still friends on Facebook.

A year or so later, on a different holiday with the family, I was wandering round a 'lovely' village, which was the most boring experience of my life at the time. A girl walked a horse from the road into a large property with stables - which is just as well because it would have been weird if she'd been walking it into a terraced two up, two down. I was in love immediately. Again.

That night I wrote to her. I've no idea what I said, but I probably addressed the letter to The Girl On The Horse. Very early, before dawn the next morning, I crept from our holiday cottage and walked half an hour in the dark, down a lonely country road, to put the letter into the stone gatepost where I'd seen her go.

Not through a letterbox, literally stuck between two stones in the wall to what I hoped was her house. It was the bravest thing I had ever done.

The sun was barely up when I got there and although I had not seen a single soul on my early morning travels, as I left the card, at that exact same moment, my hand still on the letter, the girl on the horse, literally on her horse again, appeared through the same gates. She looked at me. Not in a 'who the hell are you?!' kind of way, but in a 'Christ I could have trampled that kid to death' kind of way. They're similar looks, yet subtly different.

Naturally this was my perfect chance to say hello. But did I? Of course not. Instead, I spun in place and strode off as though I'd been caught peeing against the wall. Strangely, she wrote back to me too. But letters were not natural between us and after a few we tailed off. But what I remember most about the whole experience was the feeling of utter exhilaration as I walked, on air, all the way back to where we were staying. I had set out to do a thing, a romance-seeking thing, and as lame and cowardly as I'd been in her presence - I'd still done it!

I spent the next 30-odd years hoping to feel like that again, and although there were moments, it wasn't until I saw a woman looking at a dog called Murphy that I truly knew I would walk any lane at any time of the day or night, to pop a note into her letter-box. So to speak.

Sarah and a friend once left an anonymous letter on a bus for any boy who might find it. Again it was a search for a romantic connection, not a pen pal, but as you can see, back then Sarah and I had different attitudes to romance. I was looking for the absolute soulmate discovered in the glow of a grand gesture. Sarah was looking for anyone who rode the top deck of the 316 to Margate.

But the question is not whether Sarah and I are available to the romance of an unexpected connection, but rather - is Bryan?

Hang on a minute. I've just noticed, Bryan with a 'y' signs himself Brian with an 'i'!! I mean, he can have as many spellings of his own name as he likes - but if Mr. Evans is unclear of his 'i' or 'y' status, are we absolutely certain this is the right guy? The postcard went to the right address - to his Mum, at the 1985 address, so you really have to assume it's the right Brian or Bryan. But every third person in Wales is called Evans - and neither Bryan or Brian are the most unusual of names. Now, if it were Matt's friend Delpherine who was checking in, I'd feel more confident. Delpherine Evanses are a lot thinner on the ground I'll bet.

There's only one way to get to the bottom of the Brian/Bryan Evans enigma...

Us: Hi Bryan,

How fantastic to hear from you! I assume you got the postcard we sent to your old address, but when did you get the initial letter?

Although from Manchester I've always had a strong pull to Wales - I went to Aberystwyth University, lived in Llanelli for the best part of a decade and my parents retired to Prestatyn. It's such a beautiful place, top to bottom. Anyway, we're thrilled you've got in touch. And yes, absolutely, if you have questions, ask away. All the questions we had were really in the letter and we'd love to read your replies, when you have the time.

We're hearing from new RSVPeople all the time - it's turning out to be a really fun project. Hope you're well.

Suddenly, sending actual words to Bryan feels fine. (I bet he just Anglicises his name because too many of us plebs can't deal with it? Well rest easy, not here Bryan, here in RSVP-land we're more than glücklich to call you by your proper Welsh spelled name.) He's not stand-offish, he's simply cautious. He doesn't know who we are, he's probably had a long day, his Mum may have been bending his ear about his post at her address and he just wants to put his feet up in front of the TV. We hear you Bryan, we hear you. And when you get the time, we'll be equally thrilled to hear from you again.

Sarah sends me this profound thought on our WhatsApp group.

Sarah: How much of this quest is for us - feeding Paul and Sarah's romance junkie souls - and how much is a genuine pang at the sight of 24 missed opportunities spotted on Christmas Day, 35 years late..?

You know the wide-eyed, straight mouthed, slightly embarrassed emoji? The one that looks like the little yellow fella broke wind and is unsure whether he got more than he bargained for? Course you do. That's the face I'm pulling now - without being in the least bit windy. The realisation of the truth of the first half of Sarah's question is almost embarrassing in its obviousness, but I don't think I realised it at all. But of course it is. It's both those things combined: the 24 are the fuel to our romantic fire, a fire we both yearn for. Not to mention it's great fun throwing strangers onto a metaphorical bonfire.

A third possibility is that being a detective is really exciting. And just now LinkedIn suggests the Detective maybe being detected!

LinkedIn: Who's viewed your profile:

*** Donald Gerrish.**

*** Someone in the Investment Management industry from London.**

Two things to note here. Donald Gerrish is not Mark Gerrish, but the likelihood of two Gerrishes crossing our path at the same time feels very unlikely.

Hang. On.

Donald Gerrish checks out my profile after a Mark Gerrish at the address our Smash Hits 'Donald' lived at is in touch?

That's our Donald. Must be. He's Donald Gerrish.

And he's not bothering to cover his tracks, he's not walked backwards through the snow in his own footsteps - like the kid at the end of The Shining (#spoiler) being pursued by Jack Nicholson in the maze - is he?

Not like 'someone in the investment Management Industry from London'. Hiding as a mere 'someone', they creep around the Internet with the stealth of a tiger. That could be anyone - it could even be William. He works in Investment Management. In London. And is very possibly a tiger! Oooh. What fun!

Friday 26th February 2021

We finally write to First Responder Andy. It's been way too long - Sarah and I have been a couple of slatterns and no mistake. We must never forget that it's Andy who first showed us that The RSVPeople can be found and they jolly well enjoy the idea of sharing letters with us. Andy was the first, Mandy (Custard) the second and now we know for certain another two letters are on the way to us - Matt's might arrive today, Russell's will take considerably longer from Canada.

Alongside letter arrival, we're also holding our breath for several contacts. People saying, 'Yes, you've found me, hurrah!' Jane hasn't responded to my direct message. Neither Mark nor Donald Gerrish have responded or reacted to recent contacts. Bryan with a 'y' is yet to respond to yesterday's email. Johnny should have received his letter courtesy of Alison of the Appleton Massive...

Massive? Do people even say that anymore? And what did it even mean back when they said it, if in fact they even ever did?

My eldest son says things are 'dead' at the moment. A few years ago negative words were used to express positives but today he assures me this current favourite, 'dead' is definitely a negative.

Me: *How was school, son?*
Son: *...Dead...*
Me: *Right, excellent.*

Language, like methods of communication, is ever-evolving. Hopefully we will see more faith in the letter as time goes on.

One thing a person should always have faith in, is an Andy. Andy was our first. And no one forgets their first. But there's also been a second Andy. Admin Andy. He runs an actual Ashworth group online. Not the Derbyshire one, the right one. In Bradford. Called The Ashworth Estate Group. I messaged him to join the group and asked if it was OK to post an enquiry about Becki. He said it was, so I did.

But this request peeked his curiosity and when he saw Becki's road name, Woodside Avenue, he got back in touch and said he grew up around there and although he didn't remember Becki himself, he has a sister the same age as her. It was a huge slice of luck. I mean, who would ever forget an Aero-eating fan of The Cure and Simple Minds who lived close by 35 years ago? Admin Andy said he would contact his sister immediately! Another helpful soul aiding us with our quest. I thought of suggesting he change his name to Amazing Admin Andy or Astonishing Admin Andy..?

Or, as of ten minutes ago, Andy The Admin With The Sister The Same Age As Becki Who Doesn't Think Becki's Name Rings A Bell. Granted, it makes for an unbearably long signature, but it's true.

It was good of Admin Andy to check and it's not his or his sister's fault that Becki can't be found or remembered via this route. But even though not part of the problem, I sense the enormity of his disappointment at not being part of the solution.

Andys are like that. They focus, they hone in, they strike and in a flash they are victorious. Oh no, that's the sparrow-hawk. Andys write letters and run Facebook groups. Admin Andy asked if we'd got any responses from his group. When I told him there hadn't been a single comment or anything, I could sense he was as downcast as us.

Admin Andy: Did you get any responses off the group?
Me: Absolutely nothing…
Admin Andy: ☹

That's not an emoji, that's an outpouring of grief. That's a soul in damnation, broken, destroyed, desolate, without hope.

You can almost hear him writing his resignation letter to the Ashworth Estate Group. It's clear in that distraught little emoji face. I didn't expect him to take it so hard. Like a string of strong and encouraging RSVPeople angels in the last few weeks, I feel I now also owe the discovery of Becki to Admin Andy. Where else could we look? When I can't find the TV remote I look down the back of the sofa cushions, but, what with Becki being an Aero-obsessed ex-teenager, I feel that course of action might just be wasting my time.

Hang on a mo. Ashworth doesn't only have a wrong group in Derbyshire and a right group in Bradford. It also has a second right group in Bradford. A reunion group. With almost 1000 members. And an admin called Chris.

Legwork might be the answer. Not actual legwork, obviously, what with the lockdown and Bradford being over 200 miles away, which, might I add, is almost half way to Monika's old address in Germany - and a 65 hour walk. I don't mind hard work but, well, no.

Legwork at home means an office chair and a search engine. I have both. And a few minutes later I have a rather splendid realisation…

You know when you set up a new business or a website and very soon Google finds you and then there's the all-important moment of searching for your business - and there you are, on page four. It doesn't feel too far away and it's early days - you'll get onto the first page once you've had a few customers. It's a great start. Then you search for what a potential customer might search for. Something like handmade homemade biscuits… and finally find yourself, two hours later on page 739. It's a nightmare and suddenly you're buying books on Search Engine Optimisation (SEO) and trying to calm down.

Well, even without a single second of SEO work, The RSVPeople is not only on the first page - but in poll position! Out of 11,400 hits. Quite a feat, and what an accolade.

Search: Ashworth estate Bradford "Becki"
About 11,400 results (0.36 seconds)
www.facebook.com - groups
Ashworth Estate - Bradford, UK Public Group / Facebook
Hi, I wonder if anyone remembers a "Becki" who lived at 10 Woodside Ave, Ashworth in the mid '80s? I have a letter I'm trying to forward to her…

Yep, if you search Ashworth Estate Bradford and Becki, you get me - asking if anyone knows Becki. It's not quite on a par with beating

Amazon for the search term 'books', but there's a feeling of warmth spreading through my borderline asthmatic chest.

Saturday 27th February 2021

My sister turns 50 today. I sent her a card, of course I did. But, as she lives in Australia, I maybe should have sent it three weeks earlier than I did. But I didn't. So it'll be a nice surprise in April some time. She's away for her birthday weekend, so that gives me a couple more days' grace for her not to realise I've been a bit rubbish with her card. Although, she has met me, so a late card will do nothing to change her opinion of her big brother.

I tell you who would have sent a card on time: Chris, the Ashworth Reunion group admin I contacted yesterday.

Bespectacled and smiley, Reunion Chris is the nicest man on the Internet. First he lets me join the group - a closed group that exists entirely because people who lived in Ashworth, or still live there, want to talk to people who used to, or still, live there. I had never heard of the place until a couple of months ago.

I'd heard of Bradford, obviously, but for only two reasons. First, the brilliant band New Model Army are from there, and secondly I once performed in an early round talent show in Bradford - early round meaning the whole thing was only watched by the organisers and the other acts. It was me, my oldest friend Martin and a cardboard box. We went by the name The False Alarms. It was anarchic, original, under-rehearsed and we didn't make the cut. I was gutted. Bradford has made me uneasy ever since.

Until Reunion Chris! So, someone wants to share my post asking for help locating Becki. But they can't. Chris suggests I look at my settings on both the post and my personal Facebook account. I can't find anything on either allowing or prohibiting sharing. Sarah wonders if it's the fact someone is trying to share from a private group? Chris agrees this might be the case.

Not to be thwarted, he writes a new post wrangling the Ashworth Reunion group to dig deeper, think harder and help me get my 'nice' letter to Becki. There's a moment when another Paul, who lived on the same street as Becki, but doesn't remember her, mistakenly becomes me-Paul. Wrong-Paul is asked questions he can't possibly answer because he simply read a post, lived on a road and doesn't remember a person. However, I can't answer them either - because I've simply read a magazine, posted a post and lived miles away. It's a proper dilemma. Unanswered questions.

A chap called Bruce asks if Becki is mixed-race. A good question, it might narrow down the search. But I don't know. And somehow not knowing her ethnicity but knowing she liked Spear of Destiny and Aeros will take a hell of a lot of explaining. So I sit back, I don't engage. I feel like a fraud. I want to tell the whole of Bradford they no longer need to define me by some ill-thought through box-comedy act, but by The RSVPeople! But I can't. We have rules. Sarah's very keen on them. So am I. But when a group wants surnames and details of her family tree and all I can offer is confectionary preferences, it makes me feel redundant.

I frown and turn my phone off. This is exactly how I felt when The False Alarms smashed up a big cardboard box in the name of comedy and almost no one laughed.

Sunday 28th February 2021

The Internet is down. Not depressed or feeling a bit under par, oh that it were. No, today the Internet is actually dead. Probably not all of it, but definitely the bit I want to use. And when the Internet goes away, the world disappears. We all know that. Sure, there's the TV, papers, books, people etc. But there's no Internet. It's like the world - but it's rubbish.

It's the end of reality as we know it. No more cat videos, no more screaming and being vile to strangers because of different political views, supporting different teams or just having a very small penis. No more likes or hearts or, 'Aw babes', or shares of meaningless photos that falsely get everyone believing anyone gives a shit! That's all gone. All of it. Back to basics, back to the Stone Age, back to the beginning of time. Is there even any point in being alive anymore?

Sarah: *The Internet's working in the house.*

Oh. Just not in the shed. So it's only me the great God of The Internet hates? Just me. Typical.

Sarah thinks a day off might do me good. And that it's not my job to fix the Internet, either for the world or the shed. She thinks maybe it'll come back all by itself…

By itself? How ridiculous! Stupid nonsense! Obviously I don't actually say this. Not out loud. Instead, I smile, say yes I'd love a coffee and thank her for loving me. A day off ensues.

In the evening we watch '1917', which is great for a whole bunch of reasons - I'm a huge fan of Benedict Cumberbatch and Mark Strong and have a proud and open man-crush on the simply sublime Andrew Scott (I mean, yeah, he's great as the Sexy Priest, but my adoration runs so much deeper). But as the young soldiers in the film face death at every turn and danger in every heartbeat, I can't help but think: yeah, I'm really glad I've never had to go through all that, but let's face it - they never had to face a day without the Internet. Swings and roundabouts.

Monday (pinch-punch-first-of-the-month) 1st March 2021

Stand down, everyone, the Internet's fixed.

Shall I tell you what I did to fix it? Nothing. It just worked. I wandered down to the shed, knowing full well it was like entering a time void before information sharing existed. In fact, the office was no longer an office. It was a cave. I couldn't do any proper work so maybe I'd scrawl a really bad painting of a bison on the wall or something - maybe in the actual blood of the actual bison I'd just killed with my bare hands and a broken bit of Palaeolithic pot. R.E.Ms 'It's The End Of The World As We Know It' was on repeat in my head.

I thought, for a laugh, I'd plug the Ethernet cable back in, like I hadn't already done that 50 times yesterday. All the while muttering the adage about repeated behaviour and different expected outcomes and madness. But the adage was proved wrong. I plugged in. Hello Internet. Immediately. The bison painting will have to wait.

But with the return of modern existence in the shed, there naturally follows the demise of modern life at the Post Office. Sarah is, quite rightly, furious again. Our redirection has stopped working altogether. We have three pieces of post at the old address. The redirection service didn't catch any of them. 70-odd quid to have letters go exactly where they would have gone without paying 70-odd quid doesn't seem the greatest modern financial transaction. But where the Internet simply fixed itself, this letter problem had better watch out - because Sarah's determined to fix it herself.

How, you might ask? Good question. She plans to go to the local sorting office and bloody well tell them what a bloody atrocious service we're bloody well getting and what the bloody-bloody-bloody are they going to bloody do about it!?

Being a soldier in The Second World War, facing the murderous intentions of Nazis, was literally nothing compared with the force of nature stomping down to see the local posties in their local postie stronghold. God help them…

When Sarah, sooner than expected, returns home, I realise God is less about finding lost post than He is about stopping Sarah-induced carnage at a sorting office. So God, rather disappointingly, did help them. He made the office be closed. That's fine, it gives Sarah 24 hours to calm down, rather than create a painting on the office walls of a postman, maybe in the actual blood of the actual postman she'd just dispatched with her bare hands and a paper-cut-worthy edge of an envelope.

I know what you're thinking. I'm thinking it too. Never mind WHY the letters aren't being delivered, what ARE the letters that aren't being delivered? Sarah's on it in an instant. Messaging both Andi (upstairs at the old address) and Anna (new tenant in our old flat) asking about mail. Yes! The mail is still there, they could redirect it, no problem - but I'm not chancing it. I say I'll be right over, even though it seems Andi's already popped one in the post. Efficient. Oh well, that still leaves two to pick up.

I head out to get them. Borderline asthma rears its ugly head, but I'm driven on by a higher power - a divine power, capable of closing sorting offices on a whim.

I knock on the door I used to have a key for. Feels strangely odd. Anna answers, she's fine, thanks, and hands me two envelopes…

She doesn't hand me them on a piece of carpet, obviously, this photo is from later.

The red (dark grey) envelope is proof the Swedish postal service is as efficient as the German one.

'Nayumi's' returned letter - when she lived in the wrong town, on the wrong road and with the wrong name.

Damn, if it had come back a week earlier we could have sent it, exactly as it was, to Mayumi, but never mind.

The second one surely has to be Matt. The only reply to his 1985 ad. A unique moment. Brilliant.

In the letter, Matt goes on about replying to people. Replying? He clearly told his social media friends one thing and us, his wannabe friends, another. This is most unexpected. Then I see the Simon Le Bon mention and my brain does 11 million calculations while Sarah looks at the surname again.

Us: (in unison) *It's not Matt - it's Johnny!*

We've arrived at the exact same place in the universe, at the exact same time, although I've worked 10,999,999 times harder than Sarah to get there.

Johnny is brilliant. His letter is sublime. He was 'deluged' with letters for months. About 100 letters a day for the first few days. He only replied to girls who sent photos - probably of them looking at dogs - but confesses he just couldn't keep up. After a couple of months he stopped. He was looking for a girlfriend, and she apparently was waiting for him in Wales, not by the letterbox.

He tells us he was once in the music industry himself 'for five minutes' but when recession hit, that was that. Although he does still make music independently. Interesting.

He remembers 1985 as a 'magical' year and wishes his kids could experience something similar to that year 'when everything really did seem possible'. He's friendly, excited, and willing to tell us anything else we might like to know.

> **Johnny**: Thanks for the huge nostalgia trip!

Joy of joys! This is why The RSVPeople Project exists - to spread joy.

We have to say that, just in case there are any RSVPeople out there worrying Sarah and I paint cave walls with the blood of things we've killed with our hands. (It's honestly ages since either of us have done that.) RSVPeople like Donald. And Bryan with a 'y'. And Fran Hargarden. And possibly Becki - hiding away on a Facebook group, trying to work out the cut of our jib.

Donald, Bryan and Fran are at least 'found'. The ball is definitely in their courts. But what they do next remains to be seen. Becki, however, is still MIA. Once again I travel the lonely journey back to the scene of my cardboard box anxieties: Bradford. I open up the door to social media hell.

Do you know what a redundant comedy talent-show failure needs at a time like this? A Reunion Chris. And luckily I have one. And while I've been languishing in an Internet-less nightmare he's excelled himself. Literally 'on it' - like a car bonnet.

Suggestions and comments come thick and fast. Bruce, who asked about Becki's ethnicity, suggests a surname! Like a whippet up an analogously incorrect drainpipe, Chris is on it. It feels like most of

Bradford and the surrounding areas have turned their TVs down and are giving Chris their full attention. Right now in Bradford you could hear a cardboard box drop.

'Berns' is suggested. Becki Berns. Wow, that might be our 'weird hair styles' loving Becki. But Chris wants more. He doesn't run this group just to scratch the surface of things. Hell no. He's right back at Bruce: he wants to know if this 'Berns' lady of whom Bruce speaks, is on Facebook? Bruce doesn't know - what is he, Becki's keeper? No he is not. But information cannot stay buried under Chris' laser gaze, so Bruce, unprovoked, tells us the place Becki works. A nursery. (Again, I can't help wondering - how do people know so much about other people's business, but not about their actual whereabouts?)

And at the mention of the nursery, it's as if a tree has been shaken, and what should fall out? A fact-wielding Celia: but she's going with Burns, not Berns. Interesting.

Celia Grant: Yes I know Rebecca Burns, her auntie lives opposite me.

Here we go - Celia knows her (whether it's the right Becki remains to be seen) and she knows her auntie, who literally lives opposite Celia - they probably wave at each other out the front window.

That's amazing. But it's not enough for Chris.

Chris: What's her auntie's name please? Are they on FB?
Celia: No, don't think they're on FB.
Chris: Could you get a message to them? Paul Connell has a nice letter for Rebecca.
Celia: Yes, will do.

He wants names, he wants pledges of action. And, dammit, he gets them - even if the cost is the misspelling of my name

If the government had put Chris in charge of PPE last March, everyone would have had a hazmat suit by the first weekend of the pandemic.

Chris. Gets. Shit. Done. And he's polite with it too. No doubt he's off to end world famine this afternoon, excavate an ancient civilisation tomorrow and later in the week write our False Alarms material so we get through to the next round of the Bradford talent competition. (That last one's a joke - Chris is a genius, not a miracle worker.)

Rebecca Burns, or Berns. Either/or. I'm going with Celia's Burns. When you're a window-waving neighbour to an auntie, it's a well-known fact you pay more attention to spellings.

Hang on. Chris steps forward. Cool as you like. Another hush falls. Then comes the ultimate question, the one last asked by Old Girls George. The one that can bring the whole world crashing down on our unworthy heads.

Chris: There is a lead, sounds promising, I've asked if she knows you, what is the connection with the letter, please?

Damn. To tell or not to tell? We have to tell, don't we, there's no other way? Vagueness here is our enemy. Chris is an RSVPeople Person, absolutely, but is he ready to learn that Santa actually exists? That behind the curtain is an actual wizard? And that the new clothes the Emperor's wearing are absolutely bloody lovely? Chris trusts us. We must trust Chris.

So we message him the truth: the magazine, the pen pals, the project, the hope. And we wait…

And breathe! We've got Chris' blessing…

> **Chris**: Wow it sounds great, I'm waiting for the auntie to get to me. Once she has I will forward your message and see what she says.

It's on a par with a Papal decree, a President's last minute reprieve or a VAR penalty let-off. Like a future father-in-law waking you up, a double-barrelled shotgun in your face, only to joke it's not loaded, we have passed the Reunion Chris test.

Tuesday 2nd March 2021

I'm woken up by Kate Bush's favourite singer. What a beautiful sound. A blackbird. Sitting on next door's chimney pot. Sarah and I sleep right at the top of the house with beautiful views of lovely houses and trees and green that's going to be really special when spring arrives. We feel very lucky.

But less so this morning. It's 6am. And although still lovely and impressive, it's not quite how we'd choose to experience it. Like a parent, mid potty-training of their small person, would much rather experience their first full success one afternoon, rather than waking to the sprinkle of pee on their duvet and the presentation of a plastic bowl at four in the morning. And then having to be pleased about it, rather than making the toddler wear his offering as a hat.

The blackbird is remarkable. The song is ever-changing. Sometimes it's tweet-tweet-tweet-tweet. Other times it's tweet-warble-tweet-warble. No wonder Kate Bush is a fan.

By seven o'clock the sound is rather more like TWEET-TWEET-TWEET-MWAMWAMWA-TWEET-TWEET and I'm hoping Kate Bush's friend falls off the roof.

I'm tired all morning. Well, tired until Jim the postman pushes the post through. Something interesting. Matt (of Matt & Dave)? Nope. Sally (of Sally & Emma)? Nope. Oli (of Oli)? Don't be ridiculous.

A letter from Canada! With a Christmas stamp.

Russell!

Wow, that's arrived really quickly. I was expecting weeks and it was eight days or something, wasn't it? Actually, I'm not sure, I'm lacking the capability to understand the passing of time today.

Thanks Mr. Blackbird.

Russell's letter is great! He's a man who loves his LOLs. And why not? Laughter is the best medicine after all. Though for headaches I prefer paracetamol. And for sleepless nights I'm wondering about a shotgun. Russell also received 'thousands of replies' and his 1985 postman asked his Mum if someone famous lived at his house. Russell might not actually be famous - but he's definitely fabulous!

He had people track down his phone number and was inundated with calls too. That's weird - imagine people trying to locate you, sending a letter, then trying to chase you up for a reply!

Oh.

He had one unsuccessful date at a 'roller disco' and one longer correspondence with a girl in Hawaii due to their shared love of Five Star and other slightly 'not cool' music. Russell still loves '80s music. You can take the man out of Knaphill and all that.

And with a serendipity that seems pre-planned, he did his hairdressing training in the same town Five Star lived and once or twice saw their Lamborghinis pull into the local Waitrose, at which point he volunteered to get everyone's lunches, just to be that little bit closer to his idols.

He's a genuinely nice chap and Sarah and I feel thrilled he's one of The RSVPeople. We will give him a few days, so we don't seem too eager - we're very eager - before we reply.

Nothing yet from Reunion Chris or the aunt across the road or Becki herself. Of course, we still don't know if this is the right Becki. However, having Googled the 'Rebecca' all of Ashworth is talking about, I certainly hope it's her - because she sounds like a brilliant, inspiring woman, a very successful business woman - exactly the sort of woman who most definitely should be an RSVPeople Person.

Wednesday 3rd March 2021

What fresh, black feathered, hell is this! It's not even 6am and he's on his chimney - singing Wuthering Heights or something. If this were Kate Bush's house - and we had permission to be here, we hadn't just crept in and started living in her attic - and she was woken every morning by her 'favourite singer', I think she might be on the dark web right now trying to get an Uzi.

Although, shooting may be too good for our feathered friend, so between 6am and whenever I finally decide that sleep is over, I concoct a different plan. If Kate's such a big fan of his, I'm going to wait till Mr. and Mrs. Blackbird have their babies and then I'm going to play Babooshka at top volume out the window, see how they like that. Not the song, the lack of sleep caused by the song.

Sarah has a self-penned one woman show called 'An Evening Without Kate Bush'. Maybe I'll write a companion show called a Very Early Morning Without Sleep.

I may need a nap. The Internet's broken again. I'm too tired to be furious. Sophie called a nice electrician called Miles. Miles might be available next week to have a poke around if it's not righted itself. Thanks Miles…

…ZZZZZZZZzzzzzzz…..

Friday 5th March 2021

As soon as I hear tweeting, I'm tense. If it's 6am again, Mr. Blackbird and I are definitely going to come to blows. Useful in these situations is, what's commonly termed, 'a clock'. Sarah and I have both taken to charging our phones on the other side of the room - for reasons that make us feel a little bit 'progressive' without fully understanding why. But it means I can't check the time on mine. Rather than investing in a small alarm clock for the bedside, we brought the clock that used to be on the wall above the door through to the kitchen at the old flat. It's about a foot across. You probably don't remember it, but as we've been chatting like this almost every day of the year so far, I feel you appreciate the details.

So the clock is at the end of the room, where Sarah works during the day. But I can't see it. And not because it's dark. It isn't. Instead there's a bloody great bunch of daffodils in front of it. I bought the daffodils as a little room brightener for Sarah because she doesn't get to walk down the garden to the office like I do. And they've been gorgeous. But they're always in front of the clock. I mentioned this to Sarah a few days ago and she said, a little abruptly if I'm going to be completely honest...

Sarah: *You could move them.*

Exactly - is that any way to speak to a borderline asthmatic?

Unfortunately, the job of moving the daffs only comes into my head when I'm lying in bed trying to see the clock. And once I'm up, and can see the clock, the daff-moving is forgotten, until the next morning. And the call of the blackbird.

So I lean right out of bed, almost falling out, before I can tell it's 21 minutes past something. I do some quick logic wrangling. I can't see any of the little hand. So it's not 21 past four or five, but the light in the room sort of tells me that anyway. The next number I can see above the slightly drooping daff heads, is ten. I know for a fact Sarah is running with the British Military Fitness this morning (I know, what a show off!) so the alarm is set for eight. So it's 21 past seven or 21 past six. It's almost sad to think the life of one of our beautiful feathered friends lies in the simple truth hiding behind bright yellow blooms.

I lean out more - if I pull something, I swear I'll scream - and glimpse it's 7.21am. Hallelujah! I could close my eyes again, but I've already done as much thinking this morning as Einstein managed in half his whole life, so I'm wide awake.

It's clear to me that I've trained him. With my mind. Incredible really. Obviously, after taking yesterday to have a long hard think about whether 6am singing is conducive to remaining alive, Mr. Blackbird postponed his warbling till this respectable 7.21am. Which you might call 'meeting half way'. But I call it what it is: mind control.

Shower, nice. Peak flow test, poor but steady. Brown steroid inhaler, with face mask, faintly ridiculous. Mouth rinse and tooth brushing - imperative! (Oral thrush can be a side effect of the inhaler, I've seen pics, it looks like no one's idea of fun.)

Sarah's still asleep. That's unusual. Maybe the clock's wrong. Nope. Maybe I've perfected the power of utter silence in all I do? Or, what if this is an alternative reality, where time will be perpetually at 7.21am, freezing all other beings on earth, except me and the bird? Stranger things have happened. Even asleep, I can hear Sarah scolding me, once again, that they haven't.

It's 7.42am now. I've had a thought. I mean, I've had a few, but I want to ask Sarah about one in particular. Although it's not really a question, it's more that I want to say the words out loud. And she's fast asleep - although she has poked a strangely Wicked Witch of the West finger out from under the duvet, and sort of left it there, just hanging.

A moment later she wakes. I put the cymbals back under the bed and pretend I haven't heard a thing. Once the lovely 'thank heavens neither of us died or moved out during the night'-esque chat is done, I say what I need to say:

Me: *Some of them aren't going to get in touch.*

I can't remember the actual sentence in our conversation that preceded this, but I'm fairly sure my segue was entirely without preamble. But Sarah is up to speed in an instant. I can tell by the way she mumbles.

Sarah: *Mm?*

In my head I'm creating this list, the one right here:
Heard From: Andy, Russell, Johnny, Custard.
Optimistic: Emma, Mayumi, Matt, Donald.

Ongoing: Becki, Sally, Lars, Dave, Monika, Faheen, Louise, Adam, Richard, Delilah.
Voids of Misery and Emptiness: Oli, Jane, William, Fran, Bryan, Roobarb.

We have coffee and breakfast and Sarah goes out to be shouted at for an hour by ex-soldiers. Horses for courses.

I'm concerned by that list. It's not as positive as I expected. Seeing it all in such clarity perturbs me. Strictly speaking, we know Matt is a definite. The only reason his letter hasn't arrived - aside from the almost unfathomable disinterest of our redirection service to do its very simple and extraordinarily self-explanatory job - is that our previous upstairs neighbour, instead of forwarding, like she said she had, had actually put the letter in her bag and forgotten about it. An accident for sure, but I may request Monsignor Merle (or Monsignor Noir-Oiseau, to give him his Garden of Eden birth name, though I can see why he changed it) pay a little visit to a bedroom window just a few minutes flap away, maybe at 5.30ish. Reduced sleep helps keep you sharp - said no one ever.

Anyway, it means Matt's letter may arrive today and the 'heard from' part of the list will look much healthier. But those in the other sections? Where do we go from here? Let's take a look.

I contacted Oli yesterday - remember him? Mum scanned the letter and emailed it to The States? Never replied to our questions? Come on, keep up!

Now, you may have realised by now that I am not always at home to succinctness. I am oft wont to paddle in streams rather more multiloquent, ambagious and pleonastic. (Yep, I used a thesaurus.) But when I wrote to Oli, it seemed just the right number of words.

Us: Hi Oli, hope you're well.

We've now managed to make contact with more than half of your fellow 1985 pen pal seekers, and a friend suggested it might be interesting to ask everyone the same brief questions about their experience and compare the answers - especially as not everyone has the time or the inclination for writing actual letters. So, if you've got a few minutes, we'd love to hear the answers to the following questions (feel free to write as much or as little as you like).

1. Can you remember, roughly, how many replies you got?
2. Did any of them become a friend and are you still in touch?
3. Did you get what you hoped from the experience?
4. What music do you listen to now?
5. Most importantly, if you were to write a pen pal ad now, what would it be?

We look forward to hearing from you.

Seeing it today, it feels like a seminar.

And do you know what there is, right down at the bottom? No? Let me tell you. It's the death nell to modern communication; the Gates of Hell clanging behind you when all you thought you'd done was buy a ticket on the Brighton Pier Ghost Train; the 'whatever' of the Internet: a tiny circle containing Oli's face. Which means Mr. Oli has seen the message - and immediately found better things to do with his time.

It isn't for me to say that Oli doesn't have better things to do with his time, but he doesn't. Do you know how often a letter arrives from 35 years ago? (Unless, of course, it's taken out a Postal

Redirection, in which case I'd imagine it's two or three times a week.) Never. Never, ever, ever.

Sarah suggests that he may yet reply. It was only yesterday he got it, and he's on the other side of the world and time-differences and stuff. Damn, she's good.

Roobarb was approached by Custard, Mandy told us as much, but she feigned indifference, claiming she didn't really remember posting an ad. WTAF? (I think that's what the kids write?) But not knowing Roobarb's name or address, at any time, and Mandy having told us that her old friend has wiped the whole event from her mind, I think we must call Roobarb our first failure. Sad face.

Fran is an interesting one. Disappeared from the face of the earth, but her Mum sent her our letter. We can't chase or nudge Fran in any way. We can only nudge her Mum. And Mum-nudging isn't really what Sarah and I signed up for. We'll have to hope Fran decides a letter to us is the very best thing that's happened for a while (ever!) and chooses to say hello. We'd like that. We hope you would too, Fran.

Jane and William are similar in that I've contacted both of them directly through social media channels. And I've heard nothing. It's very odd. If it were me, my curiosity would be off the scale. I mentioned this to Sophie this morning and she said she really wasn't a very curious person. Oh.

I'll test this. Next time she bakes a cake I'll eat it, clear up perfectly and see how curious she becomes about its whereabouts. And don't come all 'gaslighting' with me, I knew about gaslighting long before the Internet began wielding it like a broadsword. I knew about it when it was still a play by Patrick Hamilton. My Grandfather played the lead in a production of it before I was born, and apparently got very 'Method' and was, I believe, not easy to live with until the run was over. But I digress (in a multiloquent way).

William is the right person. I know he is, I have no doubts. He doesn't yet know what this 'mysterious letter' is about. This is the final attempt at connecting with him we have left:

Us: *Oi, Billy-boy, you were looking for a pen friend, here we are, lots of fun, bish, bash, bosh.*

I'll probably reword that, before sending, but you get the idea. Ultimately, if a person's curiosity doesn't get them to respond, we can, as a last resort, simply tell them, spoil the surprise in order to see whether we can squeeze blood from their stones. As it were.

Jane might not be the right person. She might just be a Jane, who the people of Hemswell believe to be RSVPeople Jane. But I've more faith in the people of Hemswell. However, I messaged her directly and she hasn't replied. What should be the next step? The RSVPeople Project doesn't stop unless there are no more avenues to explore, or until restraining orders are received.

Which leaves only Bryan-with-a-'y'. He's had the letter. He told us. He's had the postcard. He told us. So he has our street and email addresses. He can contact us in many ways. He said he had questions. No questions have been asked. He said we probably had questions and I'd gently nudged him towards the questions in the letter, which are, after all, questions, with actual question marks and everything. But, since then, nothing. Maybe Bryan is just too busy or just too sensible to pop this new request high enough on his to-do list, for it ever, you know, to actually get done.

So what about the 'ongoings'?

Becki.
So much detective work, tendrils extended out in the world, we must be patient. Next step could be emailing her business directly (but the company website says emails that aren't asking about the work will be blocked) and that would be a nightmare. So we wait.

Sally (of Sally & Emma).
I contacted Emma yesterday and she said she'll reply in the next week or two. That's a distinct reduction in excitement from the Emma who ran screaming with glee through the Old Girls group page over a month ago. 'Week or two'. It's definitely better than 'bog off, weirdo', but it's in a ballpark only a couple of postcodes over from that ballpark. But what of Sally? It seems that if you didn't live at the original address, or aren't the first name in the ad then you're not as engaged with the arrival of our letters. They all seem to be behaving like the letter wasn't actually for them, or that Matt, Donald, Custard and Emma are the ones in charge of replying.

No one has asked the question whether Matt, Emma, Custard and Donald are keeping Dave, Sally, Roobarb and Richard in cages, feeding them scraps and making them listen to the droning noise of thousands of '80s pen friends introductory letters. I'm just saying.

Of course, Sally was actually the first name of the two, and she lived at the same address (the convent school) so my dissection of the facts is a little off, but I'm confident we're onto something here - why is no one else asking these difficult questions?

Lars.
Still an enigma. We await an email response to our postcard.

Dave.
Hopefully escaped from Matt's cage now, and well worth a prod and a suggestion that maybe he'd like his very own copy of the letter? It's against the original rules, but Dave's had a hard life, who knows how many months or years he's been Matt's prisoner?

Monika.
Awaiting the postcard reply, but what with the Berlin Wall coming down and the reunification of Germany somewhat scuppering our

attempts, I think further detective skills are required. I wonder how many Monika Meyers there are in the world?

Faheen.
More postcard waiting and when lockdown lifts over in Malaysia, Sarah has friends who live nearby who are actually willing to go and knock on his door.

Louise.
Postcard then detective work. Spinkhill and Bucks Fizz - how many Louise Fairstone's can possibly fit that profile?

Adam.
He was the youngest RSVPeople Person - I'm fairly sure he still is. When we find him we'll check. Fact-checking is so very important in the world today. It really is. I checked. It's a fact.

Richard.
May still be in his cage. He may have grown to like it.

Delilah.
Grimsargh. I can't remember whether we've made any enquiries about her yet. I was in love with a girl called Delilah from the age of about 12 to 14. I think it damaged me. It's left me a bit queasy about anyone called Delilah. Not their fault, obviously, but I think I'll feel better if I go and sit in my cage for a while.

Saturday 6th March 2021

Matt's letter arrived! It wasn't an anti-climax, it truly wasn't, but because we had already tip-toed through his Facebook chats about getting it and what his experience was 35 years ago, his letter told us a lot of stuff we already knew.

> **Matt**: For a few days you brought some much-needed humour and light - both for me and many friends on Facebook who thought it was hilarious. Thank you.

Still pretty awesome to see it written by his own hand though...

Matt discovered Smash Hits via a discarded copy he found at school. This is innocuous enough, but he remembers it was a 4th year student who discarded it and that this was in 1983, which suggests to me a framed copy above his mantlepiece - how else could he remember such details?

> **Matt**: Thank you for your letter - a brilliant 'interruption' into this Covid madness and, if you look at my Facebook page, you will see it brought immense amusement to many others as well.

We have, Matt, but we will again - this time with permission.

Monday 8th March 2021

While walking my borderline asthmatic self to the post office to post one of the papery eBay items that may also be causing the borderline situation, I decide to walk across the common. My body feels like it needs to walk without talking at the moment, the air much better spent solely keeping me oxygenated, rather than expelling words. Unfortunately for my lungs, Sarah and I are unable to walk for more than a few seconds without nattering. Until my borderline, it was one of my greatest joys of being outside - walking and blathering.

That's not to say my walks are silent. I'm more than capable of holding an eight-way conversation in my head that's only slightly less exhausting than the real thing would be. But one of the first things I see on my walk is something you see all over South London, it's literally everywhere and way more exhausting than voices in your head: people exercising. I head towards four people jumping up and down, generally behaving in a way as unnatural to humans as flying. But nevertheless, judging by the way they're all kitted out, and failing to see guns or other signs of coercion, I can only assume this is something they've chosen, and no doubt paid, to do.

I think what they're doing is known as burpees. Burpees? That word was surely created by twee parents trying to get a new-born to bring up the air, and most of the milk they've just consumed, and gleefully telling the baby well done for covering their back with warm wallpaper paste, no? If either a parent or an exercise instructor were ever to mix up those two definitions, one would attract a very niche cliental on the common, the other would have a hell of a time explaining themselves to social services. Maybe the only reason the exercise is called a burpee is because the people doing them are fit enough to do them and the worst that might happen with all that jumping around nonsense, would be the audible escape of air, as opposed to the projectile vomiting the rest of us would experience before being whisked away in an ambulance.

Another irony of the people exercising on the common is that they're all already fit! Fit and healthy people pretending to be out of condition so they can run around in skin-tight lycra. And they're all young. And it makes me feel old. And I don't need anyone new to make me feel old - not since my hairdresser first asked, about 12 moths ago, whether I'd like my eyebrows trimmed. Ever since then, age has been like an advancing army, even greater in number than exercisers in London.

But hang on, rather peculiarly, one of the very young lycra people is jogging away from the throng and towards me. And suddenly I realise that as one ages, it's not just the body that gets out of condition, the eyes start to deceive too. And I don't mean, that as the figure approaches they're not slim and in fantastic condition, they most certainly are, but the person has to get much nearer to me than I'd thought necessary before I realise it's Sarah! Sarah doing an incredible impression of a 19 year old! I thought, well if we're doing impressions… and I immediately do my party piece impression of the luckiest man on earth, which requires no effort whatsoever.

Sarah, realising the lucky, old, wheezy bloke has seen *and* recognised her, waves and returns to the voluntary physical abuse she pays for by standing order and I take a deep breath and extend my walk. I pass lots more joggers and burpers and realise yet another thing they all have in common - a look of abject misery. As though the exercise is killing them. I make a mental note never to join in.

Instead, I get to thinking about The RSVPeople. I wonder if they work out? Whether they burp or vomit - and where are all the ones we've yet to touch base with? I mentioned earlier, there's room for many voices in my head, so while I walk with the ex-pen pals, the burpers and my borderline concerns, I remember this is my Mum's birthday. She would have been 85. I would have called her today, I would have sent flowers or maybe written her a poem in a card.

Instead I'll call my Dad and we'll know we're talking specifically today because I can't wish Mum a Happy Birthday and he can't take her down to the beach to see the sea and then on to a restaurant, where Mum, after much deliberation, would pick precisely what she had the last time she ate there. But we won't talk about it, because knowing neither of us will ever talk her through a menu again is too painful to bear. Instead we'll talk about the football, whether the other siblings have been in touch and more ordinary stuff. But we'll both know. And we'll be glad we do.

It's also International Women's Day; Megan, Harry And Oprah Day; Kids Going Back To School Day and also Me Having An Actual Appointment With A Doctor Day. Even with the mess of voices in my head, I have room for one more. And today that's a blonde woman I've been seeing for days, without ever actually seeing her. Her face is on every bus stop and lamp post because she's missing. I haven't seen her, but I wish I had. I wish I could phone the number on all the posters and say I've just seen her, maybe feeding the ducks or sitting on a bench. I'd like to ask her if she's OK. I hope she's OK.

Life isn't simply a road, a three score and ten Route 66, that you start at one end and just keep going for as long as you can manage. It's more like a bowl of spag bol. You start on a pasta path and constantly get choices to stay on the spaghetti worm you're on or choose another one. Constantly leaping from strand to strand, never quite sure where it's going or when the next will arrive. Some strands take you to a hospital bed, with your family around you, just shy of your 84th birthday, others put you on national TV, talking to Oprah, trying to 'set the record straight' whilst really only guaranteeing you'll be adored by some and despised by others. And some paths end up with your face all over a South London suburb.

It's a sobering thought.

What's odd about trying to find 24 strangers from 1985 is that as the quest develops and we invest time into each one of them, they actually cease to be strangers. Because of social media, we know what a lot of them look like. And then a jigsaw of information arrives the longer you look - maybe not a 1000 piece jigsaw, but one of those 24 piece ones, that makes you scoff at how much better you are than your two year old at putting the sky together.

But with each and every 'yes, that's me' we get, there's a peculiar relief that these strangers are OK. I know how ridiculous that sounds but we're all in that giant pan of pasta, grabbing on to slippery choices, never quite knowing where we'll end up. Since 1985 we've taken so many spaghetti choices - we're all drenched in tomato sauce.

Becoming a pen pal ad hopeful was a choice those people made. Smash Hits decided if they got into print, and every reader, whether to respond. Likewise, being contacted by Sarah and me wasn't a choice they made any time recently, but rather they found themselves inside a huge pasta lasso - and whether they hold on, say hello, write a letter or prefer to slip through, is entirely out of our hands.

Tuesday 9th March 2021

The sun's shining. On a very long and pleasant walk to have blood taken, I leave a message for a dear friend. On the way back, I have new medicine helping me breathe more easily. The morning was a good morning and no mistake.

But now I'm home and looking at a Messenger reply from Delilah! Hurrah. But something doesn't feel right. I can't put my finger on it, but something, non-asthma related is coiled in my chest. Sarah's right next to me and excitedly asks that we read the message together…

Well, it's definitely Delilah. She hellos me with being 'insistent'. She received our original letter and had always planned to reply but now feels sort of harried by my endeavours to make contact. And she is very unhappy about me using the local Grimsargh community group to help find her. She asks for the post to be removed and mentions privacy a lot. A lot.

Oh dear. I told you I have a tricky relationship with Delilahs.

We immediately remove the post, of course, and apologise for any upset we've caused. We explain that our assumption was she still knew nothing of our letter - hence trying other ways of touching base with her. It didn't feel intrusive when we thought she didn't know we were out there. It seems she may have got the letter, received the postcard, seen the LinkedIn message and now been made aware of the enquiry on the community group. If we'd done all that on the same Tuesday morning, I too would have balked at the attention. But the original letter was eight weeks ago - the assumption Delilah knew nothing of it seemed better than likely.

But what we might have described as 'over-eager', Delilah labels 'unprofessional'. On the one hand, being thought of as unprofessional does rather require us to be 'professional' somethings and we rather like the idea of being professional pen pal seekers, but on the other hand, we've upset someone and that makes us feel really bad.

Delilah truly feels that trying to locate her by mentioning her 1985 address online was an invasion of privacy. I'm very nearly certain it isn't, but she and I disagree on that. Delilah is entitled to feel any way she likes about absolutely anything. As are we. And in that frame of mind we know we meant no harm, didn't do a single thing that we wished we'd done differently. We feel we did nothing at all wrong, in fact. But Delilah feels differently. And that has to be absolutely fine even if it really stings.

No matter how innocent and earnest your intentions, if a person doesn't want to play, you cannot, nor should you want to, make them. Our intention was always to try and find the writers of those ads and to see if they wanted to reply. Delilah didn't want to. Fair enough. We wish her well.

(However, we really, really, really, really hope she changes her mind and writes us a letter, if for no other reason than she's a brilliant artist and when The RSVPeople is looking for a flag or a coat of arms, I reckon hiring her to design it would be a match made in Smash Hits heaven!)

And even if we've been a bit stupid - that's what your teenage self was looking for - 'a bit stupid (as in a bit mad and zany)'. That's us, Delilah. Kind of.

Whenever you re-find your inner teenager, we're here for you.

In the meantime, Adam. Or Adam The Younger-er-est, as he shall forever be known. He lived in a place called Peatesby. How to find an Adam in a place I've never heard of? Tricky, but if you recall, we've got form here - when absolutely no one had ever heard of Sweden, Sarah and I still managed to find it.

Another nice back and forth with a very amenable admin chap called Duncan. His response to my request to try and find Adam via the group is…

> **Duncan**: Okay - I think the chance of someone having a problem with it is near to zero - so I would say, just post it and see if you can track down who you're after ☺
> And good luck with any responses ☺

A man built of the same optimistic stuff as Sarah and me, and not afraid to show his double smiley side, either.

It takes five minutes to join the group and write a post.

Peatesby is waiting.

Linda Milton: Adam or Young Adam their son?

Me: The Adam I'm hoping to get in touch with would be in his mid 40s now, so Young Adam?

Linda Milton: Adam Lucas.

Me: Oh, wow, thank you so much!

Linda Milton: No problem, I grew up on the same road.

Five minutes later, we're pointed to the right Adam: Young Adam.

Calling him Adam The Younger-er-est was a little joke about him being the youngest pen pal person but now it turns out to be true. Young Adam is how he is universally known - no matter how old he gets! Brilliant.

Is this a first - asking the identified RSVPeople Person where to send a letter? What if he's already had it and chosen to ignore it? As one door closes, another opens. Thanks Peatesby!

Wednesday 10th March 2021

Kate Bush has dreadful taste in music.

From 3.59am I listen to her favourite singer 'perform'. As the endless minutes creak by I find less and less to like as the incessant warbler sings and sings and sings and sings. Of course, it isn't singing. It's tweeting.

It's like listening to the worst performance on The X-Factor ever:

Simon: *And you are?*
BB: *Blackbird.*
Simon: *Great. And what are you going to sing for us today?*
BB: *The titles of every song I've ever heard ever. Twice.*
Simon: *Right - that isn't really what we do here.*
BB: *Happy Birthday To You. Happy Birthday To You. Rehab. Rehab. When I'm Cleaning Windows. When I'm Cleaning Windows. Wherever I Lay My Hat. Wherever I Lay My Hat. I've Been Flushed From The Bathroom Of Your Heart. I've Been Flushed From The Bathroom Of Your Heart...*
Simon: ... (sound of the large red X doing its thing.)

Of course this wouldn't stop the bird - it would simply fly up into the lighting rig and sing everything from Eminem to Elvis to Wham! - well, not Wham!, obviously, everyone draws the line somewhere. For hours, without pausing for breath.

And from 3.59am to 7am my South London blackbird does just that. What an utter shit.

Whilst abluting I finally stop thinking of ways to kill my feathered nemesis and instead get to thinking about privacy. Upsetting Delilah yesterday had a very negative effect on both Sarah and me. There's probably some trauma from a long-forgotten school telling off or some attempt to do a nice thing and it backfiring, leading to embarrassment and shame. We probably all have those memories - but not too easily accessible, so it's hard to work on them. Instead they fester out of sight, like a haddock down the back of a radiator.

Privacy. My earliest memory, as a small boy, of invading someone's privacy, was when I almost walked in on my Mum on the loo. The toilet was essentially just a cubicle at the top of the stairs. No sink - that was a few long strides across the landing - just a loo. The door wasn't locked, so I pushed the door and Mum's foot came up to keep it closed from the inside. Privacy was entirely intact. I apologised and that was that. Or maybe it was the time I walked into my parents' bedroom and Dad was having a smoke. I didn't know he smoked. But he was holding it behind his back because he didn't want me to see it. At least I imagined he was smoking, he may have actually been on fire, which, now I think about it, I should probably have mentioned.

Neither time was earth shattering, although, the clarity with which I remember both those events suggests a sliver of more importance to me than to either of my parents.

When we began The RSVPeople Project we wondered about privacy and how much things have changed in the world regarding our obsession with protecting our 'data'. I'm just as bad - when we moved I cut the addresses and the numbers and the account details from every bank related piece of paper that might have been an invitation to the 'Bad People' to steal everything I own. But why?

First, who are the Bad People? Well, I suppose if we knew that we'd just arrest them and the world would be a better place. But they're the fear aren't they? Bad People. It's because of Bad People we lock our doors - because Bad People have been known, since forever, to come into other people's houses and take their stuff. We don't give our bank details to people over the phone, or online, because if they're Bad People they'll take all our money. We don't let our kids walk home alone because there may be Bad People around with insidious intent. I understand all these things. My family home was burgled, my eBay account was once hijacked and we've all heard way too many stories about stranger danger.

Back in the good ol' days, when 'you could leave your door unlocked all day round here', was that because Bad People hadn't thought of robbing houses? Or were there fewer of them? I doubt it. There's probably evidence that in every group of random people there are X number of Bad People. So why were doors kept open then but not now? Was it community? You knew everyone local and trusted them and believed criminals didn't travel for work?

Was it because of, 'I know your Dad', and back then Dads were more frightening than policemen? Or was it because we didn't have as much stuff worth stealing? I don't know the answers.

And, of course, we don't give our bank details out to people - other than every single person we invoice for a service. We don't balk at doing that. And every employee at every bank and credit card office has access to at least some of our personal data, but we don't mind that, and they're strangers aren't they? Could it be that those people don't have our passwords? They don't know the three figure number on the back of our cards? Or just because we sort of know them: *Hello is that Barclaycard? Yes it is. Great.* And in that moment we're sure we're talking to someone on our side, even if they are fleecing us with interest. They're not Bad People, they're Barclaycard.

OK, maybe that's not the best example, but you get the idea.

And stranger danger. Don't get me wrong, I don't think for a second there isn't danger on our streets. There is. But is there more danger today than 50 years ago? I don't know if there is. It's probably another fraction of society. X% are wrong-uns, always have been, always will be. There might be more of them because the population has increased, but the percentage is probably similar?

So what's the difference today? Is it the press? Always telling us every piece of horrible scary news they can? 'Back in the day' (what on earth does that even mean?) we didn't have 24 hour news so 'crime' didn't feel like it was everywhere and constant? Or is it the obsession that 'foreigners' aren't as 'good' somehow, as us? And all our neighbourhoods are more cosmopolitan than they used to be - because we all move around more. So is it simply suspicion of people we don't know? And suspicion, (unless fuelled by isms, or phobias) comes from a place of 'better safe than sorry', doesn't it? So the large gang heading our way on a dark, empty street, all shouting and being 'rowdy' are probably just football fans celebrating a good result, but the adrenal gland suggests they might just as easily be axe-wielding maniacs on a head-chopping-off spree, so we go the long way home instead, just in case. That's perfectly understandable, isn't it? Better to be safe?

But online data and privacy - what's all that about? Every single website today flashes a warning that they're using cookies to 'improve our viewing experience'. That means 'collecting our data', doesn't it? But regardless of what it means we all click the yes/agree/happy button without reading any of the small print stating the website now owns our first-born and all our old copies of Smash Hits. Because we don't care, we haven't time, we need to buy stuff or read stuff or find stuff and we need to do it right now. So we click the button. We don't care.

But someone, I don't know who, once cared enough to change the rules. And they told us to be wary. They told us that using cookies was infringing something and so the sites all had to tell us what they were doing, rather than just doing it without telling us. So now everyone using tracking cookies, which is everyone, has to tell us. And they do. And we still don't care. Not one bit.

Because after all - what data are they collecting? Isn't it mostly Google Analytics logging who visits the site? And recording when and from where and how long they stayed and how many of them didn't engage with the 'call to action' and therefore maybe upping our advertising budget tenfold might be a good idea? Isn't it that? Or advertisers? You look for socks on one site, the advert for the very same socks that you looked at, didn't want, moved on from, appears on every single page you look at for the next three days. You didn't want them then, you don't want them now, you don't buy them. I think advertisers are fooling themselves that an advert these days makes anyone buy anything. But I might be wrong. That happens sometimes.

All this brings me back to Delilah. Not the Michael Praed desiring Delilah, but the issue she flagged: putting an address online is not OK. I'm not suggesting she's wrong. In fact, I even sort of agree with her, deep in the pit of my stomach. But I don't know why.

If all our concerns are about trying to stay ahead of Bad People then what's the issue? We had Delilah's address from 35 years ago. She wrote it in a magazine with a circulation of hundreds of thousands. And her parents must have known. And her parents didn't mind. No one's did. So, there, on page 21 of Smash Hits were the names of 24 children and the addresses where they could be found. And every Bad Person on earth could lurk near any one of those houses with their nefarious plan. But none of those parents thought the magazine caused a problem. And none of those grown-ups today worry that Smash Hits back issues still present their data to anyone who grabs a copy off eBay. It seems almost ridiculous to care.

But somehow, that very same address when placed online, causes concern. And, again, I feel the same discomfort. But why? Do we think Bad People are scouring the Internet for addresses? And if they are, what are they doing with them? Phone books are full of addresses. And phone numbers. And names. You can buy them. Addresses exist on every road you walk down:

Anyone: *Oh look, I'm on Kingsbrook Road and there's number 9 Kingsbrook Road and there's number 11 Kingsbrook Road right next to it, who knew?*

So what?

An address appears online. With no details other than the enquiry that a person (Sarah and me, existing here as a single entity) is trying to get a letter to someone who used to live there. It's not like the address didn't exist until we wrote it down. It's been there as long as the house. It's an address. We've all got them. But online, does it suggest to a Bad Person a thought of criminal activity they otherwise wouldn't have been undertaking? Or does it create a Bad Person, from an otherwise Good Person? Do random addresses have that power?

So, a Vicar is looking through the local community group on Facebook. He sees an address. Maybe he knows the street already, maybe he doesn't. But suddenly, just because the Vicar saw it, he now has an uncontrollable urge to send unwanted pizzas round, or jump over the front garden wall and deadhead the roses or pee in the birdbath? Is that what we're afraid of - Vicars peeing in our birdbaths?

I mean, don't get me wrong, I don't want the Vicar peeing in my birdbath and I certainly don't want to be responsible for the Vicar peeing in your birdbath either, but I really don't think he's going to - and categorically not because he saw your address written down. So I can't believe that it's that. What am I missing?

Could it be that we have stopped thinking for ourselves? What do I mean by that? (That's not a question for you by the way, I'm talking to myself.)

We live in The Age of Sharing, so our social media streams are chocker with articles our friends have shared, with earth-shattering comments like 'This', or 'What he said'. Or, often, nothing. There's no discussion, probably because no one's had time to actually read the article, but the headlines need immediate attention or fury or rebellion. And piece by piece our echo chamber encourages us to think a certain way. Because you have to think 'a certain way' depending on the club colours you've signed up to. So if you're a member of whatever club, you have to sign up to this, this and this - while the 'others' are all in favour of that, that and that. Not only is fence-sitting not allowed, neither is having a toe in each camp. You're either one of us, or you're one of them. For us or against. It's absolute nonsense.

Thanks social media - I'm pretty sure you're responsible for more misery than literally anything else on earth, well done, I hope you're proud of yourself.

One of the reasons we have so many appalling people in the House of Commons is that many constituencies will vote the same way, for the same party, even if a suitcase full of dog poo bags stands for election. And the evidence for this is just how many full dog poo bags are currently MPs. I rest my case.

So when we were told everyone was stealing our data was it true or did we just say: *Really? Baton down the hatches, run, run - protect the data, protect the data* - whilst obviously, still posting pics of our kids, our holidays, our views, our rants and our dinner and all without bothering to check our security settings - because, still, most people don't care.

But has it made us paranoid? People knowing things about us = bad. Because when people know things about us… they..? I don't know, what will they do? Call us? Then block them. Email us? Straight into spam. Try and 'friend' us? Say no. Try and follow us? (Online, not in the aisles of Tesco.) Well that's what we want! We've no problem with every single Bad Person from here to eternity following us on social media if it makes our numbers look good!

Most of us would take Satan as a follower to boost our numbers. And then check to see if he also has accounts in the names of Beelzebub, The Devil, Lucifer and Mephistopheles that might like to follow us too.

So when a thing is Bad, because we've been told it's Bad, it's just Bad, is it? Without thought or consideration? So, personal details online are Bad. Simply because they are. And we're no longer a society that asks 'why' anymore? I don't know why we don't, but we don't. We don't question anything anymore, we just already know what we think about everything then oppose and abuse everyone who disagrees. We're great at being vile, not so good at pondering, questioning or explaining.

So, I fully understand that a certain action can offend someone. When that Vicar pees in my birdbath I'm not going to be happy. But it's not the end of the world. Similarly, an address online might make us a little uneasy - but not for any actual reason I can think of - other than society has battered it into us that it's something we need to fear.

And breathe.

I was raised a Catholic. I was an altar boy. And one day I considered whether I believed in transubstantiation - that bread and wine actually become the body and blood of Jesus. And I decided I didn't. I'd sort of believed it because I'd been told it was true. But I'd also been taught to think for myself, to question things. And that's what I did, and technically in that moment I stopped being a Catholic. And that's OK - I'm still, mostly a nice person. But the reason I didn't believe in transubstantiation any more was because it's entirely based on the literal interpretation of Jesus saying, 'This is my body, this is my blood'. I'm no Bible scholar but I just thought to myself: I don't think that's what He meant, not literally?

Data sharing and bread and wine becoming actual flesh and blood of The Saviour Of All Mankind are not necessarily comparable, I get that. But I think if we believe putting innocent personal details online is intrinsically going to bring Badness or Bad People into our lives, we have to first ask ourselves an honest 'why?' And if after answering that we still think it's the case, well, fine - but it makes me sad that our lives are so full of worry.

Monday 15th March 2021

I'm just going to leave this here.

See that chimney?

This is 6am.

I'm mentioning no names - he knows who he is!

Mark Gerrish knows who he is too - Donald's Dad!

Mark: Hi Paul & Sarah,
Have received the letter and passed it on to Donald. He may have Richard's email in Oz, I'm not sure. Donald is my son by the way. I remember well the tons of letters which arrived back then, you'd never believe it. At the peak, the Post Office were delivering 2 or 3 sacks a day in the mail van. Amazing how long ago it was.
Best regards, Mark.

Mark was there back in 1985. He saw the sacks, marvelled at the letters - maybe even gave the postie the number of his osteopath? We can't cross Donald off the list yet in the way we'd like - but here, in this email, we revisit the past. Thanks Mark.

Yesterday was Mother's Day. Sarah had a long chat with hers and I called my Dad. Even though we didn't even mention Mum, just like on her birthday, we both knew specifically why we were chatting. Communication, with love at its core, is surely one of the most valuable things there is.

Another thing that happened yesterday was discovering Simon Le Bon look-a-like Johnny Carter as 'Badrat'. Discovered him on Spotify. He's great. Proper eclectic music. Very cool.

Do be careful though, the bass is sometimes enough to literally move things along a desk. Or maybe I have a poltergeist?

But he's not just a one rat band, no indeed. He's one half of a 'pair of sonic mischief makers'. I highly recommend them!

Not just for the music, but also because there aren't many people who can pull off a shades/beanie/mules combo like that, but Johnny was never afraid to express himself: his ad said he liked Billy Idol and Dire Straits. The man knows his own mind - and recognises the importance of keeping it warm.

I mean, I'm assuming Johnny is in the hat. If not, then I have to beg him for his skincare regime because the other guy doesn't look like he was even nearly alive in 1985.

So, the chap in the hoody must be Yssip. Other than a Badrat collaborator I know nothing of him. I'd also need take a moment before pronouncing his name. The Chameleon/Lizard thing may be why Yssip is armed. That scaly fella looks mean.

It was brilliant to get a peek through the window of Badrat's creative output, but we almost forgot we have letters to reply to, and Johnny is top of the list. 'Top of the list' meaning: 'the one we've been most tardy about'.

It's important to point out that when first reading Johnny's wonderful letter neither of us fully appreciated he signed himself off as 'Robert Johnny'. There's absolutely nothing wrong with choosing your middle name over your first name, but was it the name he went by as a teenager or a 'maybe don't put your full name' warning from someone? Although, simply giving your middle name isn't exactly 'security-conscious'. In our letter we ask him. Maybe there's a story? Maybe he wanted to be JR at school, especially as there was the hit TV show Dallas around back them? So many questions.

We also write to Russell. As far as we're aware he's never used a musical moniker. But what he has definitely done, is train to do hair and wigs for TV & Film, as a means to earning a living during the pandemic. I worked in the theatre for years and knew a lot of wiggies - a lot of them also work in the Film & TV industry. Maybe Russell will end up working with someone I know? Stranger things have happened - Sarah's letting me have that - they probably have.

We have a few dead ends now. We remain ever-optimistic of finding Lars and Monika, but it's the cold contacts that are problematic. Delilah opened our eyes to the fact that non-communication does not mean we haven't been knocking on the right door. And intentional hassling is not what we're about. Tricky. There are quite a few RSVPeople that we think we've found, have put out feelers for and have even contacted in person, but we are still, to each of those people, just strangers asking for an address.

My feeling is that we may have to send letters out again - individuals might, understandably not want to connect with an online request without more information. And even though we wanted to keep them in suspense to get the surprise of opening the envelope and being taken back to 1985, we may have to say pish to that idea. And if we approach, assuming they've no idea what this is about, we have to risk people thinking us pushy.

We're ok with 'pushy'- so long as it's unintentional pushy.

It's a real minefield:

Got letter from: Andy, Russell, Johnny, Custard, Matt.
Have received our letter: Emma (waiting for letter); Donald (hoping for letter); Sally (nudge through Emma); Dave (nudge through Facebook?); Delilah (X); Oli (...); Fran (...); Bryan (...); Roobarb (X).
Contacted but don't know if they've seen our letter: Becki (send letter to work); Adam (???); Jane (???); William (???)
Unsure if they even know we exist: Mayumi (hoping for letter); Lars (???); Monika (try and locate); Faheen (???); Louise (try and find through FB); Richard (try to locate through Donald).

Judging by this latest, cutting-edge, scientifically collected data splurge, we still have nine RSVPeople to connect with. Nine!

Tuesday 16th March 2021

Sarah's 'gone to work'. Now, what I mean by 'gone to work' is that she's 'not in a shed at the bottom of the garden, trying to get in touch with 1985'. She's doing 'proper' work. Now, what I mean by 'proper' work, is she's 'not in a shed at the bottom of the garden, trying to get in touch with 1985!' She's workshopping a new play. And by 'workshopping', yeah, you know what I mean. She will be Covid tested, made to stand in her own personal, taped square area on the floor and probably hosed down with something usually used to get the barnacles off the bottom of boats.

Damn, she gets all the fun.

I, however, have been writing letters. Johnny, Russell and now Matt. I know I didn't write the first two today, but where I'm scoring points with 'writing' I'm losing them in the area of 'posting'.

For heaven's sake, who writes letters these days anyway?

Oh.

Also, it's not like I write a letter then sit in the shed drinking coffee and eating Mr. Kipling apple pies! I write a letter, sit in the shed, eat apple pies and don the deerstalker. I've never appreciated the 'stalker' in there with the deer. Ah well, it is the hat of detectives and I've been detecting.

Let me say straight up that I've found a Monika Meyer who went to university in Leipzig at the right time to be our Monika. She has a work address but, as with Matt who pointed out his work has been shut for a while, I decide to contact her directly on LinkedIn. I offer to send it to her work, or wherever she wants, without telling her it's post in a time machine.

Invite Monika to connect

Me: Hi Monika, are you by any chance the same Monika who lived at..? If so, I have a (nice) letter to forward to you - maybe I could send it c/o your work address? If that's not you, apologies for the intrusion. Thanks. Paul.

I've also been scratching my head after yesterday's 'where we're up to' table…

I'm simply not happy with our William progress. I very much equate William with Matt - both got proper jobs after leaving their boarding schools and even though they differ in their attitudes towards that Queen of Pop, Madonna, they strike me as being cut from similar cloth. And now that we know Matt to be a super-human, super-hero, capable of distributing sacks and sacks of post around a library with his bare hands, I have a tremble in my stomach suggesting a) William will be an RSVPeople Person very soon or b) that apple pie was only disguised as a gorgeous snack, and was in fact little more than a fistful of sugar. I think the former.

As the beastly monsters at his old school didn't deign to help, and Nick (at William's old work address) went over and above the call of duty, I decide the time has come to approach the man himself.

We pondered whether William took a peek at my LinkedIn profile a little while ago, which should have allayed all fears about me being anything other than the utterly harmless, devilishly attractive, chap that I am. Let me show you what I mean…

Here I am on LinkedIn.

OK, so that's a slightly sinister looking backdrop, I forget why I chose it, but look at that cheeky-chappie face! That's a face that screams out…

Me: *Write to me, I'm harmless… until I take you up this hillside, hollow out your head and wear it as a hat.*

Mm, might need to rethink the photo?

But too late for that now. I've messaged William. I'm almost as excited as he'll be when he reads it.

> **Me**: Hi William, apologies for the intrusion, but since the start of January I've been trying to send you a letter. Absolutely nothing unpleasant, I promise you, and I'm not selling anything (I'm a writer, I have nothing to sell you!)
>
> The letter is best described as a 'blast from the past'.
>
> The first attempt at your old school was returned, the second attempt, a nice chap at your old work address, called Nick was unable to help, so with no other leads, I decided to contact you here.

Me: *(cont…)* Your letter was always supposed to be a surprise (hence trying to get it to you without contacting you first) and it would be great if it still could be, but you don't know me, and I completely respect that, but if there was somewhere, anywhere, I could send it for you, that would be great.

Failing that I could photograph the letter and send it as an attachment - it would take the surprise away, but at least you'd have it.

Apologies for the cloak and dagger.
I look forward to hearing from you.

Look at that!

Friendly, informative, even a tiny bit whiny, that although he owns the ball, I'd very much like to play my game, my way. Exactly as I planned.

This is a departure for the project, of course, the offer of a photo of our letter. Maybe I should have said 'scan' instead. The word 'photo' does rather make you think of my LinkedIn photo and the sinister land of 'scooping out heads' which it suggests as my preferred holiday location.

I didn't even know 'scooping out heads' was a thing until I saw that moody photo and the words just seeped out - into a putrid puddle of gore on the floor. Stop it! Honestly, I'm a nice person, and I'm not even sure if we have an ice-cream scoop. I shall check, and if we do, I will bury it in the back garden - to be on the safe side.

If William chooses not to engage I will have no choice but to come into a huge amount of money and employ him for his investment skills. Failing that - no idea.

Next I invoke the combined spirits of Bucks Fizz and the Spinkhill community in search of Louise. And Spinkhill, as all the local communities do, immediately comes good. A chap messages me directly with a possible email address for Louise - seems his wife is a distant relative. He couldn't say if the email address was still current though.

Mm, emailing someone at an address that might be no longer in use, and if it is, still not being sure if it's the right person, could make for a trickily worded message. However, her email address is her full name - and she's no longer a Fairstone.

Having a new name to search for makes the next few steps straightforward. Email-Louise is on FB. And there's mention of the Spinkhill area. And also the family name - Fairstone.

Email-Louise is RSVPeople Louise! Fact.

Thursday 18th March 2021

Four things of significant note happen today. Followed by another one. Making five.

Five things of significant note happen today.

1. We post a letter to Russell.
2. We post a letter to Matt.
3. We post a letter to Badrat.
4. I'm asked to go for my vaccine - asthma unveiling its solitary benefit. Nearest centre means a wait of a week. A little further away, half hour walk, and I can book it for tomorrow. So that's what I do.

5. Monikagetsintouch!

Sorry, what was that? Yeah, Monika, or rather 'Nika', sends a message! Precisely like this…

Monika Meyer:

Hi Paul, what a surprise. I am the Monika who lived in Leipzig. I went to University there. The street name should have read Lertheaustr, not …ster, it was printed wrong in the Smash Hits pen pal pages.

I am currently on furlough so not at work, but would love to see that letter. How did you get hold of it?

Nika.

Let's look at this scientifically.

First let's look at the top: Monika.
Now let's look at the bottom: Nika.

Exactly! We've gone from LinkedIn formal, to bestest buddies in less time than it takes to run down to the pool and pop a towel on a sun lounger at 5am. (That, I'm aware, is a German stereotype, a cliché that might cause a micro amount of annoyance, but in 1985 it was simply a joke, so I'm relaxed about it.)

In fact, more than that, I'm OK with it. It's a compliment. And the thing is about compliments, we take them wherever we can get them. And if you want a sun lounger and you're prepared to get up at the crack to park your towel, then more power to you. And if you're not doing that but I'm still dishing that out as a compliment, just take it. Even more power to you for not dashing my illusion about your resourcefulness.

And, as if to underline in a dozen different ways that the Germans are also known for efficiency - five minutes! Five minutes it took Nika to reply - and that includes reading and writing time too. And let's not forget that as it's Monika, she's filtering every word through 83 different languages, a veritable computer of translation.

But let's not ignore the single piece of information that no other RSVPer has uttered - that she already, somehow, knows this is about her pen pal ad in Smash Hits - without us uttering a word about it. Clearly she's a psychic? Or a witch? And, sigh, not in a derogatory way - in a: *hurrah, wow, brilliant mind-reading, caldrons and bats and broomsticks and please don't turn me into a newt,* way.

I'm not sure witches can actually get furloughed though - I've always thought of them as rather more self-employed than employed? Sure, sure, sure, maybe there's a more reasonable reason than witchery. I'll ask…

Me: Hi Nika, how lovely to hear back from you, and I'm so glad you're the 'right' Monika. But I'm intrigued - how did you know this had anything to do with Smash Hits? Are you psychic? ☺

Monika: Not psychic, I lived at the address for 4 years and remember very clearly when the letters started dropping in. Although I must have had a couple of thousand replies to that little pen pal advert and they were the only ones that misspelt the street name. It did not stop them passing it on to other magazines, though, notably a magazine in Greece, as I suddenly received a couple of hundred replies from there…

Monika: *(cont...)* It's totally weirded me out that you contacted me as only the other week I was reminiscing on my time at Uni and that I never did anything with my Scandinavian studies, instead ended up in England.

In the same way it's not wizards or mysticism that make impressively reliable German cars, but straight-thinking, intelligent, skilled engineers basing their work on their talents and experience, Nika draws open the curtains on my small-minded stupidity.

Smash Hits spelled her address wrong. She got a 'couple of thousand' wrongly addressed letters - and, let me tell you, German or not, you don't forget the same mistake befalling you 2000+ times over a few months.

And not just from the UK, from Greece too! Smash Hits has a lot to answer for. Speling is veri inportent.

It's totally weirded me out that you contacted me...

Just for a second a sort of Delilah-shaped shiver runs up our spines. Oh no, please don't be cross/offended/upset/insulted. But it's a simple serendipitous moment that's got Nika 'weirded'. Phew.

However. She knows this is Smash Hits related. There's no point trying to pretend it isn't. Gosh, for the first time since we started this I feel I'm the one playing catch up, wondering what's going on, what's going to happen next. Nika needs the story. She needs it more than she needs a 5am sun-lounger...

So we tell her the whole story. Cat. Bag. Everything out. It feels so, so good to get all this out in the open right from the start. Everything off the chest is a good way to be. Especially a chest that's recently been diagnosed with asthma! It feels really good. The openness, not the asthma.

But she doesn't reply…

Friday 19th March 2021

I have The Fear. That's what it is. It can be nothing else. The Fear.

What exactly the fear is, is not easy to define. Is it when you wonder if a line has been crossed? That someone else's Detective Stalker Moment has discovered something they find unsavoury? Possibly a child, my child, making an accidental (but hilarious) finger gesture from his high chair on Facebook? Has this triggered something in the seeker because they find toddlers accidentally being puerile a step too far? Maybe the cut of one's jib is seen as a jibbing step too far? Or has a friend warned against all contact with all people who haven't had a police check and given a TED talk? Any, or all, of these are entirely plausible. Sarah's not sure if they are, but she hasn't come up with a better explanation.

With little else to do for the moment I do the only thing I can do - I walk to a chemist and get my vaccine. The instructions (yes, there are instructions - it's not just 'roll up your sleeve' during a global pandemic!) state I may have an appointment that lasts as long as 45 minutes! That's almost two episodes of Schitt's Creek! I take a book.

However, I arrive, I get jabbed and I leave in just under four minutes. 2 x 35 minutes of walking for a four minute appointment and protection (in three weeks) from the nasty-nasty.

Walking home I check my phone many times. Monika is not there. Maybe she too is having her vaccine? She's a little older than me - she was the oldest of The RSVPeople back in 1985, and therefore far more deserving of early vaccine protection than some of those younger whippersnappers.

I get home to no sympathy. I mean, really? This morning I was one of the ordinary 70-ish million, now I'm one of the special 20 million. I'm a little aggrieved to not even get a sticker to commemorate this momentous day. A surprise street party might have been a little too much to ask, but would a T-shirt be out of the question? Or a guest spot in the next available panto as a V-celeb? No. No sticker. No T-shirt. No burgeoning minor celebrity career. And no sympathy for the pain in my arm which is currently 'vaguely noticeable'.

And I'm a bit tired after all that walking. Sigh. But not for long…

CLEAR!!! Monika's message is like a full-throttle chest blast from a pimped-up defibrillator!

Her pen pal experience is still crystal in her memory. Mostly.
She, not unsurprisingly (ahem) thinks the project a good idea! She's a little vague about how long it's been, which maybe means up until now it's not been one of the most life-affirming moments of her life. '30+' years ago is close, Nika, but come on: 35 years. And a quarter. 35.25 years. But, OK, we can forgive that. Eventually.

Back in 1985 she was getting 50 letters a day, from all sorts of people, even 10 year olds. And although she may have been a little hazy about the passage of time, this is entirely eclipsed by her care, attention and utter niceness. She was 21. But she didn't disregard those letters from 10 year olds. Oh no, she didn't want them to miss out on having a pen friend. So do you know what she did? She took them to her old school and gave them to her old English teacher to pass on to suitable children looking for pen friends.

I mean, they may have been a little second hand, but when you're offered a letter sent first to Monika, turning it down would be like turning down a Fabergé Egg because it wasn't made specifically for you. Thoughtful. Wonderfully thoughtful. (Unlike Matt & Dave who just 'library-dumped' the whole lot of them!)

And just when Monika thought the letters were coming to an end, Smash Hits was published again in other countries and the flood of letters began again.

Monika: Would you believe that I found my very best friend through that advert?

Sarah and I wondered right from the beginning (a ridiculously short 78 days ago) whether a handful of written words could bring a meaningful relationship into one of those young lives. And here it is: Nika's 'very best friend' came from that ad. Never mind the spelling mistakes, the address mistakes, the name mistakes, Smash Hits changed Nika's life. Oh the power of a teenage music magazine. We'll never know how differently the paths of Matt and Dave's lives might have veered had they only replied to a single one of those letters in 1985 - in the way replying to ours has (ahem, again) changed their lives in 2021.

Nika, thank heavens, acknowledges that there are no secrets online and finding a way to contact a person, as we've discovered, can be achieved with some digging and a bit of luck. She's happy to give us her address so we can send that original orange letter to its proper home.

LinkedIn is no place for this new friendship. We immediately give Monika an email address. Without a doubt, not unlike my experience with the vaccine, she's no longer one of the faceless, she's most definitely one of us.

Thanks Monika. What a glorious day.

There's something weird about making contact with wonderful people. When we send out enquiries, our modern minds want instant gratification. Like we're sending texts, not letters or even emails. But when we get replies, we're ashamed to say, we reply with a more old-fashioned mindset - meaning we don't reply right away. We celebrate the victory and the fact a new person wants to play. Then we forget to get back to them in a timely manner.

I wonder if it will happen with this latest unexpected piece of the puzzle..?

You: *Eh? What's that? Has something unexpected happen?*

Yes it has!

Out of the blue. We got an email. And it wasn't even from an RSVPeople Person. It was from… (drum roll please…) Mrs. Badrat!

She calls her husband Johnny. I wonder if she knows he signs off as a Robert? Awkward. We don't know each other even half well enough for us to drop the bombshell that her husband, Johnny-Robert-Badrat-JR-Larry Hagman clearly has a shoebox filled with passports and foreign currency buried under that weird creature in his album photo by the table. But that's information he'll need to share himself when the time is right - maybe after some overseas assassination trip that goes particularly well?

Oh my goodness - she went to the same clubs as me in Manchester. And she has a friend who was going to do a Kate Bush show - Sarah has a Kate Bush show! She sailed to Aberystwyth from Aberdaron - I've been to Aberdaron and went to university in Aberystwyth and once dated a woman in the ABBA musical Mama Mia. All the Abers!

You know what this means?

Me: *I've got a stalker!*
Sarah: *You haven't got a stalker.*

Well she would say that - she's not the one whose partner has a Kate Bush show, is she?

There's another spooky thing - the one and only time I went to Aberdaron, to that static caravan (the one bigger than most London flats), when my friend Mark and I were thrown out of that pub for being too stupid to smuggle in the right beer cans, yeah? Well Mark and his family just so happened to live in Hale Barnes. And, as you know, I, spookily referenced that trip on the 20th of February! So these 'coincidences' suddenly feel a little closer to home…

Is it possible Mrs. Badrat is actually Sarah, but in a beanie and dark glasses?! Sarah says no.

Well, of course she does, because you know what, if she were Mrs. Badrat, that's exactly what I'd expect her to say!

Wednesday 31st March 2021

This is the end of the longest gap between entries in The RSVPeople journey so far. It's not like we haven't been busy. We've developed an idea for a musical into something a bit more coherent after being longlisted for a competition. We also find ourselves looking forward, wondering about the nation's 'road map' out of lockdown. The return to the normal future we all hope for, being dangled like a carrot. But who knows what the carrot looks like? When it arrives will it be the colour carrots used to be? Will it have the texture carrots are famous for? And if we lean in close and listen and find the carrot mumbling to itself, what accent will it have? A carrot accent? Or a post-lockdown accent?

Sarah's not sure this helps to explain, well, anything. She suggests coffee. I never turn down coffee. No matter what accent it brews in. But the future is gaining focus today. We talk about a holiday. Not to anywhere or at any time in particular, but the notion of being able to leave the country like people used to. We talk about a dinner party, with people who have not been allowed in the same room for a long time. Sarah talks about gigging again, actually facing an audience no longer wrapped in masks and sitting at tables almost a peanut-flick away. We talk about getting my boys and my Dad all together in the same place at the same time. We talk about cinema, theatre, picnics, beer gardens, meals out and even haircuts.

I desperately need a haircut. My hair looks like it once lived on Boris Johnson's head but was evicted for really letting itself go.

But we're also thinking about The RSVPeople. They're all thinking these same thoughts. Maybe not the hair thing, but most of the others, I'm sure. Being locked down during a pandemic allows way more time for reminiscing the actions and experiences of our teenage selves; way more time to fill; way more time to maybe, oh I don't know, write a letter or two.

Those we've actively heard from: Andy, Mandy, Matt, Russell, Monika, Badrat - a more wonderful and eclectic bunch of people you could not hope to meet.

It's as though we knocked on their doors…

Us: *Hello, do you want to come out and play down Memory Lane?*
Them: *Yes!* (As they wipe imaginary chocolate from around their imaginary mouths with imaginary sleeves).

And we played out and Memory Lane was warm and fun. Even the odd scuffed knee or dropped sweet was not a problem, just being out there, reliving a special time, put smiles on all our faces.

We did that. Sarah and I grin and bask in the special sunlight that only truly exists in memories and episodes of Midsommer Murders. Then, a little while later we're knocking on the doors again…

Us: *It's us again!*
Them: *Right, hi, yeah…*
Us: *Remember how much fun Memory Lane was?*
Them: *Yes. Yes, indeed, it was great. I think we said how grateful we all are that you reopened that memory. Really great.*
Us: *You're welcome. Want to play out again?*
Them: *Again?*
Us: *On Memory Lane. It was so much fun, remember?*
Them: *Right, no, absolutely… it's just the dog needs walking…*
Us: *Bring the dog!*
Them: *Right, no, but I walk the dog while I jog and listen to a podcast about present day things, very much anchored in, well, Today, so…*
Us: *Jogging and podcasts isn't really what Memory Lane is for.*
Them: *No, you're right, which is why I'm going to the park.*
Us: *Not Memory Lane?*
Them: *No. Sorry.*
Us: *Oh. Right. Maybe another time?*
Them: *Yes, another time, absolutely.*
Us: *Great.*
…
Us: *Great. When?*
Them: *I have to get my trainers on, so…*
Us: *Of course, great, well, enjoy the park.*
Them: *Thanks, take care.*
…
The door closes. Sarah and I sigh. It feels like a failure…

But it isn't. Every single letter we've written has taken us ages to get round to, because there have been other things to do, and not just RSVPeople things. It's no different for anyone else. They have kids and work and families and picking up after their dogs in the park to do.

After the first trip to Memory Lane, the next visit for The RSVPeople has one foot planted firmly in Today Town. Today Town is right outside their front door. In their porch. In the drawer where the poo-bags live, next to batteries and bits of string. Time is precious.

The sunlight in Today Town is real and random and often scarce. And it makes weirdos at your door look a smidge weirder than in the dappled glow of Memory Lane.

So, we've accepted we've touched base with this Smash Hits half dozen and any contact beyond that is entirely in their hands. Nothing to be done. And. That. Is. Perfectly. OK.

That's not to say there's *not* other work to be done. There is. Lots. We've almost completely forgotten about Louise from The Land of Make Believe (see what I did?) There was the distant relative email address. A way in. A door to knock on. Maybe an address to send Memory Lane to? I don't know why Bucks Fizz Louise wasn't emailed weeks ago? There was probably a reason. I've forgotten the reason. Luckily, though, I've not forgotten how to write an email...

Me: Hi Louise, I was trying to locate a Louise who lived in Spinkhill in the '80s and so I posted on a FB group of the area to see if anyone could help. A chap who said his wife was a distant relative of yours gave me this address. I'm hoping you might be the right Louise? If so, would it be OK to forward a letter on to you?

I realise you don't know me but this is not an unpleasant letter in any way - and I'm absolutely not trying to sell you anything! I very much hope it will be a surprise that puts a smile on your face. If there's an address I can send it to, please let me know and I'll pop it in the post.
I look forward to hearing from you.

There it is. An email.

As we worried from the very start, it's not easy, in fact it's impossible, to know how any collection of words will be received by a person who doesn't know you. I'm certain Bucks Fizz Louise is much more evolved than this, but here's how my email might be interpreted by someone on the paranoid side of privacy and spam and all that:

'Hi Louise' - means nothing, anyone can get a first name, in fact maybe I'm about to be buttered up and I'm all about low cholesterol greetings. I'm instantly on guard.

'Locate' - you mean 'find' - which easily becomes 'track down' which is only a telescope up a tree away from 'stalk'.

'Distant relative' - vague, might as well say 'drunk bloke I got chatting to during a lock-in'.

'Would it be OK..?' - makes it all sound so innocent: 'OK' - putting all the onus on me. I mean, it's like saying - *If I say it's OK, then anything that happens after I open those floodgates to hell, is entirely on me.* OK!? As innocent as teenage friends agreeing to push each other on the swings, but hiding the adult strangers waiting to push you off a cliff!

'You don't know me... unpleasant' - impossible not to notice how close those two bits are. Me + unpleasant = unpleasant me! Sender doesn't grasp they're subliminally outing themselves as a monster.

'Pop it in the post' - might as well read 'cut your head off with the edge of some very cutty paper and then go into the hills for some scooping?' No thank you, no thank you at all!

'Kind regards' - nice, friendly, I think I'll reply - NOT!!

It's harder to be normal than I thought it was.

> **Louise**: Hi Paul,
> Thanks for your surprise email. I am the Louise you are looking for. I don't recognise your name though, sorry, or your photo. What is the letter regarding? Is it sealed or opened, can you give me some indication what this is regarding please? I'm not sure which FB group you posted on, could you tell me please? Sorry about all the questions, you have to be so careful giving personal details out nowadays.

Within moments Bucks Fizz Louise reveals she's not as paranoid a lunatic as my wild imagination had painted her. In fact, she's precisely the right amount of cautious and interested. Sounds exactly how an RSVPeople Person would be.

As we worried from the very start, it's not easy, in fact it's impossible, to know how any collection of words will be received by a person who doesn't know you. (Is there an echo..?)

So here's the translation of Bucks Fizz Louise's email into RSVPeople Speak.

'Hi Paul' - my very favourite name in the world! Paul Newman. Paul Young. Paul King. That bloke who won Britain's Got Talent. Pope Paul the All Of Them!

'Thanks' - Louise: polite, well raised, good stock.

'I am the Louise you are looking for' - a little bit like a lyric from a 1980s ballad, but bringing with it all the choruses of heaven in a Hallelujah - which, if you listen to it through an audio microscope, you'll hear that hallelujah is made entirely from the sound of another RSVPeople tick!

Bucks Fizz Louise is one of us. She will get the letter. She will return to that 1985 pen pal fold. It's another glorious day.

Friday 9th April 2021

The last few days have been amazing. For many reasons. Good reasons. And rubbish reasons. Where to start..?

Let's start with the blackbird. I've now listened to the language of blackbirds more than any other being on earth. I'm almost fluent in blackbird - without understanding a single word. And I don't know what he's on about. I mean, is it a song for a mate? Surely he's got to face it - he's been trying unsuccessfully all this time, he's just not what the discerning South London Lady Blackbird is looking for. It's a shame, but shut up about it already! If this is the blackbird's reality, is the continuous warbling a final, desperate, 'PLEASE CHOOSE ME!' before all the nest building material's been nabbed?

I'm pretty sure it's too late for that. So maybe he found his Lady Blackbird? I've never seen her. She may be sitting on eggs, but even a busy nesting Lady Blackbird needs to stretch her wings now and then, doesn't she? And if this is what's happened, she must be as sick of her husband's singing as I am. Because what is he singing?

'I've got a Lady Blackbird and she's sitting on some eggs!' Who cares? All the birds are in the process of nests and egg sitting. It's not like it's a special blackbird thing - and if this particular blackbird doesn't know that, well, he's an idiot.

Humans are famous for their idiocy. But evolution, a relatively caring society and a million drugs and lifestyle choices have allowed even the biggest idiots of humanity to have a fairly good chance of survival. In the animal kingdom, if you mess up, you're something else's dinner. If Mr. Blackbird is an idiot he probably shouldn't have made it this far.

So, name calling aside, let's assume my nemesis is not an idiot and is in possession of a full set of blackbird faculties, honed with Darwinian precision. So, once more, what the hell is the singing about?

Territory marking? Unable to cock his leg against every tree and bush in the neighbourhood, is he letting all the other birds know this is his patch? Maybe. Although yesterday he was singing in a big tree, and, defying every law of physics, a big fat Bertie Wood Pigeon was sitting on an insubstantial twig 18 inches away, looking at him. Utterly unbothered by the threats of violence in the blackbird's song. I imagine the wood pigeon, famed for repeating the same few notes over and over and over again, was tweeting the mantra, 'Or what? Or what? Or what?'

Blackbird: *Leave my Kingdom!*
Pigeon: *Or what?*
Blackbird: *This is my turf, I rule, begone oh lesser being!*
Pigeon: *Or what?*
Blackbird: *I rule. I have bagsied this area, it's mine, move away!*
Pigeon: *Or what?*
Blackbird: *Oh shut up!*
Pigeon: *Or what?*

I was expecting my hate/hate relationship with this feathered 'friend' to be drawing to a close. Our bedroom is undergoing the insertion of new windows. Perfectly fitting windows removing all unwanted breezes and irritating singing.

In order for the windows to be replaced we pushed the bed into the middle of the room. The job was to take a couple of days. The first night I woke in the dark to very faint singing. Yes! Even being a few feet away from the old windows reduced the volume. The new windows will deliver me the best night's sleep I've had in weeks.

I nip to the loo.

The singing is twice as loud! The blackbird, for the first time, has moved his stage to RIGHT ABOVE MY HEAD! But for the sloping roof, I'm sure I could reach up and poke him right in the eye. At least I know now why Mr. Blackbird is doing it. To ruin my life. Put on earth to ruin my life. There's literally no other explanation!

So I'm both exhausted and reeling from this new, nightmare realisation. I pick up the asthma peak flow tube thing, and with even more gusto than normal, take a huge breath in and blow with all my might, hoping to reveal the yin of the blackbird is at least balanced by the yang of being cured of asthma.

I blow. I put my back out.

I've put my back out many times. I'm tall and don't always sit properly/lift properly/blow into a peak flow metre thing properly. But I know the process. A twinge, a slow tensing of every muscle in my back. A leaning over to the right like an Italian tower. Finally - surprisingly searing pain.

Just brilliant. Some might say it's ludicrous to blame a blackbird for a back injury. Not me.

For the first time in ages, Sarah and I have a well-ventilated lunch date in the diary. She's very kindly offered to postpone it due to my back. But, I'm feeling particularly 'blokey' and therefore am blessed with the knowledge that what I need, beyond a shadow of doubt, is a 25 minute walk on the coldest April day since the last Ice Age, followed by a social afternoon, sitting in the same cold, followed by an even colder walk home later on.

But it's been such a long time since we last saw our friends. In fact the last time was before New Year, when we told them about a certain imminent project, involving a certain copy of a pop mag.

Our friends, Kate and Andrew are wonderful hosts. They're great fun, always make delicious food and never let our glasses run dry. They also have a great line in French muscle relaxant tablets. I can't understand a word on the packet but they assure me they're just what I need.

Andrew is one of those incredibly social people who can, and does, talk to anyone. Reminds me of my Mum. Dad always said if they went out for the day and Mum nipped to the loo - she'd always come out in conversation with a stranger. I don't know how Andrew conducts himself in public loos, but I do know he has a spooky ability to discover connections between people. He'll meet people who used to live on his street or who know his old English teacher, that kind of thing.

Now pay attention…

Andrew is about to be the best man for his best friend, David. He's talking about his speech. The fact my Dad was a GP comes up, I forget why, but Andrew asks what part of Manchester my Dad's practice was in. I tell him. Andrew mentions a name, asking if it means anything to me. Strangely enough, it does. It's the name of a partner at my Dad's old surgery. I'd known him as a child - a terrifically smiley Doctor. Andrew's best friend David is his son!

Andrew's best friend's Dad and my Dad both went to work through the same front door every day for years! What a ridiculously small world! It turns out my Dad was at David's Bar Mitzvah!

We all chat non-stop. I don't know if the French drugs do anything but at one point I laugh so hard I almost wet myself.

Wet myself and end up in hospital! Almost. Debbie Harry, on the wall looks concerned.

When we get round to discussing The RSVPeople, Kate and Andrew follow the twists and turns with glee. We explain the folk we've contacted, the folk who've replied, the one's yet to be in touch. It's supremely exciting to recount the adventure - and a surprise to see how much detail we have at our fingertips.

We tell them everything, ending with Fran's mysterious disappearance. Fran. I'm sad to think there's nothing else we can do to nudge a response from her. But like Bryan (with a y) and William, some of The RSVPeople have been passed the ball and decided not to play. Instead of that being a failure, Sarah and I are just accepting it as part of the story.

We stay at Kate and Andrew's for a long time. My back doesn't improve but it's great fun. The walk home is tricky, I walk gingerly - a term I've never understood - how exactly does one do something as though with reddish hair?

Home, I'm wondering how I might sleep, move and not be in constant pain. Is it cold or heat that I'm supposed to apply? Or both?

Me: *What?*

Sarah's grinning at me.

Momentarily all the pain in my back disappears, replaced entirely by the joy of realising we've had not one, but two new letters!

Like buses - but much smaller and made out of paper. And with stamps on them.

But who? One is the new address, one the old address. Old address with the re-direction STILL not bloody well working!! Stone cold sober and without acute pain, mildly dulled with mysterious French witchcraft, I might have been able to rattle off the list of possible RSVPeople in those envelopes. But I can't.

We start with the oldest one. And you won't believe it: it's only Fran Hargarden! And it's quite a story.

It's fair to say that Fran's life has taken some twists and turns most of us should be grateful not to have experienced. Her letter is candid and after a tentative apology for not knowing quite how to approach the 'elephant in the room', she shares the story of her life, her RSVPeople experience and her hopes for the future.

The elephant she spoke of was the fact that for the next 36 weeks her address is a women's prison.

This explains her social media disappearance, but it's still quite a shock. The reasons for her incarceration are a mystery, but as far as we're concerned it's not our business to know. The woman herself, who put pen to paper and bravely introduced herself, is a supremely articulate and creative person - and still very much a fan of music!

Her RSVPeople experience included a chap from Milton Keynes who bought 'a) expensive and b) disgusting' perfume for her. Quite the offer from one stranger to another.

I've never bought a scent for anyone without a conversation with them first:

Me: *This one? You're sure? Better than the other eight on these little white sticks? Great. What do you mean do I like it?* (Christ, I've absolutely no idea, I really just need some fresh air or car fumes to clear my head of all these) - *I mean, YES! I love it! Let's get it. Right now. Now!*

Mr. Milton Keynes was a braver man than I.

Fran was quite the rock chick in her teens and tells us she saw ZZ Top, Bon Jovi and Guns N' Roses - don't Rock Bands have weird names? I prefer Indie bands - they leave it to music: The Smiths, New Order, Blur, Oasis, The Jesus & Mary Chain. See? Oh.

Fran also sings and recently came second in a prison talent show performing 'Yesterday'. And she writes poetry. Life might not have gone exactly to plan since placing the pen pal ad, but Fran has a creative streak running through her and an honesty that brings tears to our eyes and the same thought simultaneously into our heads - we really like her, immediately and enormously.

Full disclosure, that's not a unique response to a new RSVPeople Person. I mean, they're all brilliant, but they did also all write to us. We like people who write to us. Are we really as shallow as that? Is it shallow? If it is, then we are. It doesn't bear thinking about what Sarah and I would have been like if faced with a thousand letters from strangers with whom we shared only the vaguest of interests in music - at a time and age when new bands were arriving weekly and old favourites were dropped at the drop of a dropped hat.

We'd either have gone bankrupt trying to let everyone know their letter was important to us or we'd have done a Matt & Dave and enjoyed the letters and not replied. We are either brilliant or terrible people, I'm not quite sure which.

One person who was loyal to only one band was Louise. Bucks Fizz Louise. Oh, she didn't bother with newer or cooler bands, she had definitely done her Making Her Mind Up (see what I did?) And hers was the other letter we got with Fran's.

Bucks Fizz Louise is great! She's chatty, has a twinkle and suggests she might only give us half the story of her RSVP adventure so we have to await her second letter as 'a taste of being an '80s pen pal'. If she were 12 we might call her cheeky - in a fun and funny way. We like Louise - also immediately and enormously!

She, like Russ before her, refers to her reaction to re-seeing her ad as 'cringe'. But goes on to describe a new sensation - fear. Of rejection. Getting a single letter through her door was the first she knew about her ad having appeared. It was only then that she rushed to her newsagent and bought a copy of the magazine. But do you know what her first thought was? 'What if I only have the one reply?' I mean, having only put a single band down to attract pen pals, and having decided that band would be Bucks Fizz, I can see how she might think she were appealing to a rather thin slice of the UK teenage music mag buying population. But her worries were unfounded - she got 400 replies, which, if I'm not mistaken is actually every single Bucks Fizz fan on earth writing several times over!

Only joshing, Louise. Bucks Fizz were huge for a while, whilst also being the only band of the era ripping each other's clothes off as part of their dance routine, whilst all sporting the same hairstyle. They had their share of fans too and, if you don't mind me saying it - they were lucky to have you, Bucks Fizz Louise.

As promised, Louise is going to tell us more next time. But she loves the name The RSVPeople. Thanks Louise - and we're very glad you're one of them.

Wow, two new people on the same day.

As we fold into bed, albeit with quite some considerable back pain on my part, we are grinning at these two new successes. Fran and Louise, Louise and Fran. Two new RSVPeople.

Saturday 10th April 2021

At 5.45am I am woken once again by the blackbird. He's on next door's chimney again. He's singing all the old classics plus some new tunes for his fans. Of which there are none. I have virtually no sideways movement due to my back, but when you've gotta go...

I move inch by inch, more in expectation of pain than in actual pain. But, don't get me wrong, there's still pain. I have a flash of understanding about the blackbird. A new thought that isn't simply a unique way to end his warbling forever. I realise he isn't trying to ruin my life, or even my sleep. There is, if you can believe it, a possibility he has only the faintest notion that I exist at all. What he wants is to be heard. That's all. Whether by a romantic other or to ward off troublemakers, or because he's always wanted to be a singer in a band, or maybe because he simply wants to connect... Yep, that's it - he simply wants to be heard.

For the first time in a very long time, I lie here as dawn yawns into life and I listen to him. It's rather pleasant, actually. I hear you Mr. Blackbird. I am here. I am witness to you and your song. You annoying, sleep-stealing little shit.

It's morning now. Proper morning, not blackbird morning. And I'd like to request a moment of reverential silence if you will - The RSVPeople is officially 100 days old today.

100 days!

I can't be absolutely sure, as all the data is not yet in, but if every single letter sent to our RSVPeople was put in a box - the box a medium-sized family car might come in, for instance, and all those letters were put into similarly sized piles and then delivered to Sarah and me on a daily basis for the last 100 days - not via the postal redirection service, obviously, or we'd get about eight of them - we'd get somewhere in the region, and this is a conservative estimate, of around 250 letters per day. Per day! 25,000-ish! That's how much post was generated by a half page feature in a music magazine 35 years ago.

I'm fairly sure, not counting Birthday or Christmas cards, I've not received 200 letters in the last 35 years! Although, because of The RSVPeople, more actual letters have come through the front door in the last hundred days than in the last couple of years.

In today's money, if we chose to reply to each and every one of those letters, it would cost £13,200 - and that's second class! If we were trying to appear posh and went with first class we'd be looking at a cool £17,000. And of course, that's just replying. Add on the stamps on the letters sent in the first place and, second class that's £26,400. Smash Hits came out every two weeks, 26 copies a year. That means, were it published today, and were the RSVP feature still included and email and the Internet had never been invented and people weren't worried about cutting down trees to make paper and folk actually still listened to music and bought records - that would amount to £686,400 in post generated in a year!

Maybe if the Post Office were still getting that extra revenue they'd have a few extra quid to bung at, oh I don't know, let's say the redirection part of their organisation, making it work a bit, if not a lot, better. I think I'm blaming Smash Hits for our postal issues..?

Of course, not all of those letters received a reply. We can discount the sizeable chunk sent to Matt and Dave - and when you look at the PhD level mathematical calculations above you can see why teenage boys would have felt out of their depth with what little pocket money they had at boarding school.

Anyway, that's a lot of thinking for a Saturday morning. Especially when I have a plethora of other things going on.

Things going on:

* My lingering hangover.
* My trip to the Osteopath - literally 15 steps away across the road.
* More painkillers.
* A thought or two about French tablets, then a decision not to touch them today. Honestly, after Brexit, who even knows if they're legal?
* And a third letter from Mandy.

Lovely Mandy. A tonic on a day when everything hurts. A glass of bubbles on a cold April morning. A snifter of reality in a world gone mad. I think my hangover can only blabber in booze metaphors.

She, Mandy, always starts with an apology for tardy replies. We agree, she is tardy when it comes to replying to us. At least by dictionary definition, but no more so than is entirely expected in 2021 when pop star leaning pen pal requests are so far down everybody's list of priorities as to be off the actual paper available for the list. And no more tardy than us.

She has a surname now too. Carter. There are a number of Carters who spring to mind. Jimmy - my American politics knowledge is almost as complete as my blackbird language understanding so apologies if Carter was a wrong-un. I could check, but, well I think he was a peanut farmer? And there's never been a horror film where the lead character was a peanut farmer, so I'm thinking - there alone is enough evidence to hope he was one of the semi-good ones?

Michael Caine of course, tried a similar project to ours back in the '60s - his film Get Carter is no doubt based upon his exploits in the pen pal tracing world.

But the Carter who springs into my mind most clearly is Lynda. No idea what happened to her post '90s, but to my mind she is still, albeit inappropriately dressed for a kids' show, 'Wonder Woman'. In the same way Mandy is an RSVPeople Wonder Woman - however she decides to dress. In any case it's a big step up from Custard.

She's definitely our kind of woman - not only really busy but already thinking ahead as to how she's going to get through her jobs list when the pubs open! 'Pass Out To Help Out', or whatever the government are calling it this time.

But Mandy really endears herself to us because she recognises the pain, the sacrifices we've made in the pursuit of 24 people who last wanted contact from strangers more than 35 years ago.

'It must be very time consuming', she says. Yes! Yes Mandy, thank you. The time. It doesn't bear thinking about. So much time. All the time. Yes, Mandy, thank you. You noticed, you're the best. Wonder Woman without a doubt!

She also thinks it's sad 'everyone is always wary of other people nowadays'. And she's right again... (but why is she saying that? What does she want? What is she after? Hello, hello, police please,

I'd like to report a strange woman dressed as Wonder Woman, sending things to my house!)

She would love to come and see Sarah in her Kate Bush show. Excellent. And drag the hubby along too. Right there, might this be where The RSVPeople becomes a social, face-to-face experience?

Mandy has some concerns for when the country eases its lockdown on Monday. And they're the sort of concerns that current reporting has missed. Firstly: 'Don't know how I'm going to fit everything in when the pubs reopen'. Yes indeed, there's a big chunk of time well spent right there. But her main concern, and it's one Sarah has shared privately with me: 'One of my biggest worries about going out after all this time is being able to fit in any of my old clothes.'

I have a feeling, Mandy, that all that walking to and from pubs and Kate Bush shows will shift any unwanted millimetres in no time. If we get the chance to meet Mandy, we'll jump at it. She sounds fun!

You'll be pleased to hear my back is a little improved, but I still have bad nights and like the blackbird a little less for it, even though I'm now much more in tune with his song.

Sunday 11th April 2021

Half way through today my back improves a lot. But later, after two hours of watching Netflix's new version of 'Pet Sematary', I know I'll suffer tomorrow. The film also made me look at our cats, Frank and Lily, with a new suspicion they might be possessed of something more sinister than just sleepiness and the need to tell everyone when it's tea time...

Monday 12th April 2021

The pubs are open! I can almost hear Mandy scampering to her local in her pyjamas! And the hairdressers are open too!

I head down the high street and there are huge queues on the pavements of people waiting to have their barnets done. I can't be bothered waiting - especially as every single person is getting the same haircut, and it's one that wouldn't suit me.

I'll try again tomorrow - I mean, do I even need a haircut?

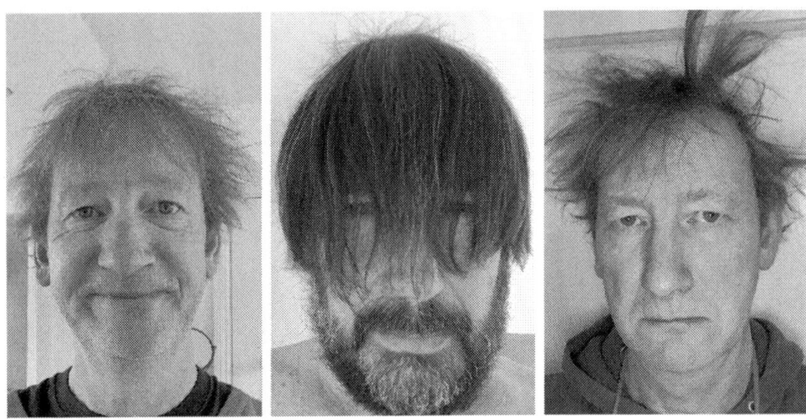

You'll have noticed the one in the middle isn't me. And possibly not even human. That's our friend Andrew.

He looks ridiculous, doesn't he? What a disgrace.

On the next page you'll see Sarah. From the front. We need to talk about her brushing technique, it's not serving her terribly well.

When she gets hers cut, she's sending most of it off to The Little Princess Trust, who make wigs for kids with cancer.

Great idea, great charity.

When I get mine cut, it's all going in the bin. Or maybe I'll collect it up, pop it in an envelope and push it through Andrew's door?

Decisions, decisions.

Today, with the UK looking a step closer to something vaguely familiar - Mandy in a pub etc. - we get a move on and get letters in the post to both Fran and Bucks Fizz Louise.

And a card to my youngest for his birthday. It didn't have money in it so no doubt the loving Father to Son message will be ignored. But the pressies are on their way too - so that's something. My son is not an RSVPeople Person, he's only 10 and has barely any concept of communication that isn't instant and filled with emojis. I mostly mention his birthday so that when this is published, I'll be able to send him a copy of the book as a present and he'll be vaguely interested he's had a mention.

The last year has been hideous, tragic, awful, worrying etc. for everyone, but one thing that's been very odd is how it's been for Dads who don't live near enough to their kids to keep up visits without breaking lockdown rules.

We've managed, of course, we've sent loads of messages and initiated dozens of video chats - that the kids have been too busy, lazy, unbothered to engage with. Ah well, I wouldn't want them to miss me too much.

But it must have been so much harder for parents alone with children - no nurseries or schools or the usual help and support. People often think of single-parenting as being the experience of Mums, but we'll be able to find out first-hand how a Dad copes under the same circumstances. How? I hear you ask. Well, let me tell you a very short story.

Remember Donald? (Frankie, Madonna, King.) Richard's friend?

We'd had several messages from Donald's Dad, Mark, telling us Donald was planning to reply, but nothing so far. Because of this I decide to drop Mark a message.

Us: Hi Mark,

Just a quick message. As we haven't yet heard from Donald, which is perfectly fine and understandable (we know how busy everyone is), we were wondering whether you might give us Richard's surname, please? You mentioned he was in Australia as far as you knew - with a surname we might just be able to locate him and send him the same letter we sent to Donald? It's a long shot but we'd like to give it a go.

Hope all's well with you.

We didn't want to appear pushy, but only a couple of hours later, just after dinner actually, I spot the following…

Donald: Hi Paul and Sarah,

Well excuse me for keeping you waiting so long…

My stomach turns over and flops to the floor.

It's a second rejection. Not Bucks Fizz Louise teenage rejection, but grown-up, should take it squarely on the chin but instead hark back to some pre-Delilah shame again for stealing the farmer's apples or smashing a window in the deserted creepy house at the end of the road in some childhood memory. That sort of rejection. I'm managing both my shame and my disappointment when…

Sarah: *What's he says next?*

Next?

Wow, Sarah's become thick skinned. Just roll right on in there, no matter the veiled insults and wrist slapping for over-stepping an invisible line somewhere. She must be desensitised to it.

Oh, I bet the Pet Sematary cats have eaten her soul and replaced it with this iron-clad, unfeeling, Terminator-esque killing machine incapable of human emotion.

Best not upset it. I read on.

> **Donald**: Hi Paul and Sarah,
>
> Well excuse me for keeping you waiting so long but it seems the years have got to me! ☺

Oh. That's a smiley face then? And a non-sarcastic use of 'excuse me'. I think it's the French drugs, they've made me tense - what else could it be?

Donald: As you will see I originally wrote to you 4 weeks ago now and made a typing error in the email address, so no wonder you never received it. It also left me wondering as I hadn't received any form of response. I must say well done for your efforts as I have only just realised my stupidity after my dad emailed me following your email a short while ago! So let's try again!

Ah, that's brilliant! I have a ridiculously easy surname to spell wrong. But Donald spelled Gmail wrong. A simple typo - probably caused by uncontrollable excitement at joining The RSVPeople. Easily done. I'd have done the same: Do^@!d@geemayal.cottoncom. That's the best I'd have managed.

I thought he hated us, but it was only a little typo. And the instant we emailed Mark, he messaged his son and a most glorious email arrived soon after.

The one above? Oh no, no, no. That was just the explanation of the typo holding things up. What followed was a huge tome of detail, energy and the sort of chatty chat that goes on in our house. Donald was born to be one of The RSVPeople!

If you remember, he didn't get the initial letter, so his first toe-dip into The RSVPeople Pond was our postcard. Without the letter, Donald was very confused. He used familiar detective skills to find Sarah and me (what a stalker!) and couldn't fathom any time our paths had crossed. He and I went both to the same university, but five years apart, so Donald, wracked his brain in case I'd been an older student who stayed in the town after graduating. But shortly after we sent the letter out again, as an email, to his Dad, all the glorious RSVPeople truth was revealed.

Donald feels, no doubt in his waters, there's more than pure chance in the crossing of our paths…

> **Donald**: But this feeling of meaning, the time the ad featured, the timing of you receiving the vintage copy and making contact make me think possibly there is something more than chance/coincidence. I suppose we will find that out through discussions. So actually it doesn't feel strange at all, quite the opposite, it seems wonderfully interesting! ☺

Wonderfully interesting! Clearly Donald's waters run deep.

He tells us Richard was a neighbour, and although they were friends back then, the ad was really just him - he added Richard's name out of fear of striding into Pen Pal Land alone.

His initial intention to reply to everyone went out the window as his postman began delivering them, literally by the sack full.

> **Donald**: I received thousands upon thousands of letters from pretty much every corner of the world!

Interestingly, Donald had only a vague recollection of the advert, until we, via his Dad, jiggled his memory.

His email is wonderful, filled with his life, his highs and lows and lots and lots of, well, Donald. He confesses he can talk for days. Sarah glances over at me, maybe we have discovered a chatterbox, kindred spirit? Once again, we like him immediately and enormously.

When we started this, Sarah and I never thought much about whether we might genuinely like the people we found 35 years the other side of their pen pal ads, but some of these folk, most definitely including Donald, are wonderfully extraordinary human beings.

Wednesday 14th April 2021

It's been a heck of a few days in RSVPeople Land. Fran. Donald. Louise. Mandy. They all sent letters. Old Girls George was in touch again, always lovely to hear from her. And Monika needed a reply that got missed in a cloud of back pain and blackbird tweeting. We sent it ASAP.

Being Monika, she wasted no time in acknowledging our reply…

…with this photo and the simple, honest and efficient reply, 'Will reply ASAP…'

Can't say fairer than that.

Mandy needs a reply, so too, George. I'm really finding myself empathising with those 1985 teenagers. If we were replying to everyone with a pen, rather than by keyboard, I imagine the replies we sent would all be a little less detailed - there's only so much time in the day after all.

Last Christmas all The RSVPeople were aged between 11 and 21 to us. They had names, addresses and dubious tastes in music. Nothing more. Now they're between 46 and 56 and more than half of them have faces and pens and pieces of paper that they've used to make words to send to us. Or they've typed - but it doesn't sound quite so romantic.

We know about their jobs and families and the experiences they had, inundated with pen pal replies. We know the differences between them in tone and humour. We have a sense of them. It's nice.

Thursday 15th April 2021

One of the people we have no sense of is Lars. Mostly because he's one of the few people who have remained entirely anonymous and undiscoverable. Nothing from the letter. Nothing from the postcard. There's also the issue of Lars not being as rare a name as, let's say, Mayumi. And no surname. The piece of information making him stand apart is his liking for Vince Clarke.

Depeche Mode, Yazoo, Erasure, The Assembly, Vince Clarke. I was a fan of all of those bands in the '80s. So Lars and I have two things in common - the music and not knowing each other in the slightest.

The area he's from in Sweden has no Facebook group. So I can't pick their brains. In fact the place, Storvreta, barely comes up on Facebook at all. I look on Trip Advisor, hoping for a long established hotel that might remember the Electro-synth-indie looking teenager who maybe collected glasses there during the '80s, but to no avail.

So, Vince Clarke. He's 60. During his 60 years he's only smiled about six times - probably when Lars sent him fan mail. But he had a lot of fans I'll bet, even if he never smiled at them. Mm. The Vince Clark route might not be the most fruitful way to find Lars.

I'm momentarily thrown off the scent by a Storvreta in Norway. Which is not Sweden, but when the first person named Lars that

Google thrusts at me is Lars Ulrich, the Metallica drummer, my confusion increases. Because he's Norwegian.

Me: *Sarah, you can surely see my dilemma?*
Sarah: (not geographically challenged) *Nope, I can't see it.*

Oh. Right.

There seems to be absolutely nothing in Storvreta. Well not nothing. There's a church and some houses - one of which ignored a letter and a postcard from RSVPeople Land. And I found a photo of some ducks in the grounds of a hotel which seems a long way from Storvreta according to online maps.

The name of the hotel is in Swedish. I've learnt from my Swedish friend, Fred, that the Swedes are like that - evidently they insist on using Swedish for describing things in Sweden. I know! Selfish is what I call that. The Swedes would insist on calling it 'självisk', which I think proves my point? I could ask Monika to translate it for me - maybe it translates as 'Lars' Vince Clarke Themed Hotel.' Or croissant. I'll investigate further.

There are literally no other web-based shops or temples or airports or volcanoes of any description in the area of Storvreta. Very odd.

I refuse to accept this is a non-starter. I search for his road - oh, and a business appears. Almost spitting distance from Lars' address. Maybe it's been there for 35 years and the owner remembers Lars' Vince Clarke-esque hair when he earned a few extra krona helping them move in? They might also remember him saying he needed money for stamps - he was writing a lot of letters? They might.

Only one way to find out. The business, and possibly the business *owner*, is 'AuntyCaroline'. I explain to her she's registered on the same road Lars lived on...

AuntyCaroline: Hi unfortunately I moved here 3 years ago but I can check with my neighbours ☺ You don't have a last name?

I most certainly do, and I tell her so…

Me: Hi, thanks for getting back to me so quickly. My name is Paul Chronnell. No one on the road will know me though. It's actually regarding a pen pal ad Lars posted in Smash Hits in the '80s.

My partner and I are trying to locate all the people who placed ads in the same particular copy of the magazine. It started as a lockdown project but has turned into something bigger… if it's not too much trouble to ask your neighbours that would be brilliant. Thank you so much.

AuntyCaroline: Haha what a lovely lockdown project. I've sent the info to my neighbour now ☺

Me: Thank you so much! I've just realised - you meant don't I have a last name for Lars, not for me! Oops! I'm afraid not, his ad simply said Lars. Thanks again.

AuntyCaroline: Haha yes ☺

And that, my friends (based entirely on the above evidence and the music of Abba) is why Sweden is universally loved by everyone on earth.

Clearly, I was feeling a little ego-centric half way through that exchange. AuntyCaroline couldn't have cared less what my last name was. She wanted Lars' surname. Sarah was out when I made my error, but she corrected it the moment I told her of my progress. So the 'I've just realised' bit is a total lie. I didn't realise anything. Sarah did. That 'Haha yes', suggests AuntyCaroline has already decided I'm an idiot. Mm. Sweden? Silly place. (Based on nothing but the above evidence and the music of Abba.)

Of course, asking the neighbours may reveal they got the letter and the postcard and simply couldn't be bothered engaging. Or maybe they don't speak English? Sarah thinks everyone in Sweden speaks better English than most of us English. We'll have to wait and see.

I twiddle my fingers for a couple of hours and realise something. You know, there's a chance the neighbours won't help AuntyCaroline anyway. They may not know her. Although maybe she doesn't mean neighbours either side of Lars' address, just neighbours who've lived there for a long time?

Thinking outside the box, I wonder if Lars hero worshipped Vince Clarke to such a degree that he runs his fan club? Or is famous for having the ex-Yazoo man's face tattooed on his chest?

I briefly dated a girl in Manchester who was the biggest Marc Almond fan in the world. A proper fan - every issue of every record, went to all the gigs, dressed in black all the time. Years later, when the Internet had catalogued every single piece of information about everyone, I used her name and Marc Almond as Google search terms, trying to see what had become of her. And, would you believe it - I discovered absolutely nothing.

So, logic suggests, using similar criteria here will give a much more positive outcome. And that's maths!

So, 'Lars' and 'Vince Clarke'...

Lars Persson. Nah, can't be, this is just too weird: a synth musician who captures 'the melodic spirit of Vince Clarke'. He's Swedish. He looks about the right age. It's undeniably spooky and I have a strange tingle, but it might be shingles. I need more...

I find two interviews that both make connections between Mr. Persson and Mr. Clarke...

Interviewer: I have to bring up Vince Clarke...
Lars: Sure, I don't mind the comparison at all.

And...

Lars: Happy Birthday Vince Clarke, on your 60th birthday! You're the reason I gained an interest in electronic music, which led to me starting making music myself, some 35+ years ago. Thank you for all the inspiration you've given me, and still do to this day!

Lars Persson cites Vince as the reason he got started in music! This is all flimsy but I'm wondering about setting up a joint music venture with Badrat and this Lars...

I message him. Lars, not Vince.

During dinner Sarah and I explore all the likelihoods of Vince Clarke Lars being RSVPeople Lars and about how he is sort of famous and that would be such an exciting addition to the whole RSVPeople Project.

We're still pondering this as we sit down to a couple of episodes of Schitt's Creek, when my phone pings...

Lars: Hi Paul, sorry I am not that guy. I lived in Karlskoga, Sweden in the '80s.

Oh, Schitt. It shouldn't have been a surprise, but Lars is not our guy.

His niche musical tastes are overshadowing the fact Lars is a very, very common name in Sweden. I don't know how I'll break it to Badrat the joint gig is off…

The other reason I really, really wanted this Lars to be the right Lars, is because we're running out of avenues to explore. The neighbours in Storvreta may remember Lars from 35 years ago, but maybe not. Lars may still live there and has simply ignored everything we've sent him and is waiting for a third contact so when it arrives he can drag the postman inside, shave his head to make yet another Vince Clarke wig out of the cuttings.

It's certainly possible.

Sarah: *Everything else in existence in the whole world is more possible than that.*

Which is interesting wording for her to choose, as the very next thing I do produces something even more impossible than the most impossible thing on earth..!

I search for Lars' 1985 street name: Hövägen. And the area: Storvreta. I'm sure I must have done this before - how else could I have discovered the issues with the post code when he sent out the postcards? I must have done.

But that was a while ago - a while before the impossible became possible...

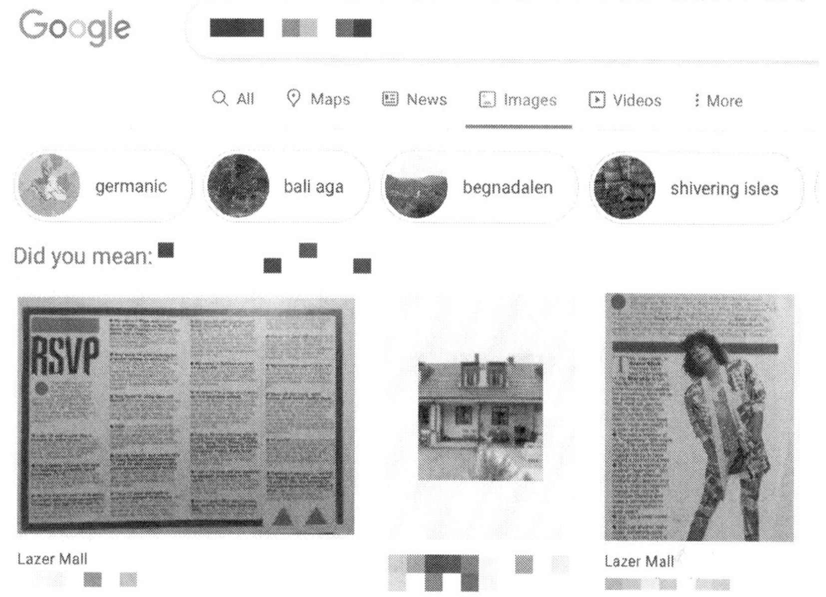

What?!

Yes, exactly, how is that possible? A search for a little known Swedish village, with a population of around 2000 if memory serves, coupled with an even less well known street in that little known village, that's what I wrote and what did the great God Google throw back?

THE RSVP SECTION FROM OUR COPY OF SMASH HITS!!!!!!!!!

Everything, and I mean everything, that I've previously caveated with 'stranger things have happened' (and Sarah has given me withering looks about) is now right back on the table as a thing that might happen, has happened or might even be happening right now - because a photo of the RSVP section of our Smash Hits is staring at me when the likelihood of that was and is nil. It's impossible. Impossible.

Lazer Mall?

I'm fairly sure no parents looked down at their new-born and plucked that out of the air as the name they would ruin their new child's life with. Would they? Well, quite literally stranger things have definitely happened - see above!

The only way to get to the bottom of this is to follow the money. Of which there is none. So, next best thing is to follow the Lazer…

Searching 'Lazer Mall', rather than taking me to the Tumblr account I was expecting, as suggested by Google, in fact leads here. To a rat on an egg. Angry rat too (maybe a Badrat?) And with a tail that must give him all sorts of problems in the tripping up department.

Filthy Loot publish books. Excellent, I like them already - certainly more than their rat friend. But what does this publisher have to do with Lazer Mall..? Wow. And blimey.

Just when you thought it was safe to go to the mall…
Three authors (Katy Michelle Quinn, Joe Quenell, Sam Richard) of the strange, the unsettling, and the bizarre each conjure their own vision of lazer-infused mall-horror. From queer mall-goths fighting for their lives against androids with explosive genitals, the American propaganda machine using coerced shock-rocker punk musicians to fight Soviet Communism, to the mall security officer high on the power of robots who seeks to crush the women who've scorned him. We have it all, and more…

A book by three authors, or more probably three stories under the one title of Lazermall?

'Explosive genitals' is the stand out back page quote there. It's an oft ignored medical condition, but with this book I'm glad those genitals are getting the airing they deserve.

Could Tumblr Lazer Mall be connected to 'queer mall-goths fighting for their lives'? I literally have no idea. Only one way to find out.

So, Tumblr. I've heard of it, but I don't really know what it is. I should ask my kids, they'll know - and laugh at me for not knowing. Kids can be cruel. Sod them, I'm doing it myself. I need an account to connect with anyone. Right. Oh, great, that took literally one minute. So now I am in possession of yet another social media account. I think. Is Tumblr social media? Not sure. I think it's a platform? Like a shoe? It doesn't matter, I won't be on it long.

RSVP

Anyone need a pen pal from the 80s?

From Smash Hits Magazine 1985.

Extraordinary.

'Anyone need a pen pal from the '80s?' That's the sort of thing Sarah and I might have said to each other at the start of the year.

Or if we'd seen that post back in 2016, we might have started The RSVPeople Project 5 years ago - although Sarah and I hadn't met at the time which would have made things complicated.

Tumblr doesn't do accounts and profiles as such, so I'm no nearer to learning anything else about Lazer Mall. Until this…

> Lisa Eilbacher, '80s mega babe known for An Officer and a Gentleman, Beverly Hills Cop and Leviathan.
> Big hair, big sweater, what's not to like?

This comment under a photo of Lisa Eilbacher suggests a male identity behind the Lazer? I write to him on Tumblr, but I'm not terribly optimistic. The Lazer Mall moniker isn't repeated anywhere else so I'm stuck and dead-ended if the big-sweater fancier doesn't respond.

I try adding 'Lars' to the road and town search that lead me to Tumblr - and look!

Men in suits - AND our RSVPeople advert - from Lazer Mall's Tumblr account. My head hurts. It doesn't make sense. For the moment I can't think of any other way to search for a new 'in'.

Maybe it's lunch time? It's lunch time.

Lunch is an omelette. Followed by some admin - not to eat but to do, address changes and the like. Then a walk just as the sun goes down. And now - now I have a hopeful glance at my phone...

Nothing from Lazer Mall. Sigh.

Saturday 17th April 2021

This morning the blackbird is noticeable by his absence. I thought I heard him at some ungodly hour, but fell asleep again until a much more agreeable 8.00am. Yesterday evening I took the liberty of recording his song in the garden. Technically I didn't have his consent so maybe he's talking to a solicitor, which explains his absence. It was an incredible recording though. I played it to Frank and Lily...

They thought it was garbage.

Another absentee is Lazer Mall. Like the blackbird, Mr. Mall appeared while I slept, viewed my message, then disappeared.

I really am very disappointed in people sometimes. Maybe disappointed isn't the right word - but I'm certainly surprised when people aren't curious enough to reply immediately. Especially when a very short reply is all that's required.

Me: *Hello Lazer Chops, do you have links to a street in Sweden?*

That was essentially all I asked. If he doesn't, a simple 'No' covers it and he'd never need to think about me again. If the answer is 'Yes' then you'd imagine he'd be intrigued - especially as my interest clearly isn't him, but the strange way Google decided his photo of Smash Hits pen pal requests was relevant in my search for Lars' address.

Or maybe I've stumbled on something much stranger, involving exploding genitals?

My imagination instantly pictures a spy or someone in witness protection shaving their head, inserting coloured contact lenses, adopting a fake limp as they disappear up into some desolate hills with nothing more than a tent and an old satellite phone.

Lazer Mall would love an old satellite phone, I'm sure - which just adds to my curiosity about why he's not engaged his own curiosity and replied immediately.

Maybe telling him I'd only joined Tumblr to send him that message is verging on creepy? Or is it, in fact, the very definition of creepy? I don't think so - I only mentioned it so he'd understand why my brand new profile has nothing on it. It was said so as *not* to seem creepy. But creepy is in the eye of the beholder - as they spot you at the end of their garden in a cowl, carrying a scythe.

Instead of scratching my head all morning, which while carrying a scythe is a dangerous business, I decide to revisit the challenge to locate Faheen. Like with Lars, there's only a first name. I Google, what I assumed I'd Googled in the first place: Faheen and the town…

And suddenly there's a Faheen listed as a graduate of an Open University. Faheen Yap Zhang Choi. He's a mature student of the right age. And he lives in Ipoh. Which was where RSVPeople Faheen lived!

FINALLY FULFILLING HIS DREAM OF AN ACCOUNTING DEGREE

Although has had substantial work experience in management and accounting for some years he missed having a suitable degree qualification to augment his professional functions. It was therefore a special moment when the 48-year-old who lives in graduated with a Bachelor of Business (Hons) in Accounting degree from

has been working as an Implementation and Support Manager at a software company for about three years, and before that he was a Senior Accounts Executive in a manufacturing company. He presently manages clients' complaints and training when customers purchase software from his company.

"It was my dream to get an accounting degree because I had previously worked for many years in the accounting line," he said. He deals with financial software in his current job. "The learning experience has made me more confident in speaking to clients as I am equipped with the knowledge besides the practical experience," he added.

"Education is very important," he said in explaining his drive to study. "We must embrace lifelong learning, being motivated always to upgrade, to equip ourselves with as much knowledge as possible, in any field of interest."

Could this be an ex-teenage Kate Bush fan? Would he know all the words to Babooshka? (Sarah knows all the words to Babooshka in Russian. She sings them in her show. It's brilliant. And weird.)

You have to admire his dedication to gaining a degree in his late 40s, very impressive - does it top learning pop songs from the '80s in Russian? It's certainly very close.

But is Faheen's additional impressiveness a whole level up from that? Is he one of The RSVPeople? No idea. Yet.

Sarah and I confer.

We still don't really understand the richness and complexities of Malaysian name structure. After much research, I'm still not certain whether Faheen is even a first name (the article above suggests his 'first' name is Yap). What we need is help. Malaysian help.

From this man…

Pun Kai Loon.

He doesn't live very far from where Faheen lived. He's offered to do a little digging when lockdown ends. I'm assuming that doesn't mean he's a part time grave-robber but rather that when thrown a deerstalker hat by his old friend Sarah, he's happy to accept our challenge to become a Malaysian Sherlock Holmes.

He's smiling now - he may not be when he realises what tough taskmasters we are.

But before sending him out on missions, the most obvious way to proceed, before Kai Loon undertakes the full transformation into an opium-smoking, violin-playing super sleuth, is to message the Open University and see if the recently graduated Yap was once the Smash Hits Faheen...

Me: Hi, I was wondering if you know any way I might get a message to a recent graduate of yours? Faheen Yap Zhang Choi. He was featured in your online brochure.

I don't expect you to give out personal information of course, but I am simply trying to get a message to him. Maybe if I were to email the message to you, would you be able to pass it on to him?

Any help in this matter would be much appreciated.

Sunday 18th April 2021

The very nice people at the Open University reply before I wake.

OU Careline: Dear Paul,
You may send us the message and we shall forward it to him.

Great stuff. And I reply just as quickly. After a shower. And some stretching - the back wasn't happy yesterday. And some coffee. And some high-bran cereal. And some more coffee. And a cuddle with Frank. And after removing Frank from the kitchen table where he protested after I stopped cuddling him. Virtually instantly.

Me: Hi, My name is Paul Chronnell and the very nice people at the OU offered to forward this message on to you on my behalf…

My partner and I are trying to locate a 'Faheen' who lived at 41 Jalan SS 82/5C, Ipoh in 1985. A search for your name and that address gave us your graduation feature at the OU and we wondered if you might be the right person?

If so we have a letter for you (happy to scan and email it). If not, we would be grateful if you would let us know, and thank you for your time.

Kind regards, Paul (& Sarah)

See? 'Very nice people' - I'm not just telling you, I'm telling everyone!

We shall have to see what excitement awaits us when that email is delivered. They don't waste any time!

> **OU Careline**: Dear Paul,
> We have forwarded your email to the email address according to his profile. I hope you get a reply from him soon. Warms regards.

I have a feeling 'warms regards' isn't their usual sign off.

That's probably just for us?

Tuesday 20th April 2021

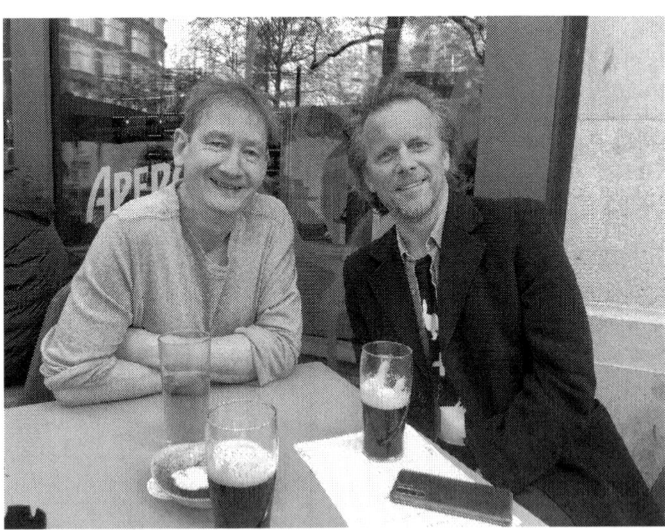

Last night we went for our first drink out in the big wide, eased-lockdown world with our friend Russell. I dressed for the late afternoon, when it was gloriously sunny. By the time we'd sat in Leicester Square in the shade for a couple of hours, I was freezing…

At some point Sarah was rescued from an incident at sea, and I was used (and abused) as a dressing-up doll. In the end I nipped into a shop and bought a jumper.

It was a pricey evening - we'd all forgotten that everything is about 4 x more expensive when you go out in Central London, as opposed to when you stay home and get your drinks from your own fridge. The hangover is similar though. But we were celebrating. And not just celebrating lockdown easing, we were also celebrating this…

MAYUMI REPLIED!

Wrong name, wrong address but we found her. She even sent a photo of who she was when she posted the ad. There's no way her hair could have been from anywhere but the '80s!

Mayumi - even with the wrong name and address still managed to get more than 200 replies. She replied to a respectable 5-7 and became 'good friends' with two of them - a guy in Liverpool and a girl in London. London? That's where we live! We probably know her. She's probably still got '80s hair!

Although difficult to locate, Mayumi still lives only a three minute walk from her 1985 address. And she thinks it would be nice to exchange a letter or card sometimes. So do we, Mayumi, so do we!

There's a real warmth from all the people who have replied (ten now!) A genuine appreciation for the trip down memory lane, and maybe more surprising, a real feeling of connection with this couple who undertook a lockdown project to find them.

All The RSVPeople are fabulous - but I feel a special affection for Mayumi because all the odds were against even being able to find her. I remember discovering her photo through the translating site and realising all the research, all the time spent gently trying to work out how much of her ad was incorrect, was all worth it, whether we heard from her or not. And now here she is: An RSVPeople Person through and through.

Mayumi, come on in, you are so welcome.

But, I'm still dealing with a hangover. I'd forgotten what they're like to be honest. But, if you've ever forgotten what a hangover feels like, you'll know, should you get another one, that no matter how long it's been, the memory comes flooding back like a sack of potatoes. So it's with foggy headedness that I open another 'Paul & Sarah' letter. I might have had a stab at guessing who it was from, had I not been fighting the urge to lie down again from the moment I'd got up.

Here's a clue… there's yet another photo of a teenage young lady from 1985. Any guesses? No? Let me help you out - there's a rather large poster behind her: Bucks Fizz.

IT'S 1985 BUCKS FIZZ LOUISE!

Early on, Sarah and I talked about whether sharing photos from back then might be interesting to everyone. But we thought actually asking for those photos might be a 'friendly-step-too-far'. But within a 24 hour period we get two. Mayumi and Bucks Fizz Louise are made of similar stuff. And they both hoard very old photos.

Buck Fizz Louise's letter stretches to three pages and it's as much a rollercoaster of fun as her first! No - do you know what it's like? It's like a bubbly Bucks Fizz!

Bucks Fizz Louise paints a wonderful picture of a time gone by. She reminds us about notepaper! I wasn't aware I'd forgotten about it, but yes - remember pages with clip-art-type pictures in the corner? Bucks Fizz Louise does! She remembers 'flowers, football teams, animals, cartoon characters, visitor attractions and holiday destinations'. She even remembers the 'clear acetate box' that housed those writing sets. Maybe she has a time machine? Maybe the reason Bucks Fizz Louise remembers 35 years ago like it was yesterday is because, for her, it was. Maybe she popped back to her old room, re-stuck the curling corner of her beloved Bucks Fizz poster and propped her time travelled phone on a shelf and took the photo she sent us?

That's literally what must have happened. Sarah says not. Bucks Fizz Louise says not too. Such negativity! However, the photo she sent is one of the actual photos she had a friend take back in '85 to send out to pen pals. She kept a few photos back, clearly anticipating our letter arriving decades later.

Little did we know that drawing a small cocktail glass at the end of a letter was the 'Bucks Fizzer way to sign off'. Bucks Fizz Louise still does!

Bucks Fizz Louise admits she was no novice at pen pal ads. She'd written one a few months earlier which hadn't been published - no doubt Neil Tennant had just announced he was going to be a massively successful pop star and some basics of the magazine got neglected.

But second time round she hit all the right notes for the magazine and she was in.

She got 20 letters a day. Mostly from the UK but also from Germany, Holland, Denmark and Cyprus, if she 'remembers correctly'. I've no doubt Bucks Fizz Louise remembers - anyone who can recall that many types of writing paper and the boxes they came in, will remember things so much bigger - if you can remember a box, you'll have no trouble remembering a country, now will you?

She also had some letters from HM Prisons. Her Mum wouldn't let her reply to those. The letters kept coming - the last couple more than a year after her ad appeared.

In true Bucks Fizz Louise style she's going to carry on her pen pal saga in her 'next letter'. Louise's commitment is second to none.

She was not a fan of The Smiths or The Cure, as Sarah and I were, and still are. She reckons because of that we must have been 'fashionable teens'. I'm certain Sarah was - I'm not sure I can claim that accolade - although I did frequent the Hacienda and various other indie clubs in Manchester in my teens. Which makes me fashionable-ish?

Bucks Fizz Louise is the first person to show actual interest in The RSVPeople Project as a thing outside of themselves. Everyone else has been lovely telling us about their experiences, but Louise wants to get into the mechanics of how we work together. Do we write the letters together or split them up? I'll have to tell her, gently, that Sarah is a complete slattern and doesn't write any of the letters. We did write them more jointly at the beginning, but discovered, as I'm at my keyboard most days, it's easier for me to reply and then read them to Sarah, to see if she's happy to have her name added to whatever nonsense I've written. Then, if she wants to add anything, she writes it by hand on the bottom.

There's a very clear disparity between the work hours we put into this project - but she also has to put up with me, so I figure things are pretty even.

Fogginess, caused by the near freezing to death experience last night, is sticking around much longer than I thought it would - it's almost like I'm not living in the '80s anymore… But through the mists of over-indulgence and being underdressed, I can just see another layer of mystery that may have been peeled away by the amazing AuntyCaroline, Children's Clothes Detective from Sweden. She's not certain, but…

AuntyCaroline: It could be a Lars Axelsson, but we are still investigating ☺

Me: Amazing!! Thank you so much, we're keeping our fingers crossed!

AuntyCaroline: ☺

Lars Axelsson. That's definitely a Swedish sounding name. Lars, I think is the Swedish version of 'John'. Axelsson, although spelled very differently is no doubt the Swedish equivalent of Smith.

It's still a needle in a haystack, but it's a bigger needle than we had before alcohol and the freezing wastes of Leicester Square reduced my lifeforce to that of a boiled potato.

Some days, if it weren't for the amazing support of the stranger-angels doing some of the work, this whole project would stall, sit down on the pavement and curl up into a ball. AuntyCaroline, we salute you.

Thursday 22nd April 2021

This arrived in the post today. From Becki! The wrong Becki.

Becki: Dear Paul & Sarah,

Thank you for your letter, an interesting read to find 'weird Becki'.

I'm sorry to say although I too am Becki from the same street it's not me, I lived round the corner.

I don't recall anyone of that name from that time, although I'm a little bit younger, my taste in music was similar.

I wish you all the best in your search for weird, awesome music-loving Becki.

Kind regards.

But it's such a lovely letter, I think this Becki should be inaugurated into The RSVPeople Hall of Fame anyway. Still pleased we got a reply - even a 'wrong' one.

Really not sure what the next steps are to find our Becki. So, in the meantime, let's return to Chris. Reunion Chris.

I learn something very important about Chris today. He's a woman. The photo on Chris' account appears to be her son, not her. Chris is probably Christine or Chriselda. It's an honest mistake, but all those correspondences with Chris are now filed in my head as being with a chap, a brilliantly helpful chap, who is now an equally helpful lady.

Sarah points out they might also be non-binary. (Good point.) So I check their personal pronouns and confirm Chris identifies as a woman. Sarah kisses me on the head and says thank you. Living with her is an ongoing education.

I get straight back in touch and update her about Wrong-Becki and she's more than fine with me posting again on the group, so I write an updated post - which amounts to the original post with this caveat.

Me: I posted this same request at the end of February and the group was amazingly helpful and suggested this might be Rebecca Burns, but she has been in touch and unfortunately it's not her (she lived round the corner), so I'm just trying again to see if I can jog someone's memory. Any pointers at all would be very helpful. Thank you.

I don't know what the life expectancy of one of these posts is. There were a lot of replies to it last time, but, like all Facebook posts it no doubt drops out of view fairly quickly and the majority of people don't see it?

Keeping my fingers crossed is now an almost permanent state of mind. And fingers.

So, after posting the above we are once again in the hands of the good people of the Ashworth Reunion Group. But if it doesn't lead to a positive result, what next?

Previous digging revealed Becki's old house was on sale earlier this year. Maybe it still is and maybe I can get information from the Estate Agent? I don't even know whether details about a house are private or not? Is there a list somewhere of who used to own a house? No idea.

First things first though - another search for the address…

Oh, no! No, NO, NO!!

Our Smash Hits RSVP section again!

Posted by Lazer Mall on Tumblr. This means Lazer Mall is not going to lead us to some weird and wonderful situation where he is actually Lars. He's just a guy who likes big hair, big jumpers and exploding genitals! Or was that the book?

What this shows, by some strange means I didn't know existed, wizardry probably, is that Google can read the words on a photo! I thought they couldn't and that's why we have to add meta data to have photos recognised for whatever it is they are?

Oh, double, no! You know what else this means? Every single one of those 'stranger things have happened' things that were back on the table because of Lazer Mall's extraordinary appearance in the search results, are now all off the table once again!

Worst. Day. Ever.

However, we haven't tried a search for her name and the street - remember when we did that for Faheen a few days ago and we discovered the newly graduated chap at the Open University? Well here goes nothing...

Do you know what happens now when you search for Becki at her old address? Of course you do, it hasn't changed. You still get me, still asking about Becki. But with her whole address it's just that one single hit, nothing else. One - like a single sock on a disused washing line, longing to be made a pair. Yes it is, it's precisely like that.

Hang on though, Google's omitted some results because they might be 'very similar'. Well, let's not forget Wrong-Becki was very similar, and yet completely different. Google says I can see them if I like. If I like? Well, yes, I do like! How similar can results be, I wonder?

Right. Great. Very similar. Identical, in fact - except one is Hebrew, one Korean, one Arabic, and one, Swahili. Identical. Brilliant.

Just a minute, these results aren't Chris' Ashworth Reunion Group - that Google suggests I learn four more languages to explore - it's the other one. The one run by Admin Andy. Better pop another message on there too, just in case.

Popped it on. Not holding my breath. The last post received a single like and nothing else. Funny how two groups about the same place can receive such differing levels of engagement. I think it's Chris. She's the magic that gets the Ashworth people's cogs turning.

Woah. As I arrive back at Chris' page there are now five likes on my post. (Does that mean five people like it that I can't find Becki?) No matter, it's lower down that I'm interested in. Right at the bottom…

Someone is typing…

But what they're typing is someone's name. Paul. Wrong-Paul. Poor Paul, everyone thinks he should know. He said before he lived on the same road as Becki but didn't know her. He must be famous on the street - he's everyone's first port of call. I hope he's not annoyed at being asked the same question again..?

He's not, in fact, annoyed at all. Paul suggests the wrong Becki. Everyone suggests the wrong Becki. I thank him, but kindly tell him he's wrong. Not because I think he's wrong, but because the very person he's suggesting - she told me he's wrong!

Of course, there's the possibility her name isn't Rebecca. I mean, it probably is, but there are other possibilities. What if it's short for Becheera? Or Bechan? Bechyrah? Maybe? Similar, or course, but wearing different jaunty hats?

The Ashworth Reunion Group have been wracking their brains for us, wondering if she was a teenage Goth, because of the 'black clothes' preference. A Goth - of course. The Cult, Spear of Destiny, The Cure - any self-respecting Goth might have those groups in their record collection - if they can find their record collection in their black-painted room with black curtains and black carpet and black lightbulbs? U2 and Simple Minds were the other two bands she listed in her ad - she was probably a secret fan of them - the local Goth Club would look very unfavourably at Bono and Jim Kerr.

Friday 23rd April 2021

A quiet RSVPeople day. I have to write a short script for an actress and Sarah is finishing her first week of directing a one man show about Derek Jarman.

Then we head back round to Kate and Andrew's, with better backs and fewer French painkillers than last time. It's Andrew's birthday. His big pressie is a pizza oven and we sit in his garden being fed and watered until it goes dark. Really tough day.

As we turn in for bed, Richard - from Donald and Richard fame - pings a reply…

It's honest but unenthusiastic. He's spoken to Donald but doesn't really remember anything about the ad. He lived across the road from Donald in the '80s and thinks Donald might have simply added his name. Which was nice. Then maybe kept all the letters for himself? Which is less nice. But entirely understandable. Richard didn't suggest that Donald hogged the letters, that's me wondering why Richard doesn't remember. Because who could forget an ad in Smash Hits?

But, you know what? For whatever reason, he doesn't remember. And he got in touch essentially to say he has nothing to add by way of his experience. And that's fine. No problem, thanks for letting us know, Rich. Hope all's well down under.

Saturday 24th April 2021

Sarah's having a brainwave. That's not terribly unusual. She's a brainwave kind of woman. Her brain is a thing to behold, I can assure you. But this is especially exciting because it's an RSVPeople Brainwave. They're quite something…

They look exactly like this. If you ever see Sarah looking like this, you know genius is at work within her.

As soon as I see her like this I sit back and wait for the brainwave to erupt. A few moments later, I'm not disappointed...

Sarah: *Why don't I send William a message on LinkedIn?*

You might think a brainwave that comes with an actual photo of the brainwave's birth, should be more earth-shattering? Well, you'd be wrong. Because it's genius. You see, LinkedIn allowed me to contact William in the middle of March. But he didn't reply. And if he doesn't reply the site won't let me send him another message. It's a sensible system put in place by sensible people to keep evil spammers at bay. But the Gods of LinkedIn have not anticipated The RSVPeople Project. (Which really deserves a letter to Head Office pointing out their shortcomings - but I have enough letters to be getting on with, so I'll pass, just this once.)

So, we write a new letter and Sarah sends it. Genius.

It'd be cynical of me to think a message from a more attractive face than my own might bring a response, but I'm a cynical kind of guy. Of course, Sarah is so much more than a 'pretty face' (see Brainwave photo to be reminded just how much!) But it can't hurt, can it?

Thursday 13th May 2021

I know - long break, huh? Nearly three weeks. Things have been bitty. Busy and bitty and breaky. I've no idea where time goes.

Stuff still occurred, but the stuff wasn't quite as noteworthy as we wanted. In fact, in the world of The RSVPeople it was dust bunnies rolling through a closed fun fair, the sort that's either waiting for the return of thrill seekers or serial killers dressed as clowns.

Things did happen, but nothing inspiring. It shouldn't be a surprise. When you set out looking for 24 individuals, you have 24 strands to pursue. Once you make contact, that strand disappears, job done. And if all remaining strands are waiting to hear back from people, there simply isn't much to do. Thankfully other stuff happened - things like this - like a Dr. Who at the end of his/her contract, Sarah underwent a change...

From this...

...to this!

What? No, she didn't just turn round! What sort of a change would that be - Tom Baker, John Pertwee et al, didn't simply 'turn round' did they? No, Sarah had all her locks cut off - and donated them to the Little Princess Trust - the folk who make wigs for children undergoing cancer treatment. And she raised a whole load of money for them and Cabaret vs Cancer too. She's brilliant.

We also did this…

Which I'm fairly sure speaks very clearly for itself.

Mine's a fly hat. (Obviously.)
Made out of an Amazon envelope. (Badly.)
Come on, you've never worn a homemade birthday hat before?
No? You should.

I visited Dad up in Wales and my son down in Brighton. The sun shone occasionally and plants were re-potted. And when it rained Sarah and I snuggled up both together and with the cats, waiting for something to happen.

Because, if you wait long enough, something always happens.

And it did.

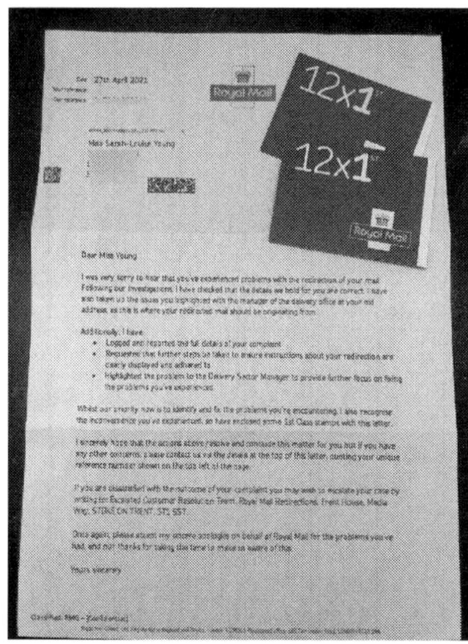
Date: 27th April 2021

Miss Sarah-Louise Young

Dear Miss Young

I was very sorry to hear that you've experienced problems with the redirection of your mail. Following our investigations I have checked that the details we hold for you are correct. I have also taken up the issues you highlighted with the manager of the delivery office at your old address, as this is where your redirected mail should be originating from.

Additionally, I have:

- Logged and reported the full details of your complaint
- Requested that further steps be taken to ensure instructions about your redirection are clearly displayed and adhered to
- Highlighted the problem to the Delivery Sector Manager to provide further focus on fixing the problems you've experienced

Whilst our priority now is to identify and fix the problems you're encountering, I also recognise the inconvenience you've experienced, so have enclosed some 1st Class stamps with this letter.

I sincerely hope that the actions above resolve and conclude this matter for you but if you have any other concerns, please contact us via the details at the top of this letter, quoting your unique reference number shown on the top left of the page.

If you are dissatisfied with the outcome of your complaint you may wish to escalate your case by writing to: Escalated Customer Resolution Team, Royal Mail Redirections, Trent House, Media Way, STOKE ON TRENT, [illegible]

Once again, please accept my sincere apologies on behalf of Royal Mail for the problems you've had, and our thanks for taking the time to make us aware of this.

Yours sincerely

The Post Office agreed they were a bit rubbish with our redirection and give us... stamps.

Stamps?!

Talk about adding insult to injury: we've been rubbish at the job of delivering your post - so why not send more letters for us to practice on!

Stamps!

Then Sarah does some maths. 24 first class stamps is not nothing, she says. I'm well aware it's something - I have a photo to prove it. But Sarah's maths discovers the stamp value equates to more than a month's worth of poor service. Not too shabby.

We send Wrong-Becki a thank you postcard. She would have made a wonderful RSVPeople Person, you can just tell. But if you're not the right Becki, you're not the right Becki, as several ancient Greek philosophers never said.

Even with the whole of Ashworth wracking their brains, there are no further thoughts how to find her.

You'll be aware by now that we don't accept defeat easily, but we can't think of any other avenue to try. I look into the possibility of acquiring details of the house deeds, but they're only available for a shocking amount of money and anyway the records don't go back to 1985. So if Becki's family moved away before 'records began' we'd be a whole mountain of first class stamps-worth out of pocket.

Sarah wonders if Becki used a fake name - maybe to protect her identity in a world where identity theft was less than the glint in a would-be hacker's eye. She's so often right, but I hope, in this case she isn't. I'll have to come up with a new idea - returning to the Ashworth Group simply to say, 'Think harder - damn you!' doesn't feel like the right thing to do.

Roobarb and Richard have removed themselves from the project by means of forgetfulness. Is Becki the first proper Dead End?

Sigh.

William may be joining her. It seems inconceivable that he's not seen at least one of our attempts to contact him. But, sadly, if he has then he's not interested in getting in touch. Or if he is interested, he's just really busy. But I'm not sure another nudge is possible. 'Get in touch - damn you!' doesn't feel like the right thing to do.

This is what the majority of the Smash Hits respondents felt like isn't it? Rejected. No matter how hard Bucks Fizz Louise and Russell tried to keep in touch with their pen pals, there were hundreds who waited by their front doors who never received a thing. Thousands who wrote to Matt & Dave felt a little down that the young men who asked for contacts, chose other people, not them. Obviously, Matt and Dave's teenage selves were useless and those thousands were flogging a dead horse with them - but those thousands didn't know that! How could they know that Matt's bar was set so high, it would take 35 years for people to match his massively high expectations in pen pals? (Ahem…)

As well as the postcard to Wrong-Becki we also sent letters to Bucks Fizz Louise and Old Girls George and Mayumi and Mandy

Custard. It took a long time. Letters should be fun - and writing them all was definitely that. But you can't rattle them off, can't cut and paste the same messages and stories and thoughts. Every person opening an envelope deserves a personal letter - otherwise it's like hearing from the bank: a computer generated missive pretending to be personal. Sarah and I are not computer generated.

Makes you wonder if someone would rather forget their childhood, or if they've lost the fun that made them write their ad, and now the idea of penning a letter never rises above work, kids, shopping, health, worries, Netflix etc. on the To-Do list of their lives?

On one level these 24 ex-teenagers are all well-practiced in the 1985 art of not answering letters because for each person they wrote to, there were hundreds, or even thousands who were ignored.

But when it feels like you're being ignored, ghosted, it smarts. It makes you ask 'why?'. Why would a person rather go to work or parent their kids, or live their lives when they could be writing to Sarah and me? See what I mean? I know! Some people are so selfish.

Sarah says I've not had enough fresh air today. I bet the missing RSVPeople are all having lots of fresh air, rather than picking up a pen! 'Oh look', they cry. 'Sky! Trees! Grass! People! Postboxes!' Yeah, you should feel guilty. Postboxes need post - it's their food - you'll miss them when they're gone.

Sarah's shaking her head. I thought it was at the missing RSVPeople, but I think it's at me.

Adam and Jane don't want to play. Emma hasn't yet been in touch. Becki's missing. Roobarb and Richard have opted out. Delilah's made her feelings clear. Dave and Sally both seem to be the second strings to Matt and Emma. But Dave did comment on Matt's Facebook page, so he's sort of engaged. And as we haven't heard from Emma yet it just feels rude to approach Sally while we're still waiting for her friend. Faheen has our email and he hasn't replied. We can't nudge him again, we can only nudge the OU. Oli and Bryan (with a 'y') can be nudged again. But it would be a second nudge because the first nudges fell flat. And second nudging, as you all know, smacks of desperation.

Maybe this is why there's been a break in The RSVPeople? Have we reached the limit of what we can do without hiring private detectives and sitting in trees with binoculars? 10 letters is great though. Isn't it? Hearing from exactly half the ads. 50/50 split. Would be really great to get just one more, though - 'more than half' sounds so much better than 'exactly half'.

And then, as if by magic, a Swede appears! LARS!!!!!!!!!!!!!!!!!!!!!!!

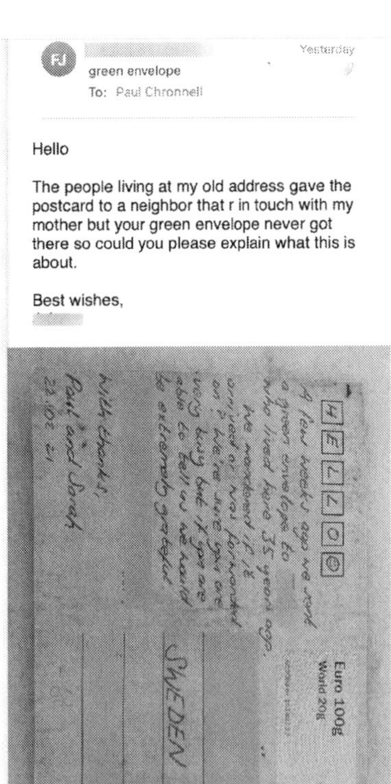

FJ
green envelope
To: Paul Chronnell
Yesterday

Hello

The people living at my old address gave the postcard to a neighbor that r in touch with my mother but your green envelope never got there so could you please explain what this is about.

Best wishes,

Out of the blue! Lars got the postcard! But not the letter - possibly due to the original letter address discrepancy.

So how did that happen - local neighbours whipped into a frenzy by our friend AuntyCaroline? Maybe her interest nudged the postcard into the hands of whoever still knows Lars' whereabouts?

We shall endeavour to find out! And in about half an hour of hearing from Lars, our original letter is scanned and en route to him the modern way. It's still the letter, of course, and we'll happily take an electronic letter in return.

I believe the kids call them emails?

Us: Hi Lars, how fantastic to hear from you, so glad the postcard finally reached you - thank you so much for getting in touch.

As for what happened to the green envelope - that remains a mystery, but we've reprinted and attached what you would have received, if it had arrived… (The green letter may have vanished because the post code numbers were not correct in the original Smash Hits advert?)

We have heard from many of the other pen pal seekers and we'd love to know about your pen pal experience 35 years ago.

Hope you're well
Paul & Sarah.

It's only polite to let AuntyCaroline know that she can re-call the dogs as Lars is found.

There's no amount of excitement and thanks that truly sums up the gratitude and warmth we have received towards our quest to find The RSVPeople. Even if we don't make contact with any of The Missing, The RSVPeople is already a huge success.

Ping!

AuntyCaroline: Wow! That's amazing! Love to help! And please update me again ☺

No, Aunty Caroline *you're* amazing!!!

England's moving closer to the final stage of lockdown easing. Sarah and I decide to put a final date in place for the end of The RSVPeople Project: 21st June. All restrictions in England are supposed to be lifted on that Monday. Once the day arrives we're hard pushed to call this a lockdown project any more. We'll still answer letters, of course, we may even try and meet some of The RSVPeople, but the search will be over. All good things must come to an end. Just like the letters coming into the homes of those teenagers, one day the last one arrived. And then there were no more. Until ours - so I suppose that's 'never say never.'

Putting it down on the page like that makes me realise that every last opportunity must be seized before the clock ticks down.

So I return to Jane. Jane whose old house is now a Wellbeing Centre, who have a pen pal group but don't answer email enquiries. Rude. I check and Jane doesn't have many friends on Facebook and rarely posts. So I find someone who liked her most recent post and send them a message. Let me introduce - Sandy.

Me: Hi Sandy, I hope you don't mind me contacting you directly, but I've been trying to contact the Jane who lived at 183 Dalmorton Street, Hemswell, in 1985. And although I've messaged her on FB, as we're not friends she might never see it. So I thought I would take the liberty of asking for your help. It's nothing unpleasant btw - it's actually regarding a pen pal ad Jane posted in Smash Hits in 1985! My partner and I are trying to locate all the people who placed ads in that same particular copy of the magazine. It started as a fun lockdown project but has turned into something a bit bigger. (We've received replies from as far away as Canada!)

Me: *(cont...)* If Jane has read my message and isn't interested in responding, that's fine, but I have no way of knowing. It's cheeky I know, but if you wouldn't mind asking her if she knows about our 'quest', I'd be very grateful - and if she doesn't, I'd love to let her know. Thanks in advance. Paul.

Sandy shares Jane's surname so it's not ridiculous to think she's family. I've given her much more information than I'd like, but time's a-wasting and if Jane hasn't heard from us, I want to make sure she does!

Oh those weeks of stagnation. It feels wonderful to be dipping the detective toe back into the detective pond! Jane's back in play, and we've possibly come up with a long-shot idea of finding Becki...

Friday 14th May 2021

We hear from Monika. A month since we last heard from her but she has life going on. And life takes time and effort and more time. As two writers/creatives/biscuit eaters who get to play at our work (before we get to panic that we'll never make another penny from it) it's easy to forget that people in the real world have jobs that require offices and workplaces to open up properly so they can get out of the damn house and get some damn routine back in their lives! And, as Monika mentions, the longer you're not going into work and work finds 'better and better' ways to get stuff done remotely, will everyone even have a job to go back to? Worrying times. Mm, that's a very real and very different sort of world to ours.

Monika's month to reply is nothing in the scheme of things, and anyway, heaven only knows how long it will take me to reply to her!

I mean, I have life going on too. I have script stuff going on in loads of different directions. Sarah's got so much going on that it's possible she's a number of different Sarahs, clones probably, all working together for the single purpose of making her work output look super-human and mine look exceedingly mortal. It would explain the haircut - I've only got her word she had it cut, this might be a second Sarah, Short-Hair Sarah, covering for her, while the Long-Hair Sarah perfects alchemy or living forever, or whatever's next on her list.

But I have script stuff. And kids' stuff. Because of the virus I haven't seen my youngest, he's 10, since The RSVPeople began! Wow, I've had more contact with a bunch of strangers than I have with my own flesh and blood.

Obviously we've talked and video called a lot. Sort of. I mean, he's sent literally dozens of 'sorry, I'm not available right now' messages when I try to Skype. I think it's brilliant he's so attuned to technology, so I feel a little mean now explaining that if he just let the call ring out, I'd assume he wasn't near his iPad, whereas hitting the 'unavailable' button means I know he's doing stuff way more interesting than talking to his old man - which could be almost anything - eating, homework, 12 months in solitary in a maximum security facility. But when we do talk it's brilliant! We have so many meaningful conversations - just the other day he was telling me about Roblox and this thing they had going on where everyone had to collect things in different games and when you had all the things you were really great and he was definitely really great because he'd collected many things really quickly, which was great. Great. I think.

But I tell you what's greater than even that greatness (and if you're reading this son, you'll notice the following bit is redacted in your copy of the book). I'm going to tell you it's a grownup thing and all the grownups reading it will find it hilarious. Don't tell me I've not thought of everything! Ha! (I'll redact that line too, and this one.)

What I have going on today is hearing properly from Lars! (So much better than collecting imaginary stuff in a daft iPad game! Ha! Redact...) He wasted no time in getting back to us. A long and astonishing email letter (I know that's what 'email' means, but in this RSVPeople case, they're actual letters without the paper - you know what I'm talking about).

The first thing Lars tells us is how much fun it was to be contacted about 'this little ad that made such a big impact on my life'. Yes, Lars, yes, right there is all the proof we need to recognise you as a 100% RSVPeople Person. Brilliant.

And with words that were Once Upon A Time-like to my ears, he went right back to the beginning of the story...

Do you know why he placed the ad? Don't worry, it's rhetorical, but you'd be forgiven for thinking it was because he wanted a girlfriend, or someone to talk to about Vince Clarke or, heaven forfend, a pen pal?

No. Not for our Lars. It was because his English teacher said he was rubbish at spelling. Getting a pen pal would help with that and so he placed an ad. By the time Smash Hits decided to make Lars an RSVPeople Person, a few months had passed so when he got home from school to find two letters, he'd almost forgotten about it.

He looked at the letters: two girls (you can almost see him stroking his chin whilst deciding which one to grace with a reply). No doubt he went to bed wondering which would help him most with his spelling - possibly the older one, or the one who had the nicest writing?

Next morning he woke up to 70 new possible pen pals. And, as we know, they just keep on coming. But what's different is Lars reckons he got 5000. FIVE THOUSAND!? If he'd had enough stamps he could have ended up being the greatest speller ever to scribble the earth.

Do you know what the chance of getting a reply from Matt & Dave was? Well prior to 2021 it was an absolute impossibility. Nada. Zilch. But this year their average, as you know, went up to 1 in 2000.

The chance of a letter from Lars was 1 in 1000. (Technically, if he got exactly 5000 letters and then got ours and replied to it, the probability improves significantly - to an impressive 1 in 833.5. Which is a pretty good improvement. You're welcome.)

So, he replied to 5 of the 5000. One from Wales, two from England, one from America and another from Greece.

Candidly he admits three of them were very good looking. Interesting that so many people sent photos when Lars didn't ask for them. But for those three lucky lasses they got Lars as a pen friend purely because of the randomness and attractiveness of their genetic makeup. But Lars had a sixth sense looking beyond prettiness. Because he only went and fell in love with the Welsh girl. Wow. All because she thought writing to a Depeche Mode fan might be a giggle. And it might be - we haven't written back yet. Falling in love with 20% of your pen pal cohort is impressive, but Lars did better than that. He went further…

The American girl caught his eye, he recalls her letter as being 'number 29'. At Christmas he got a card from her saying, 'Hey you bum, why no letter?' And it was this romantic and original nudge that, as Lars put it, got her 'the nod'.

Now, I'd probably remember the Christmas card: it's unusual and funny. But would I remember she was pen pal reply number 29? No chance. Maybe Lars is one of those special memory guys who can remember every single person's name in a theatre? Or maybe, as Sarah suggested, he remembers because he ended up marrying her..?

Yep, you heard right - HE MARRIED HIS SMASH HITS PEN PAL!

That's absolutely brilliant…

Hang on, I'm just thinking about Sarah's comment - yes, of course you're going to remember things in more detail with the pen pal who becomes your wife. But they only got together six years after the ad. Does that mean Lars had a spread sheet of 5000 names? Maybe he still has it? Sarah's full of suggestions today - must be her Suggestion-Sarah Clone and she's just suggested…

Suggestion-Sarah Clone: *That's the sort of thing you'd do…*

Me? How very dare she?!

Moving on.

He didn't feel he had much common ground with one of the English girls, so only wrote to her for 'a few years'. A few *years*?! With a person you have nothing in common with? Lars, I admire your dedication to the pen pal world, my friend.

Can't wait to get back to him, there are so many questions.

Sunday 16th May 2021

Sandy: Hello Paul, you have the right family and I passed your message on to Jane but she appears not to be interested. Sorry.

I'm sorry, what..!? *Appears not to be interested???*

I might just about have accepted 'has been sadly eaten by a giraffe' or 'aliens took her in the night and she's now Queen of a comet somewhere near the belt of Orion or somewhere' - but she appears not to be interested. How does that happen?

Could she possibly be re-enacting the famous, and ludicrous, stunt by David Blaine, of standing on top of a 90ft pole for 35 hours? If she was, and Sandy shouted up about our message, it might indeed be tricky to understand exactly Jane's response. She might have meant she didn't want anyone to speak to her because she'd added a tank of piranhas beneath the pole and a fall would be... inadvisable?

It's possible. Sarah's out of the house - that's the only reason she hasn't told me it isn't possible. So shush, it's our secret.

When Sarah comes home I tell her about Sandy's message, but not Jane's attempt to break the record for piranha avoidance standing. It's as close to a definite no as we've had without tipping into Delilah territory. We hatch a plan...

If Sandy is a sister or an auntie or cousin or even mum, then maybe she'll remember the arrival of up to 5000 pen pal letters into Jane's life. And if she does, then maybe all is not lost and we can learn something of Jane's experience without actually needing to hear from Jane? It's possible - and much more possible than us standing on a pole above piranhas for a day and a half.

Me: Hi Sandy, thank you so much for passing along my message, it's very much appreciated. Completely respect Jane's response.

Just in case you're in the dark about what we're up to, I've attached the details we would have sent - in case you're curious. Thanks again. Paul.

OK. It's a smidge sneaky. Hopefully Sandy will look at our blissfully uncomplicated, and even less threatening, correspondence and head back to the pole, kick the bottom so Jane falls into the water, then, no doubt, Sandy will scream 'SWIM, JANE! FOR THE LOVE OF GOD, SWIM!!!' and Jane will emerge damp, but unscathed and all her urges to drown Sandy with her bare hands will vanish as she sees, for the first time, that she's a bona fide RSVPeople Person.

Oh, it makes me want to spend 40-odd days in a box above the Thames with excitement!

The chances of Adam 'The Younger' performing the same trick in another part of the country are fairly slim, so the same note is sent to Adam's wife, Kim, through her Facebook page. The only cowpat in the ointment might be that Adam's page says he's married to Kim - Kim's doesn't reciprocate. It might mean nothing, and other people's relationships are entirely not my business - but if there *is* a hatchet - let's bury it in the name of The RSVPeople, yeah?

Monday 17th May 2021

We've been remiss. A long while ago we reached out to Reader Services and Lyrics Sue, who worked on our copy of Smash Hits. For all her valiant attempts she was unable to help with our questions about how the pen pal feature worked on the magazine. We made a mental note to chase down her colleagues for an insight into the RSVP world from the other side of the letterbox, as it were.

Today I set out to find them. It isn't easy. Most of them will be 35 years older than they were 35 years ago. I say 'most' just in case one of them has perfected time travel, like Bucks Fizz Louise, and sets out to sue me several years ago and take me for everything I have, before heading back into the recent past, stealing our idea, which would now be a bestseller and we'd be sitting on Christmas Day last year with Sarah's brother's copy of Smash Hits saying, 'Wish we'd thought of that'. I'm simply covering legal bases. This is 2021, after all.

In those 35 years there have been retirements and there have been some deaths. And some people have vanished off the face of the earth. And by 'vanished off the face of the earth' I mean 'I can't find them online', which amounts to very nearly the same thing.

However, I have a list of about a dozen ex-employees of Smash Hits to contact. Most of them worked there during the early years of the magazine, a couple in the early '90s. Hopefully that will lift the lid on how the feature worked.

Strangely, I have a sneaking suspicion that a woman who did work experience there between 1993-1994 might prove most useful - if you're blessed with a free employee for a while, why not have them sifting through postcards while you interview rock stars? Exactly.

The other people who would be AMAZING to hear from would be Dave Hepworth and Mark Ellen, both of whom were editors back in the '80s and now host a podcast together. They hosted Band Aid, for heaven's sake. BAND AID - 1985!! If that's not the freshest serendipity squeezed from the freshest serendipity berries, I don't know what is.

Tuesday 18th May 2021

Today is all about Becki. Again.

The idea we came up with for a new approach was to find out what schools a girl of Becki's age might have attended back in 1985 and see if they have groups online to approach. It would also give the incredible Ashworth Reunion Group a third chance to toss around their amazingly helpful memories and see if anything new shakes loose.

I start with a message that everyone who ever lived in Ashworth must now be very familiar with: *Can't find Becki - Help*! Or words to that effect. Then I ask for their assistance discovering which schools she might have attended.

People immediately suggest schools. 12 of them! 12 possible schools? I can't believe it. 'I can't believe it' translated into 'tired writer' is 'oh no, that's going to take me all day!'

And it does. But it brings moments of excitement, because there's always someone new who's been off the planet these last months and doesn't know of my Becki search…

> **Ryan Slater**: My mate Sheila Adams lived at that address and that would have been around '85, I think.

What?! Stop it!

Could Sheila be Becki? A middle name? A nickname? Could Ryan have forgotten the name of his friend? Seems unlikely, but I sometimes mix up the names of my kids. A quick exchange between Ryan and me reveals Sheila isn't on Facebook. Who isn't on Facebook? Well, Sheila isn't. But her brother is. I ask all the right permissions and contact him immediately. Like everyone in that part of the world, he wastes no time…

> **Sheila's Brother**: Hi Paul, if that's the very end house next to the hill and opposite the steps, then yes I did - sorry I can't remember the number. We moved out of there in 1983 though and don't know who moved in after, sorry.

Oh for the love of all that is holy!!!

It's not his fault, obviously, of course it isn't - but chances are the next people to move in were Becki's people. So ridiculously close, but still no.

This so-close-but-not makes the list of schools even more depressing. A dozen suggestions. But, hold on, a few are middle schools and Becki would have been too old for them, so I cross them off the list. She might have gone there a few years before but for all we know Becki moved in from another part of the country all together, or another part of the world. Cross, cross, cross, cross.

So a bit more digging and crossing leaves four schools. And they all have 'Old Pupil' groups. Who knows, in a day or two we might have four new and fantastic Georges!

Remember Andy from the Ashworth Estate page? He asked his sister if she could help and she sadly couldn't. Well he's the admin for the first school group and he has no problem with me posting another post. Two of the other three are closed groups so I fire off quick messages to the admins. It's just polite and here at RSVPeople Towers we are nothing if not polite.

Thursday 20th May 2021

Oh monkey sweat glands!! Nothing. Just messages not read or not responded to. I'm really beginning to think that Becki doesn't want to be found! Oh, or maybe *can't* be found.

And four possible schools become three because I got so excited Andy was an admin I missed the fact that his was a 'Middle School' too! Cross, cross, cross. Becki could have gone to any school. At 16 she might have left school. She might not have moved in in 1983. And, if she arrived from another city and had left school already then all this admin chasing business is a whole load of time-consuming time-wasting.

It's got me thinking about communicating. About letters. About pen pals in general. The beauty of it was the almost private and personal way you wrote your letter. You got your paper, or if you're Bucks Fizz Louise, you maybe choose from several dozen carefully stored acetate-covered writing sets, you found a space in place and time and began. You didn't try and negotiate with gatekeepers, admins or previous house owners. You sat, you wrote, you posted. And back then you didn't start stressing if a letter failed to arrive by return. You got on with other stuff. You read Smash Hits. You listened to music. You hoped and prayed there were better fashions to come in the '90s.

Back in January, I liked the fact Becki stated her interests beyond the world of music. She liked Aeros! And she wanted people to know. Who wouldn't want to write to an Aero eater? But in the pursuit of her, I'm starting to feel like a jilted partner who can't let go. One who keeps sending texts, emails, bouquets of red roses - all in the hope of one more dopamine hit while trying to kick the habit of the person who once thought about them differently.

Becki is an enigma in a way William, Jane, Adam and Faheen are not. Those four, we're pretty sure, have had our messages and are either crazy busy or not interested. And just because we don't understand why the foursome don't want to go out with us any more, they just don't. And the analogous red roses say more about us than about them.

I was going to say 'they want to move on with their lives', but that's not true - they already are moving on with their lives and have been for 35 years. They posted an ad. So what? They got loads of replies, wrote for a bit, stopped writing. So what? They don't think about it for 35 years until two strangers get excited and want them to be excited too, and they're not. So what? The undiscoverables may not be undiscoverables but rather: so what-ers?

We're going to give the school admins a few more days. Maybe they're so what-ers too?

When you're painted into a corner and can't see any way else to proceed, do you know what is always a failsafe for feeling better? Of course you do! That's right - you write to the Pet Shop Boys' very own Neil Tennant!

I've always thought he looks very approachable. I have absolutely no evidence to back that up, but if he ever reads these words he'll be happy to know that's how I feel. We will send our letter to him with hope and happiness and a jolly expectation that he will read it from a golden, diamond encrusted pop star throne like a truly 'approachable' chap.

Sarah has a contact for him. Of course she does. She emails him and asks if a letter can get to Neil's ermine-clad hand without having to go via a fan club or similar.

The contact reports the office is closed, so no. But we can email. Back in January or March we'd have been adamant this wasn't good enough and stropped around for a day or two, kicking bins and shutting doors a little more aggressively than normal. But not now. It's Neil Tennant for heaven's sake. Literal pop royalty.

If we were advised to scratch the letter into some soft cheese slices with a nail and deliver it via a recommissioned milk float, we'd give it our best shot. An email? Easy-peasy.

Us: Hi Neil,

An old copy of Smash Hits arrived in our lives randomly last Christmas. And in a locked-down world where there are 500 ways to send an emotionless emoji, we loved the idea of all those teenagers reaching out to connect - with actual letters!

What happened? Did they hear from anyone? And how many? Where are they now?

So on January 4th we decided to find out and we wrote to every last one of them. What started as a bit of lockdown fun has now turned into something much bigger.

We can't help wondering: were you aware what a huge impact that feature had on people's lives? We reckon 25,000+ wannabee pen pals responded to that one edition alone! Monika (into music, travelling and sports) met her 'best friend in the world' through her ad and Lars (Vince Clarke fans especially welcome) *married* his pen pal!

We realise that our edition was after you left the magazine, (although you're still credited as a writer) but we'd love to know what you remember about the RSVP feature.

Us: (*cont…*) Was there a system of selecting who made it to print? Did anyone in particular get tasked with dealing with it, or did everyone muck in? Did you ever hear from people *after* their ads were posted? Anything at all you could tell us would be very gratefully received.

Many thanks in advance,
Sarah & Paul.

Sarah is a professional actress, singer, director, cabaret performer, writer and Olivier award-winning improvisor. Her one woman cult-cabaret: 'An Evening Without Kate Bush' is booked for a run at The Soho Theatre, next year. She is currently directing a show about Derek Jarman.

Paul is a writer, produced screenwriter and playwright.

There we go. Neil Tennant! What a special day.

I know precisely what you're thinking - why is Sarah front and centre with me hiding behind her skirts as we stutter into the platinum palace of the Pet Shop Boys? Yeah, I'm right aren't I? And, your second thought is why does she have a CV at the bottom that reeks of super-stardom and mine reeks of a tiny bowl of star fruit soup? Is it because her credits are sexy, fun, ongoing and impressive? Yep. That's exactly why.

I'm very excited we might hear from Neil Tennant. But it might take a while. He's probably got an unnervingly long to-do list: be rich (tick), be famous (tick), be pop royalty… you get the idea, for most of us it's an impossible list, to HRH Neil, it's just tick, tick, tick. Like a dog in a meadow of long grass.

But why stop at Neil? Let's ask the others on our list.

Mark Ellen and Dave Hepworth. Both edited the magazine. And they introduced Band Aid. And they have a podcast. We send a personalised version of Neil's letter to them. Two Smash Hits editors in a single swoop.

Boom!

Lots of people worked on Smash Hits. Some are easier to find than others. Vici MacDonald worked on the magazine, let's see what she remembers. She wastes no time in responding.

> **Vici**: Hello.
> This is fascinating, but there was no image attached so I don't know what issue of Smash Hits you're referring to when you say 'the above copy'. If you could resend with the image, I'll wrack my brains for memories.
>
> Best wishes
> Vici MacDonald (ex-designer at Smash Hits)

Fascinating, she says. And she's absolutely right. And she's part of the reason it is!

I'm trying to overlook the fact there was never supposed to be an image attached and our reference to the 'above' copy simply meant the copy that the 'couple from London' received as a gift as mentioned in my letter. But I'll let it slide because it's Vici. Vici MacDonald (ex-designer at Smash Hits!!)

Before I can sort that out for Vici, a new message comes in from another of my ex-Smash Hits employee enquiries. From Trudy - the very same work-experience person I thought might come good…

Me: Hi Trudy, I'm trying to research a very niche feature of Smash Hits and have been trying to contact ex-staff to ask them a couple of questions. I gather you did work experience there and I wondered if I could send you the email. Thanks, Paul

Trudy's Store: Hey there, of course you can. You can add me as a friend on FB and I'll accept it.

Trudy's store is, as you may have guessed, not a person's name. Apart from the Trudy bit, obviously. The 'Store' bit is because she also makes rather lovely things too. It was to her store I sent the above enquiry. And, as you can see, now we're friends!

I send her the now familiar letter doing the rounds with the ex-Smash-Hitters (which you have to be very careful saying out loud).

What a great example of work experience leading young people on a road to success Trudy is. As well as being all over Etsy, she's also huge in graphical what-not stuff at the BBC. And she's on the verge of becoming an RSVPeople Person!

Ping!

Here she is. Very quick. Efficient. Excellent.

Trudy: Hey there, that all sounds fab. I was at SH a decade later so was more Take That and East 17 era, so I'm afraid I don't have a clue about the pen pals thing. All the people working in the office were in their early/late 20s at the time so I don't think any of them would remember anything that early either...

Trudy: (*cont…*) Sorry to not be much help, but it does sound like a great project and best of luck. By the way, I think I went to school with Sarah, we were in the same class! So strange! Trudy.

AT SCHOOL WITH SARAH?!!

What? What? What?!!!!

Back in January Sarah and I discussed the possibility, what with all the new people we'd be contacting, of crossing paths with someone we knew. And here we are. Trudy was at school with Sarah. Amazing.

But not the most amazing thing in the message. She remembers Sarah, but she doesn't remember pen pals or RSVP or anything of the sort during her work experience time. Eh?

So I do some checking. And the results are earth-shattering. To us. The RSVP feature wasn't there from the beginning (1978) and it didn't make it all the way to the end (2006) when Smash Hits closed. In lots of ways the RSVP feature has ended up being more important to us than it was to Smash Hits itself. Speaks volumes.

Monday 14th June 2021

As you can see. Time has passed. Lots of it. Later today we are supposed to hear, as promised, that lockdown measures will be kicked into touch in a week and a brave new world of large weddings, nightclubs and face-licking can once again be the order of the day. But, strangely, as with all government announcements, we know the contents of the announcement before it's even made. And so we're not going down the face-licking route, but instead, we're pushing it all back for a further four weeks to let more people get the vaccine and for new variants to really get their acts together, get creative, so we can continue the carousel of fun that Covid has been, for as long as possible.

On the radio there's talk about those weddings that were all set to be over 30 guests having to ring round half their family and friends and tell them they haven't made the cut - a hideous job to do I'm sure, although it would mean your sister's boyfriend, who you've never liked, could be slashed from the list without guilt - your sister will get over it, her fella was almost certainly going to leer at the other bridesmaids all day anyway.

There's brief recognition that the clubbers may have to wait a little longer before they can have a night of screaming to be heard, armpit sweat and falling asleep on the night bus - but it's difficult to sympathise in the same way as we do for the weddings.

The one area of society that isn't discussed by Boris is The RSVPeople Project. I know!

The project is drawing to a close. People have made their pen pal beds and while some are lying in them, scribbling furiously, others remain underneath them or locked in their wardrobes, or queuing outside clubs that aren't going to open any time soon.

June the 21st was the day we planned to down tools, take stock, and see what we have learnt and how far we've come in the last six months. But now it might be another four weeks! And after that maybe another four. The pandemic, the locking down, the unlocking might go on forever. The RSVPeople just can't. Begging follow-ups to the missing RSVPeople are possible but not very attractive. And here in RSVPeople Land, if nothing else, we're all about attractiveness. Well, Sarah is. I'm more about other things. Lots of them, all great and important and they absolutely exist, but I don't think now's the time or the place. Use your imaginations.

The Smash Hits ex-staff have not provided the excitement we hoped for either. Those who did get in touch definitely got nearly as excited as we did, but the majority have failed to respond.

You see, there comes a time in every RSVPeople Person's life when you have to accept you want to communicate with someone more than they want to communicate with you. Like almost all the hopefuls who wrote Smash Hits letters back in 1985 - the disappointment is part of the game. You throw out the bait you hope will catch a reply and it doesn't come. And of course you can follow up, but, 'Hey, you bum, why no letter?' doesn't work with everyone. (Try it with your bank manager while waiting to hear back about your loan application.)

No Pet Shop Boy was in touch with us. In our excitement we thought maybe a super-famous pop star would have nothing better to do. I guess he did. I wonder what his lockdown was like? Hopefully he got through it OK.

We got through it OK. While wandering the rules and restrictions of various lockdowns we started this wonderful adventure. We wrote letters and researched and discovered people and had fun. That was a rather brilliant way to spend our time. We're grateful for it. Other people had a much harder time than we did.

Maybe this book will find its way into Oli's hands, or Bryan's or Faheen's or one of the others and they'll remember getting a letter from Sarah and me and possibly they'll make contact. But for now at least, we're letting them go. Every single one of the 24 will always have a place in The RSVPeople Project and our fondness for them all will never wain.

But we're not looking anymore.

Sorry.

Late Update

When we stalled a little after Andy and Mandy's letters, I had visions of an RSVPeople Party with disco lights, a mirror ball and streamers, a buffet of finger food and a table of the four of us making small talk and looking around at all the other empty tables while the sandwiches curled…

Now though, it's the same imaginary room, but Oli's on the decks, filling in while Badrat prepares for a set duetting with Fran and Mr. Blackbird. The buffet is magnificent because George very kindly took charge of it and arranged for excellent caterers. Monika has crocheted a very cool banner, designed beautifully by Delilah, who decided she didn't want to come, but wished us all well.

Donald's here, without Mark, sadly, but someone had to look after his son. Chris has managed a night off from keeping Ashworth ticking over and is chatting to Sarah's brother, Steve, about '80s music. We had to send 1001 invites to Matt & Dave before they RSVPed and said of course they'd love to come!

Russell has brought his Yorkshire Terrier with him and has suggested that, if necessary, he'll happily cut my hair - in fact, the state of it is making him uneasy, so he's really pushing the point.

Bucks Fizz Louise and Mandy Custard are chatting about the joys of writing paper when Andy comes in, asks for quiet, dims the lights. You can hear a pin drop - before Mayumi arrives, just off a plane. She and Monika immediately start nattering in Swedish and all is well.

The others are there too, of course, all with partners, kids, dogs - all shaking hands, swapping stories and getting to know each other.

Sarah and I sit at a small table at the back, looking around, smiling. So this is what upwards of 25,000 letter recipients looks like. Sarah leans over and whispers something but I don't quite catch it - as Badrat has just started playing and everyone takes to the dance floor.

Me: *Eh?*
Sarah leans in closer.
Sarah: *Weirded Fish.*

I look in her eyes, wondering just how many shots she and Mandy shared when we first arrived. I can tell by her face that my face is not registering the correct response to what she said.

Sarah: *Did you hear what I said?*
Me: *Weirded fish?*
Sarah: *Weirded fish? What's that?*
Me: *It's what you said. Isn't it?*

Sarah laughs, it's a good thing she loves me or she might get fed up of me much, much quicker. She leans in, kisses me...

Sarah: *We did this!*

Oh. We did this...

I look around at all the wonderful people we would never have met without that old copy of Smash Hits, a strange idea and the tenacity of a Jack Russel to see it through.

Me: *We did, didn't we.*

We join the throng on the dance floor just as Club Tropicana starts to play - boos fill the air, of course, it's Wham! after all, but no one stops dancing and everyone knows all the words.

Happy Days.

The fantasy party fades into the background and I find myself blinking and yawning like a furry thing exiting his hibernation burrow, wondering where all the time has gone.

It's impossible and denies all the laws of the universe, but somehow it's September now.

We may not have had that party and we haven't heard from anyone new, but we're still writing to Mandy, Bucks Fizz Louise, Monika, Fran, Lars and Old Girls George. Our messages are no longer about Wham! or pen pals or the past. Our messages are now all about each other. About the present. We've received poems and photos. We've sent 'get well soon' flowers and 50th Birthday cards. We ask questions, we give updates, we share bits of ourselves we could never have imagined when we were deep in the 1980s.

Whenever a new letter drops onto the mat or pings into my inbox, Sarah and I grab a coffee and read it together, as excitedly now as we ever did. We love it.

We have yet to meet up with any of The RSVPeople in person, but we have watched videos of George downing shots on Facebook. And just last week she invited us to lunch, when we can all find the time. An actual face to face lunch with an actual new friend - all because of an old copy of Smash Hits that came into our lives less than a year ago.

Now, won't that be something!

A few days ago we sent out a formal message to our original RSVPeople telling them the project is now officially over. Sort of turning the sign from 'open' to 'closed' in a department store's window where 'closing down sale' signs have been on show for the last few months - just in case.

So that's it. Our RSVPeople Project from beginning to end. We hope you've enjoyed seeing what we got up to in that very odd time in 2021 when nothing was normal. Most of all, we hope you maybe seek out a piece of paper and a pen, and you write to someone. Anyone really. We guarantee they'll like it - I mean, who writes letters these days?

Well, we do, and we love it. We hope you will too.

Take care.

Kindest regards,

Paul, 53, a tall Mancunian into all sorts of music, including The Smiths, British Sea Power, Jim Bob, The Airborne Toxic Event, Kings of Leon, Black Kids, The Divine Comedy, Frank Turner, Wet Leg and The Mull Historical Society. Supports Manchester City, drinks coffee and loves a well-written sentence.

&

Sarah, 46, likes songs which tell stories and tall Mancunians. Playlist includes Martha Wainwright, Indigo Girls, Del Amitri, Tom Baxter, Kate Bush, Edith Piaf, Laura Moody and the loud purr of our cats, Frank & Lily. Lover of ambitious projects, single malt whisky, stinky cheese and a hand-written letter from a friend.

PS: If you've enjoyed this book, feel free to write and tell us at TheRSVPeople@gmail.com - there's no point us putting an actual street address for you to write us a letter, in case we've moved. And you know what the Post Office redirection service is like!

Extra Update

On Christmas Day 2021 Sarah and I exchanged gifts. She gave me another copy of Smash Hits as a joke, with the question…

Sarah: *What are you doing with the next 12 months?*

I gave her a ring with the question…

Paul: *What are you doing with the rest of your life?*

She said yes!

Looks like we have a lot of RSVPs to send.

Paul Chronnell

Paul is a produced screenwriter, has written for the stage and has seen his name fly past at the end of a variety of TV shows, including Spitting Image, Russ Abbot, Hale & Pace, Brian Conley, Talking Balls and Planet Mirth. He has had several commissioned 'web guides' published (just as Google was arriving to make such publications obsolete). He's written humorous 'Dad' articles for Mother & Baby magazine as well as put bespoke words in the mouths of dozens of Brides, Grooms and Best Men on their wedding days. He also writes original short scripts for actors to shoot for their showreels. He is a Dad of two brilliant sons, a compulsive chatterbox, and should coffee and chocolate biscuits be readily available, a companion might need to cancel the rest of their afternoon.

Paul is represented by Matt Connell at Berlin Associates for all screenwriting and scripts.

N.B. Paul is not to be confused with the sports journalist of the same name (they're actually second cousins).

Sarah-Louise Young

Sarah is a professional actress, singer, director, cabaret performer, writer and Olivier Award-winning improvisor. She has appeared in the West End with Julie Madly Deeply, Fascinating Aida, The Showstoppers! and La Soirée. She has created numerous shows and been a hugely popular addition to The Edinburgh Fringe for many years. She is one half of Roulston & Young and has gigged all over the world including Off-Broadway and 3 seasons at the prestigious Adelaide Cabaret Festival. She recently received huge plaudits for writing and performing in her one woman cult-cabaret: An Evening Without Kate Bush. She likes coffee almost as much as Paul does and reckons that £64 investment in Guardian Soulmates was the best money she ever spent.

N.B. Sarah-Louise is not to be confused with the adult entertainer of the same name - star of films such as Even Hitler Had A Girlfriend and Satanic Inferno. (They are in no way related. At all.)

Printed in Great Britain
by Amazon